For Dr. A. Denham

Wang [illegible]

Beijing, China.

THE CLASSIC OF THE *DAO*

A NEW INVESTIGATION

Wang Keping

FOREIGN LANGUAGES PRESS BEIJING 1998

First Edition 1998

Home Page:
http://www.flp.com.cn

E-mail Addresses:
info@flp.com.cn
sales@flp.com.cn

ISBN 7-119-02229-6

Published by Foreign Languages Press
24 Baiwanzhuang Road, Beijing 100037, China

Distributed by China International Book Trading Corporation
35 Chegongzhuang Xilu, Beijing 100044, China
P.O. Box 399, Beijing, China

Printed in the People's Republic of China

CONTENTS

Reference Key

DDJ = *The Dao De Jing of Lao Zi* (*Tao-Te Ching of Lao-tzu*)

* This is a newly revised edition based on recent philological studies of the *Dao De Jing* made by Chinese scholars since the discovery in 1973 of the Mawangdui versions on silk. See Appendices 1 and 2.

PREFACE

Lao Zi (c. 580-500 B.C.) and Confucius (551-479 B.C.) have traditionally been regarded as the two most celebrated thinkers in the history of Chinese philosophy. The former is considered the founder of Daoism (i.e. Taoism), and is studied worldwide, mostly by scholars, whereas the latter, the founder of Confucianism, is venerated by people of all walks of life and all over the world. As has been observed by both oriental and occidental readers (including Hegel), the ideas of Lao Zi tend to be more philosophical in the pure sense of this term when compared with those of Confucius. It is commonly acknowledged that Lao Zi's philosophizing underlies the structure or formation of the overall psychology of the Chinese people.

The Book of Lao Zi is usually divided into two parts, known as the "*Dao Jing*" (On *Dao*) and "*De Jing*" (On *De*). Hence it is also titled the "*Dao De Jing*," with such English renderings as *The Way and Its Power* or *Tao-Te Ching* (as a transliteration of its non-standard Chinese pronunciation). This book, the major Daoist classic, is composed of 81 chapters as arramged by the Daoist scholar Heshang Gong (c. 179-159 B.C.). The classification itself has all along been controversial, even though it was once officially approved by an emperor of the Tang Dynasty in 8th century. The compilation of the *Dao De Jing* by Heshang Gong features an additional subtitle for each chapter to help the reader approach the book in a more convenient and rewarding manner. This arrangement is the basis of my own methodology of rearranging all the texts thematically in order to facilitate, I hope, a more practical and fruitful reading today. This has in turn given birth to this new edition, in which philosophical and philological perspectives predominate, with particular reference to the recent findings by Chinese scholars since the discovery of the Mawangdui texts of the *Dao De Jing*. According to relevant archaeological studies, one of the Mawangdui versions may date back at least to the third century B.C., and is therefore regarded as the oldest edition found so far.

Lao Zi, as a Daoist (i.e. Taoist) philosopher, is attracting more and more attention and interest both in the East and the West. Accordingly his book enjoys a rapidly increasing number of readers today. There are, consequently, more than 20 English versions of the *Dao De Jing* (*The Book of Lao Zi*) available published in various countries. The reason why we felt it important to add one more lies in the following considerations:

(1) Lao Zi wrote the book in a poetic style based on metaphors and an expressive form of aphorisms such that many of his ideas appear to be engagingly suggestive, polysemous and somewhat ambiguous rather than articulate. Thus elaborate annotation and extended commentary are necessary for the reader to attain a justified comprehension and interpretation. As regards the straightforward translation of the book, as many English renderings are, it seems to me as though a glass of fine wine has been mixed with water, reducing it to a less tasteful cocktail.

(2) It is largely due to the favorable cultural policy introduced since China embarked on the reform policy that the studies of Lao Zi and his like have made far more progress than ever before. But most of the latest achievements in this field are missing from the versions of the *Dao De Jing* available in English and other Western languages. This edition is intended to fill this gap.

(3) Most English versions tend to employ ready-made terms to translate the ideas of Lao Zi, which I find most likely to lead the reader onto the beaten track of the occidental cultural background when it comes to cognizing what the author is supposed to say. In this case I have ventured to translate the key concepts with newly coined terminology, followed by relevant explanation. I sincerely hope that this approach will help the reader better identify what is really meant, in line with textual and contextual analysis.

(4) Previously mentioned, this version of the *Dao De Jing* is

thematically re-arranged in an attempt to facilitate a practical and fruitful reading today. The thematic arrangement as such is based not merely on the scrutiny of Lao Zi's philosophizing as a systematic whole, but also on considerations of the reading habits of the English reader. The overall aim is to obtain a more relevant understanding and effective communication with regard to the text.

(5) As can be discerned in the annotations and comments provided in the current book, what we are trying to do in most cases is to attempt to gain new insights through reviewing the old text, say, to enable the reader to rediscover the relevance and significance of Lao Zi's way of thought in view of the contemporary socio-cultural context.

(6) The present approach to the *Dao De Jing* is largely grounded on the conviction that it will be of more advantage to the reader to be directly involved in textual reading and analysis rather than to take a detour by tackling merely second-hand interpretation or reinterpretation. For it is often the case that an idiosyncratic interpreter, conceived of his own authority, gallops ahead while neglecting the reader's initiative and observation.

I must confess that whatever efforts I have to tackle this formidable project, it seems to me that I cannot hope to have succeeded completely. All too often the revision alone puts me under the impression that it is extremely difficult to transfer the thought of so lucid and poetic a writer as Lao Zi from one language into another without some damage occurring in the process. I found that the rhyming system, for instance, was almost untransferable no matter how hard I tried.

This book consists of four main parts to be dealt with by virtue of scrutinized reading, contextual analysis and systematic consideration of the *Dao De Jing* and Lao Zi's philosophizing. Part I is concerned with "The *Dao* as the Origin of All," subdivided into five topics. Part II is intended to justify "*De* as a Manifestation of the *Dao*," and subdivided into two mini-themes. Part III is designed to expose "The Human Condition in Perspective," classified into 17 sub-topics. Part V aims to illustrate "The Daoist Path to Personal Cultivation" that is, as an approach to attaining the *Dao* and *De*, categorized into four essential constituents.

In contemplating this research, I am indebted in different but important ways to ancient scholars like Heshang Gong, Wang Bi and Wang Anshi, and especially to contemporary scholars of Daoism such as Gu Di, Chen Guying, Gao Heng, Ren Jiyu, Zhang Songru, Sha Shaohai, Ai Qi and many others. Their respective approaches to the *Dao De Jing* and recent findings were of enormous help to me in my task. With regard to the English translation, my thanks are particularly due to Chan Wing-tsit, Robert G. Henricks, He Guanghu and Gao Shining.

In carrying out the actual work I have been very fortunate to receive equally generous support from Professor Herbert Mainusch of Münster University in Germany, who has all along encouraged me to complete the task. His passionate interest in the study of Chinese culture has commenced to bear noticeable fruit as is reflected in the Chinese version of his book titled *Dialogue and Distance* and in his rediscovery of Oscar Wilde against the background of early Daoism, the school of philosophy founded by Lao Zi and Zhuang Zi.

Finally, I wish to extend my sincere thanks and heartfelt admiration to my publisher and editor for their unflagging assistance.

Wang Keping
Beijing, China

Lao Zi and His Doctrine of the *Dao*

Underlying the Chinese cultural heritage are about a dozen schools of thought dating from as early as the 7th century B.C., when Guan Zhong (?-645 B.C.) and his ideas (cf. *The Book of Guan Zi*) emerged in relation to the later development of the Legalist School (*Fa Jia*).[1] The most important of these schools are known as Confucianism and Daoism (Taoism) in terms of their historical continuity and influence. The founder of Confucianism is naturally identified with Confucius, as the latinized name for Kong Fu Zi or Kong Zi (551-479 B.C.). As regards Daoism, Lao Zi (Lao Tzu) is mostly recognized as its founder despite the fact that the details of his life and work remain controversial. Here we will give a brief account of Lao Zi and his doctrine of the Dao.

I. Lao Zi's Life and Work

Almost all the different opinions about Lao Zi's life and work appear to focus on the dispute as to whether Confucius was preceded by Lao Zi or vice versa. They can thus be generalized into two main tendencies as follows: One holds that Lao Zi was an older contemporary of Confucius, who lived in the latter part of the Spring and Autumn Period (770-476 B.C.) and his doctrines are presented in his book titled the *Dao De Jing* (i.e. *The Book of Lao Zi*); the other argues that Lao Zi was born after Confucius and lived during the Warring States Period (475-221 B.C.), as there are indications in the *Dao De Jing* that was compiled in that era.

According to the biography of Lao Zi as given by Sima Qian (c. 145-86 B.C.) in his *Historical Records*,[2] "Lao Zi was a native of Qurenli Village, in Lixiang community, Kuxian district, in the State of Chu.[3] His family name was Li, his given name Er and style Dan. He once served as the head of the national library during the Eastern Zhou Dynasty (770-256 B.C.). Confucius visited the capital of the dynasty (modern Luoyang City in Henan Province), where he asked Lao Zi about the rites...." On that occasion he was advised by Lao Zi to abandon his air of pride, desire and arrogance for the sake of self-preservation. "Lao Zi practiced *Dao* and *De*," continues Sima Qian in his account, "and hence his doctrine was aimed at self-effacement and namelessness. Having resided in the capital for a long time and observed the decline of the dynasty, he resigned his office and went away westward. Upon arrival at Hanguguan Pass he was welcomed by Guan Yi, who greeted him with joy: "Write me a book, as you are going to become a recluse!" he cried. It was there that Lao Zi wrote a book in two parts and composed of over 5000 words about the meaning of *Dao* and *De*. Afterwards he left and disappeared. No one knows what became of him in the end.... Lao Zi was a gentleman recluse."[4]

Sima Qian, as a historian, adopted an individual approach intended to "convey what is authentic and to record what is doubtful." He therefore preserved two pieces of uncertain information: "Some say that a certain Lao Lai Zi was also a man of the State of Chu who produced a book in 15 chapters on the usefulness of the *Dao*, and seems to have lived at the same time as Confucius," and "Some 129 years after the death of Confucius the histories record that the historian Dan of the Zhou Dynasty had an interview with Duke Xian of Qin (384-362 B.C.).... Some say that this Dan was in fact Lao Zi, while others say he was not."[5] Many scholars agree that the opening and closing portions of Lao Zi's biography are fact, whereas the middle part is unreliable. But there is enough reliable evidence to upset this argument.

First and foremost, the fact that Confucius went to the capital of the Eastern Zhou Dynasty and asked Lao Zi about the rites is reconfirmed in the biography of Confucius according to Sima Qian in his *Historical Records*.[6] It is recorded that Confucius was seen off after the interview and advised by Lao Zi to forget himself (i.e. be selfless). On his return to his own State of Lu his immediate disciples benefitted from what he had learned from Lao Zi in the realm of the rites of the Zhou Dynasty. This is corroborated in *Zeng Zi's Questions on the Rites* (*Zeng Zi Wen*), a chapter of *The Book of Rites* (*Li Ji*), which is known as one of the Confucianist '*Five Classics*' (*Wu Jing*). It is therein stated that Confucius told his student Zeng Zi (505-436 B.C.) about how to conduct certain rites properly as guided by Lao Dan (i.e. Lao Zi, whose name is repeated in the passage as many as seven times). Moreover, in his book (i.e. *The Complete Works of Zhuang Zi*), Zhuang Zi (who is known in Western literature as Chuang Tzu, c. 369-286 B.C.) describes Lao Zi and cites his sayings 16 times, half of which concern the relationship between Lao Zi and Confucius. The similar view that Confucius learned about the rites from Lao Dan can also be found in the *Dang Ran Chapter* of the *Lü Shi Chun Qiu* edited by Lu Buwei (?-235 B.C.), and in the brick carvings of Confucius' life as displayed in the Confucian Temple (Kong Miao) located in his hometown of Qufu in modern Shandong Province. It is worthy of notice that Confucius was influenced by Lao Zi to a certain extent. Some of Lao Zi's ideas can be found in the *Analects of Confucius* (*Lun Yu*), for example, "It was, perhaps, only Emperor Shun (i.e. one of the sage rulers extolled by Confucius himself) who governed peacefully without taking any action against the natural order" (*Lun Yu*, 15:5; cf. Lao Zi's notion of "take-no-action" or "nonaction," DDJ, Ch. 48.); "A gentleman is to be grave and solemn but not to be contentious or competitive" (Ibid, 15:22; cf. Lao Zi's idea that "the *Dao* of sage is to act for others but not to compete with them," DDJ, Ch. 77.); "A benevolent man is surely courageous" (Ibid, 14:4; cf. Lao Zi's assertion that "With kindness one can become courageous," DDJ, Ch. 67.); and "What do you think of repaying resentment with virtue?" (Ibid, 14:34; cf. Lao Zi's proposed solution to "return good for evil," DDJ, Ch. 79.). It is even more interesting to point out that Confucius himself claimed to be a transmitter of the classics instead of an originator. Furthermore, he said, "I am so faithful to and so fond of ancient culture that privately I compare myself to Lao Dan (i.e. Lao Zi) and Peng Zu (i.e. a legendary figure)." (Ibid., 7:1)

Secondly, according to the *Historical Records*,[7] when confronting something confusing, Confucius would go to the capital of Zhou for Lao Zi's opinion; ...and to the State of Chu for Lao Lai Zi's opinion; ... Thus it is self-evident that Lao Zi and Lao Lai Zi were two distinct figures of Confucius' era. Hence it is fanciful to assume that they are the same person, as some scholars have insisted.

Thirdly, it is a historical fact that Confucius visited Lao Zi to clarify some of his queries related to the rites of the Zhou Dynasty as encountered in his studies and teaching practice. It was obviously impossible for Confucius to have consulted the historian Dan, who was born many years after Confucius' death. So, based on historical facts and documentary evidence, it can be safely affirmed that Lao Zi was a native of modern Luyi in Henan Province, which was part of the State of Chu in antiquity. His family name was Li, his given name Er and his style Dan. He was an older contemporary of Confucius, who once visited to ask about the rites. The tradition that he was the head of the national library of the Zhou Dynasty and that he was born about 20 to 30 years before Confucius has been widely supported by celebrated modern scholars, including Guo Moruo, Ma Shulun, Ren Jiyu, Zhan Jianfeng, Gu Di, Zhou Ying, Yan Lingfeng, Tang Yijie, Chen Guying, Ye Lang and Min Ze. As a "gentleman recluse" more than 2,500 years ago, Lao Zi's birth and death can not be pinpointed now, as is often the case with many ancient figures. However, Ren Jiyu inferred from his historical research his assumption that Lao Zi was born in approximately 580 B.C. (i.e. the 6th year of King Jian of the Zhou Dynasty) and died in 500 B.C. (i.e. the 20th year of King Jing of the Zhou Dynasty).[8] According to Zhan Jianfeng, Lao Zi was probably born around 576 B.C. and died after 478 B.C.[9] These inferences are supplied here for reference only.

As to the *Dao De Jing*, there are correspondingly distinct opinions about its emergence in view of its style and authorship. Generally speaking, some believe that it was written by Lao Zi in the late stage of the Spring and Autumn Period, whereas others maintain that it was compiled by the historian Dan in the middle of the Warring States Period; others go so far as to assume that it was based on quotations selected from such classics as *The Book of Zhuang Zi*, *Lü Shi Chun Qiu*, *The Book of Han Fei Zi* and *The Book of Yi Wen Zi*. Recent researh by contemporary Lao Zi scholars stresses the following points: (1) The *Dao De Jing* possesses an intrinsic structure and rigorous logic of its own, and therefore it is unlikely that is is merely a compilation of diverse sources. In addition, most of the authors of the abovementioned works acknowledge their debt to Lao Zi. (2) Lao Zi was not the historian Dan, as the *Dao De Jing* is a product of the late Spring and Autumn Period, as testified by its terminology and rhyming system, even though a few expressions used in it did not come into being until the Warring States Period (e.g. "ten thousand chariots"). (3) The writing style of the *Dao De Jing* as philosophical discourse features a poetic touch which corresponds to that of the *Book of Poetry* (*Shi Jing*), allegedly edited by Confucius. The former is thus considered to be a continuation and development of the latter.[10] Apart from that, its style is quite similar to that of *The Art of War* (*Sun Zi Bing F*a) written by Sun Zi in the Spring and Autumn Period. "If *The Art of War* is affirmed to be written in that period," as Zhang Dainian states, "it is not unreasonable to assume that the *Dao De Jing* was produced at the same time."[11]

In short, we conclude that the *Dao De Jing* was completed in the late Spring and Autumn Period. Nevertheless, its original text was slightly different from what it looks like today. That is owing to certain modifications and additions it underwent in the course of its history, during the Warring States Period in particular. We must keep in mind the fact that it was originally written on bamboo slips, which are notorious for a tendency to fall apart and be put back in the wrong order by careless readers. This position is even more understandable when we see with our own eyes the minor changes in wording in the two Mawangdui silk copies of the *Dao De Jing* unearthed from the same tomb and at the same time in 1973. I personally appreciate the argument that it is far more significant to read and study the book as it is.

II. Lao Zi's Doctrine of the *Dao*

As has been noted, Lao Zi is depicted in his biography quoted above as a man who "practiced *Dao* and *De*." His doctrine was then generalized into something that "aimed at self-effacement and namelessness" on the one hand, and, on the other, into something that advised people to "take no action and thus become self-transformed, and love tranquility and thus become righteous." Although it definitely gets to the point, a generalization of this kind over-simplifies what Lao Zi intended to express in over 5,000 words. Widely recognized as the founder of Daoism, Lao Zi constructs a philosophy of fertility and individuality that unfolds by virtue of his preoccupation with and formulation of the *Dao*.

Lao Zi was the first to form the special concept of the Dao, which in turn works as the keystone of Daoism as a philosophy.[12] The Chinese term *Dao* literally means "way" or "road." Based on this primary meaning, it assumed in ancient times a metaphorical sense, such as "the way of man," signifying human morality, code of conduct or essence of life, etc. But in Lao Zi's terminology the meaning of the *Dao* transcends social and ethical domains. It is then found ascribed to certain metaphysically extended implications relating to the origin of the universe, the root of all things, the law of natural change and social development, the principle of political and military affairs, and above all, the truth of human existence. The *Dao* as such can be conceived of as the constellation of Lao Zi's philosophizing. The most complicated but most fascinating of all its aspects lies, however, in the fact that its connotations vary with the different contexts in which it is used. So long as one sticks to both textual scrutiny and contextual analysis, one will be able to approach what the term *Dao* really suggests in a more justifiable fashion. Offered here is a brief discussion of the term from eight dimensions:

1. The *Dao* of the Universe

The *Dao* is looked upon as the highest category of Lao Zi's philosophy. Right at the beginning of the *Dao De Jing* it is defined as "the origin of Heaven and Earth" and "the mother of the myriad things" (Cf. *Dao De Jing*, Ch. 1. The subsequent citations are from the same source and marked with chapter numbers only). "Heaven and Earth" in Chinese culture means either nature or the universe, and by "the myriad things" is meant all beings in the world. Hence the *Dao* is often likened by modern scholars to the noumenon of the universe and the essence of all things in occidental terms.

The *Dao* itself has two essential aspects discriminated as *Wu* (Being-without-form) and *You* (Being-within-form). The former is invisible and abstract, employed by Lao Zi to indicate the state of the *Dao* before it comes down to its actuality, whilst the latter is visible and concrete, employed to indicate the outcome of the *Dao* as manifested in the things which surround us. Both of these aspects are derived from the *Dao* and are thus regarded as the two sides of one coin. The interrelationship as such seems analogically identical to that between name and object, or thinking and being.

The *Dao* as the origin of the universe and the root of all things precedes God in time (Ch. 4) and exists everywhere in space. It therefore features subtlety, profundity, eternity and indescribability as well as inexhaustibility. The coming into being of all things is characterized by a process; that is, "The *Dao* produces the One. The One turns into the Two. The Two give rise to the Three. The Three bring forth the myriad things. The myriad things contain Yin and Yang as vital forces which achieve harmony through their interactions." (Ch. 42)

The *Dao* of the universe ultimately follows "the way of spontaneity" or naturalness. It begets all things without any practical purpose. Accordingly it treats all things alike without making any distinction. And furthermore it lets all things be what they can become (Ch. 25).

2. The *Dao* of Dialectics

As has been widely noticed, the *Dao* of dialectics is one of the great contributions made by Lao Zi that marks a big leap forward in the maturity of Chinese philosophical thought. It is concisely condensed as follows:

"Reversion is the movement of the *Dao*.
Weakness is the function of the *Dao*." (Ch. 40)

Obviously the *Dao* of dialectics lies in the movement and function of the *Dao* itself. "Reversion" (*Fan*) is a dynamic term. It refers to a kind of interrelation between opposites in one sense, and a kind of return to the root known as the unity or union of opposites in another sense. The former reveals the state of being opposite, while the latter reveals the state of transformation or change. The situation may be symbolized by the traditional symbol of *Tai Ji* ("Great Acme" in literal translation) in which the two forces known as *Yin* and *Yang* are always on the move, interdependent and interacting at the same time. Lao Zi was extremely observant with regard to the changes that take place between and within things themselves. This indicates that things are inclined to reverse to their opposites in a constantly changing process. It is noticeable in both nature and human society that everything is doomed to roll downhill once it reaches the acme. As the saying goes: Things that are too lofty fall down easily; things that are too white stain easily; songs that are too pretentious have few listeners; reputations that are too high fall short of reality. All these possibilities seem to be in conformity with the Chinese conception of "inevitable reversal of the extreme" (*wu ji bi fan*).

The statement that "Weakness is the function of the *Dao*" is a further justification of the foregoing assertion that "Reversion is the movement of the *Dao*." Lao Zi was preoccupied with "keeping to the tender and weak" because he believed that "the tender and weak is bound to conquer the hard and strong." Thus he made frequent use of "water" as a simile when illustrating the potential and overwhelming power of "the tender and weak." Notwithstanding the instructiveness of Lao Zi's dialectical method, one must be highly conscious of its problematic facet that is largely due to his tendency to absolutize the function of "weakness" by cutting it off from actual and varying circumstances or conditions (Ch. 40).

The *Dao* of dialectics is also reflected in Lao Zi's notion that "Have-substance (*you*) brings advantage while have-vacuity (*wu*) creates utility" (Ch. 11). By "have-vacuity" is meant, for example, the central hole in a wheel, the empty space in a bowl, or the interior vacancy in a room. By "have-substance" is meant something concrete, such as the spokes united around the hub, the clay used to shape the bowl and the doors and windows that are cut out to form a room. Lao Zi reckons that these two aspects are seemingly opposite. However, being counterparts, they help complete each other and therefore remain inseparable and interdependent. What is instructive in this perspective is the fact that it reminds us of the importance of the inconcrete dimension of things, which we tend to neglect.

3. The *Dao* of Human Life

This form of the *Dao* is mainly concerned with the truth of human existence and the code of social conduct. In most cases it is demonstrated through the wisdom as exposed in "the three treasures" advocated by Lao Zi: The first is "kindness." The second is "frugality." The third is "to dare not be ahead of the world." It is proclaimed that "With kindness one can become courageous; with frugality one can become generous; and with not daring to be ahead of the world one can become the leader of the world" (Ch. 67). The whole idea is closely connected with Lao Zi's viewpoint of "retreat" that seems to be defensive and passive. Nevertheless, Lao Zi maintains that only the ability to fall back is bravery, the ability to shrink is to stretch; and avoiding prominence and precedence makes one the first. He is convinced that the breach of these three rules of wisdom will bring about complete failure. Moreover, it is generally acknowledged that "the three treasures" were recommended as solutions to social problems such as harsh human relations, insatiable desires and keen competition among people in general and the rich and powerful in particular.

The wisdom of life is also reflected in the sensibility and awareness of the necessity of "being contented," which is assumed to yield "constant happiness," (Ch. 46) and the necessity of "being modest" that is believed to create advantages.

Furthermore, it is also contained in the consciousness of the relativity and mutualism in respect of the interactions between the beautiful and the ugly, the good and the evil, gains and losses as well as between fortune and misfortune. According to Lao Zi, "When people in the world know the beautiful as beauty, there arises the recognition of the ugly. When they know the good as good, there arises the recognition of the evil" (Ch. 2). In our social and daily lives the beautiful and the good are what we expect, while the ugly and the evil are what we reject. They are set side by side as antithetical categories, and come into being in mutual contrast as a consequence of value judgment. Lao Zi is usually interpreted as intending to completely deny and eliminate the distinction between the above-mentioned categories. I hold that he attempted to advocate a rather indifferent stance to the distinction as such. That was because he found it impossible to improve the situation of his harsh time, when power and wealth spoke far more louder than anything else, resulting in the turning of social values upside-down.

As to the dialectical interaction between gains and losses, Lao Zi inferred from his principle of "reversion" as the movement of the *Dao* that "an excessive love of fame is bound to cause an extravagant expense; a rich hoard of wealth is bound to suffer a heavy loss" (Ch. 44). Throughout the history of human society what people have always desired and pursued are chiefly fame and wealth. They may go so far as to be alienated or enslaved by "the fetters of fame and the shackles of wealth" as the Chinese metaphor goes. Hence Lao Zi advised people to be contented with what they have on the one hand, and on the other, warned the avaricious and ambitious not to go to extremes.

As is known to all, good fortune or happiness is what people like to embrace whilst misfortune or misery is what they try to avoid. Yet, people mostly do not realize that the two opposites go hand in hand. "Misfortune is," as Lao Zi remarks, "that beside which fortune lies; fortune is that beneath which misfortune lurks." This again reveals their interrelationship of change or transformation at a certain point as they slant toward each other.

This thought naturally corresponds to Lao Zi's generalization that "Reversion is the movement of *Dao*." (Ch. 40)

Above all, the *Dao* or wisdom of human existence is fundamentally exemplified via the attitude toward life itself and its natural end —death. Almost all living beings are afraid to die, especially human beings. The love of life and fear of death seem to be connected with natural instinct in the case of mankind. Lao Zi observed that what hinders human freedom could be a double complex related to life and death. He then pronounced that life and death as phenomena are as natural as anything else in the world. "Man comes alive into the world and goes dead into the earth. Three out of ten will live a longer time. Three out of ten will live a shorter time. And three out of ten will strive for long life but meet premature death. And for what reason? It is because of excessive preservation of life. Those who don't value their lives are wiser than those who overvalue their lives" (Ch. 50). This entire statement is noticeably a presentation of Lao Zi's attitude toward life and death which are considered as natural phenomena from his Daoist naturalist perspective. Its implied message is aimed at reminding people (1) to live their lives as naturally as possible so that they can enjoy them; (2) not to be crushed by the tragic sense of death that befalls all men alike; and (3) not to overvalue life because it is in vain to strive for a long life by means of excessive preservation. Derived from the *Dao* of living is then a practical approach that lies in less clinging to life-consciousness, since only by so doing can one be "out of the range of death," according to Lao Zi.

4. The *Dao* of Heaven and Man

Lao Zi distinguished between the *Dao* of Heaven and that of man. As regards the former, it is bestowed with naturalness and selflessness, and is symbolic of equality as it treats all things alike. It is figuratively described as the drawing of a bow that aims at its target. Thus in Lao Zi's terms the *Dao* of Heaven "reduces whatever is excessive and supplements whatever is insufficient," and "benefits all things and causes no harm." On the other hand, the *Dao* of man is characterized with acquisitiveness, selfishness and inequality. It therefore "reduces the already insufficient and offers more to what is already excessive" (Ch. 77).

Lao Zi's advocacy of the *Dao* of Heaven as an ideal stands in striking contrast to his critique of the *Dao* of man as a negative product of human civilization. By reading between the lines one can discover that the *Dao* of Heaven was set as a standard with which to measure and upgrade the *Dao* of man. Observably the former is commended as an ideal model for the latter to follow and thereby remold itself. That is why Lao Zi further stressed that "The *Dao* of Heaven has no preference. It is constantly with the good man" (Ch. 79). As a result, there arises "the *Dao* of the sage" that "acts for others but does not compete with them." I personally think that the *Dao* of the sage is the fruit of the tree rooted in the *Dao* of Heaven but planted by man. It is in fact the highest form of spiritual life, resulting from the state of oneness between Heaven and man (*tian ren he yi*).

Oneness between Heaven and man can be also rendered as "Heaven-man oneness" or "nature-man oneness" according to the word order of the Chinese conception *tian ren he yi*. This key conception is a recurring thread throughout the development of Chinese thought. Its origin is usually traced back to Mencius (c.372-289 B.C.)[13] or Dong Zhongshu (179-104 B.C.).[14] I personally think that it can be dated back to Lao Zi and even further back to *The Book of Changes* (*Yi Jing* or *I Ching*).[15] As noted in the *Dao De Jing*, Lao Zi listed "four great things in the universe" —the *Dao*, Heaven, Earth and Man. "Man follows the way of Earth. Earth follows the way of Heaven. Heaven follows the way of *Dao*. And *Dao* follows the way of spontaneity' or the way of naturalness that signifies the *Dao* itself. In context, the *Dao*, or the way of spontaneity, is the highest law or hidden principle beyond sense perception; Heaven and Earth as a whole refer to nature or the universe. Man gets integrated with nature (i.e. Heaven and Earth) by acting upon directions pointed out by the *Dao*. More directly, Lao Zi expounded elsewhere that "he who seeks the *Dao* is identified with the *Dao*....He who seeks Heaven is identified with Heaven....He who is identified with the *Dao*, the *Dao* is also happy to have him....He who is identified with

Heaven, Heaven is also happy to have him" (Ch. 23). In this case "he who seeks..." apparently refers to man, and Heaven stands for nature or the universe. The identification of man with Heaven and with the *Dao* as well is surely a happy situation due to mutual receptance.

The fact of the matter is that the doctrine of Heaven-man oneness is all the more important to the Chinese people since their culture is essentially a non-religious one. Thus their pursuit of super-moral values is mostly stimulated and guided by their pursuit of the state of Heaven-man oneness as an ideal form of spiritual life. The doctrine itself has been carried on and further developed as exemplified in Neo-Daoism, Neo-Confucianism and modern schools of thought in the course of Chinese history. As far as I understand, the doctrine of Heaven-man or nature-man oneness can be rediscovered and more rewardingly approached nowadays from at least four dimensions—the spiritual, aesthetic, social, and environmental. First of all, from the spiritual dimension, the notion of nature-man oneness functions as a metaphysical bay where the anchor of the ship of life can be dropped. In other words, it is chiefly concerned with the cultivation and sublimation of human life in an ethical sense, and with the pursuit and location of man's destination in a spiritual sense. To my mind that this idea in Daoism emphasizes contentedness with the law of nature, identification with nature, unconditioned pursuit of spontaneity and absolute freedom from social ambitions. Secondly, nature-man oneness from an aesthetic viewpoint primarily refers to the inspiring interaction between the limited stream of personal life and the unlimited flow of universal change, which usually takes place in one's emotional world or at the time when one contemplates external objects. Interaction of this kind can facilitate bilateral projection, reinforcement and sublimation in a vital sense. Thirdly, in a social sense, the notion of nature-man oneness basically means the adaptation of people as individuals to the community. It can be envisaged as underlining the development of harmonious human relations. This is equivalent to the realization of unity or harmony in the sphere of human relations. Finally, with regard to the treatise of nature-man oneness from an environmental perspective, it directs man to reconsider his place in nature. It thereby consolidates his consciousness of environmental protection, and in turn ameliorates the quality of life in general.[16]

5. The *Dao* of Personal Cultivation

Daoism as a philosophy is commonly taken to be the fundamental aspect of the formation of the psychology of the Chinese people. This is due to the fact that Daoism is largely concerned with personal cultivation from within, which is then chiefly oriented to the realization of *Dao-De*.

As promulgated in the preceding section, the *Dao* of personal cultivation is a kind of principle represented in the attitude, experience, praxis and attainment in connection with the *Dao*. There are generally three different types of attitudes toward the *Dao* as categorized by Lao Zi as follows: "When the highest type of *shi* (i.e. men of learning or literati) hear of the *Dao*, they diligently practice it. When the average type of *shi* hear of the *Dao*, they half-believe it. When the lowest type of *shi* hear of the *Dao*, they laugh heartily at it. If they did not laugh at it, it would not be the *Dao*" (Ch. 41). Being positive and appropriate, the stance held by the first type of literati is most commendable and effective in view of achieving the *Dao* as the highest sphere of human life and fostering *De* as the manifestation of the *Dao* in an ethical sense.

As a natural outcome of adopting the right attitude toward the *Dao*, one would be most likely to experience sublime enlightenment, and be possessed of a mentality which is not only distinct from, but far transcends that of the ordinary person. This experience and mentality as such feature above all simplicity, tranquility, genuineness, modesty, adaptability and open-mindedness. (Cf. chs. 15 and 20.)

As articulated in chapters 7, 23 and 27, the praxis of the *Dao* and *De* involves relevant strategies. In addition, there are incredible advantages of acting upon the *Dao* as the supreme principle and nourishing *De* as the highest virtue. A wise ruler, for instance, will have all the people come to him if he holds fast to the

Dao. In the case of people in general, they will stay free from danger throughout their lives if they sincerely exercise the *Dao* and cultivate *De*.

It is discernable that Lao Zi speaks of the *Dao* from various perspectives throughout his book. All in all, the most important of the objectives lies in how to attain the *Dao* as the highest realm of human spirit. The attainment of the *Dao* is dependent on an approach as proposed by Lao Zi in his discussion. This proposal comprises six dimensional components as follows: (1) self-purification and deep contemplation; (2) plainness and simplicity; (3) vacuity and tranquility; (4) tenderness and non-competitiveness; (5) have-less-selfishness and have-few-desires; (6) naturalness and take-no-action. (Cf. chs. 10, 13, 16, 17, 22, 25, 28 and 49.)

6. The Dao of Governance

Lao Zi's political philosophy is centrally reflected in his discussion of the *Dao* of governance, or the art of leadership in modern terms. Comparatively speaking, one of its most typical traits is "take-no-action" (*wu wei*). The idea of "take-no-action" does not mean doing nothing at all. Instead it advises a ruler not to take arbitrary, unreasonable or blind actions when it comes to governing the people or conducting state affairs. In other words it demands that the governance or leadership make wise decisions and take just actions according to the *Dao* as the natural or objective law of all things. Thus it can be understood as a substitute expression for "follow the way of spontaneity" or naturalness. That is why it is respected as an ideal for political and governmental praxis, and as an instrument to facilitate smooth operation. Lao Zi himself was convinced that "the *Dao* invariably takes no action, and yet there is nothing left undone. If kings and lords are able to maintain it, all things will submit to them due to self-transformation" (Ch. 37). By the same token, Lao Zi would persuade the ruler or leader to act upon what the sage says as follows: "I take no action and the people of themselves become transformed. I love tranquility and the people of themselves become righteous. I disturb nobody and the people of themselves become prosperous. I have no desire and the people of themselves become simple" (Ch. 57). All this denotes that the ruler or leader himself must set a good example for his subordinates to follow by embracing the above-mentioned virtues. Moreover, he should not be strong-minded or persistently self-centered, just like the sage who "has no fixed personal mind" and "takes the mind of the people as his mind" (Ch. 13). In sum, as the conclusion goes, "In order to govern all under Heaven, one should adopt the policy of doing nothing. A person who likes to do anything arbitrary is not qualified to govern all under Heaven" (Ch. 48). Under such circumstances we can obtain a better understanding of one of Lao Zi's widely-quoted remarks—"Governing a large country is like cooking a small fish." (Ch. 60)

In comparison with the canon of "take-no-action," another equally enlightening aspect of the *Dao* of governing is connoted in the commitment to retreat for the sake of advance. It is stated, tactically but somewhat paradoxically, as follows: "In order to contract it, it is necessary to expand it first. In order to weaken it, it is necessary to strengthen it first. In order to destroy it, it is necessary to promote it first. In order to take it, it is necessary to give it first. This is called subtle light" (Ch. 36). This "subtle light" well represents Lao Zi's dialectical thinking as to the art of leadership. The impression it tends to leave on us is that the retreat appears, as it were, propelled by initiative, active and practically purposeful. It is aimed at harvesting a long-term gain at the expense of a short-term loss. It actually resembles drawing back the fist in order to put more power into blow.

As elaborated by Lao Zi (Cf. Chs. 3, 26, 36, 59, 60, 61, 66, 73, 74 and 75), the *Dao* of governing also features being modest as a policy to win others over, and keeping to tenderness as a strategy to overcome the strong, etc. This principle has been constantly renewed and replenished at different times and for different goals. There is no wonder that the *Dao De Jing* reveals new truths as it is read and re-read.

7. The *Dao* of War

Although he is renowned for his negative attitude toward warfare, Lao Zi never fails to see the harsh reality of frequent military conflicts launched in a diversity of names. Accordingly he gives due consideration to what people suffer from war, meanwhile offering insights into strategies and tactics connected with the employment of weapons. Lao Zi proposes a defensive policy that is firmly based on his notion of retreat as advance. Thus developed from this defensive policy are such military strategies and tactics as "wait at one's ease for an exhausted enemy," "defend in order to attack," and "retreat in order to advance," which are all aimed at "gaining mastery or winning victory by striking only after the enemy has struck." (Cf. chs. 57, 68 and 69.)

The *Dao* of warfare can, it seems to us, be generalized, if not over-simplified, into one underlying principle: "An army should be operated in an unusual way" (*yi qi yong bing*). By "unusual way" or extraordinary way (*qi*) is meant utilizing the whole gamut of secret, tricky and unexpected strategies and tactics. To be sure, military operations in an unusual way are a necessity because all warfare is grounded on deception. "Therefore," points out Sun Zi, the author of *The Art of War* (*Sun Zi Bing Fa*), "when able to attack, we must pretend to be unable; when employing our forces, we must seem inactive; when near, we must make the enemy believe we are far away; when far away, we must make him believe we are near. Offer bait to lure the enemy when he covets small advantages; strike the enemy when he is in disorder.... Launch attack where the enemy is unprepared; take action when it is unexpected. These are the keys to victory for the strategist."

The counterpart of the "unusual way" (*qi*) is the "normal way" (*zheng*). Being a pair of opposite and yet complementary categories, *qi* and *zheng* are not only recommended by Lao Zi for application in battle, but also by Sun Zi, known as the most outstanding military strategist in ancient China. In his book *The Art of War*, Sun Zi arrives at the conclusion that "it is due to the operation of *qi* (extraordinary way and force) and *zheng* (normal way and force) that the whole army can sustain an enemy's all-out attack." It is simply owing to the similarities in this particular aspect of Lao Zi and Sun Zi that the *Dao De Jing* has been proclaimed by some people (e.g. Mao Zedong) to be a book on warfare.

To be exact, that "an army should be operated in an unusual way" is a guiding principle for military actions. However, the principle itself cannot be fully effective unless it is implemented in accordance with another rule, that of non-competition for either quick victory or instant glory. This may sound paradoxical, but it can be justified as a dialectical viewpoint by a scrutiny of the message as hidden in Lao Zi's exposition as follows: "An adept commander does not display his martial prowess. An adept warrior does not become angry. An adept conqueror does not wrestle with his enemy. An adept manager of men places himself below them. This is called the virtue of non-competition. This is called the use of others' force...." (Ch. 68)

8. The Dao of Peace

Born and living in a chaotic age subject to repeated wars and conflicts among the kingdoms, Lao Zi valued peace and social order more than anything else. This is reflected in his persistent anti-war position. He looked upon weapons as instruments of evil and kept warning people of the danger in the use of military force, because "whenever great wars are over, years of famine are sure to afflict the land." Accordingly he denounced any excessive military operations and discouraged any delight in military victory. In addition, he even went so far as to advise the winning side to practice humanism by mourning all those killed in the battles. We read, for instance, in Chapter 31 of the *Dao De Jing*: "Weapons are nothing but instruments of evil. They are used only when there is no other choice. Therefore, he who wins a battle is not praiseworthy. If he thinks himself praiseworthy, he delights in the victory. He who delights in victory delights in the slaughter of men. He who delights in the slaughter of men will not succeed under Heaven. For those killed in wars, let us mourn them with sorrow and grief...." Contextually speaking, his criticism of the exultant victors has here changed into sharp and strong condemnation.

Then there arises naturally the *Dao* of peace as underlined in the statement, "He who assists the ruler with *Dao* never seeks to dominate the world with military force." The *Dao* as such is closely associated with the principle of "take-no-action." That is, it is against taking military action as a risky solution to social problems. That could be the main reason why Lao Zi insisted that "the sharp weapons of a country should not be displayed." This suggests that they should not be shown off to frighten people or utilized to destroy others. The application of the *Dao* of peace, Lao Zi imagined, would lead to the creatation of ideal states featuring small areas of territory and small populations. In such states people would have armor and weapons, but no occasion to display or use them. Plainness, simplicity and self-contentment would be characteristic of the people's way of life. Above all, neighboring states would enjoy a peaceful environment and embrace the policy of co-existence such that although they "can see one another, and the crowing roosters and barking dogs can be heard, the people may live and die without ever meeting each other" (Ch. 80). It is worth pointing out that the expression "without meeting each other" does not mean prohibition of international visits or mutual communication, as often caused by closed-door policies; rather, it means the elimination of clashes. In short, the states would be free from warfare and their peoples would live in peace.

In the final analysis, it is rationally assumed that Lao Zi's doctrine of the *Dao* can be reasonably approached and apprehended in terms of the eight dimensions explained above. It is, as it were, open to new investigation and reinterpretation by means of both textual and contextual analyses. What I can safely say is that Lao Zi as a thinker belongs to mankind as a whole, and the enlightenment to be found in his philosophizing is consequently a contribution to the enrichment of human culture the world over.

Notes:

[1] Chinese culture is renowned for its long history, based on the contributions made by "one hundred schools" of thought and their leading philosophers. The "one hundred schools" can be traced back to the centuries before the Qin Dynasty (221-207 B.C.), and down to the early Western Han Dynasty (206 B.C.-A.D. 25). They were classified by the historian Sima Tan (?-110 B.C.) into six major schools of thought, namely, the *Yin Yang Jia* (*Yin-Yang* School), *Ru Jia* (School of Literati or Confucianist School), *Mo Jia* (Mohist School or Mohism), *Ming Jia* (School of Names or Logicians), *Fa Jia* (Legalist School) and *Dao De Jia* (*Dao-De* School or Daoism) (Cf. Ch. 130 in Sima Qian's *Historical Records*). In his treatise *Zhu Zi Lue* (*Introduction to the Philosophers*), Liu Xin (c. 46 B.C.-A.D. 23) arranged the "one hundred schools" into ten main categories: the *Zong Heng Jia* (School of Diplomatists or Political Strategists), *Za Jia* (School of Eclectics or Miscellaneous School), *Nong Jia* (School of Agrarians) and *Xiao Shuo Jia* (School of Story Tellers), apart from the six schools above-mentioned. In my opinion, the *Bing Jia* (School of Military Strategists) should be included in Liu Xin's list, bringing the number of schools to 11.

[2] The *Shi Ji* (*The Historical Records*) by Sima Qian consists of 130 chapters all together. It is the first general history of China, from remote antiquity down to the reign of Emperor Wu Di (140-87 B.C.) of the Western Han Dynasty. It was commenced by Sima Tan (?-110 B.C.) and completed by his son Sima Qian (c.125-86 B.C.).

[3] Basically located in the modern Luyi district of Henan Province.

[4] Cf. Ch. 63, in the *Shi Ji*.

[5] Ibid.

[6] Ibid., Ch. 47.

[7] Ibid., Ch. 67.

[8] Cf. Ren Jiyu. *Zhong Guo Zhe Xue Shi* (*A History of Chinese Philosophy*). Beijing: People's Press, Vol. 1, 1990.

[9] Cf. Zhan Jianfeng. *Lao Zi Qi Ren Qi Shu Ji Qi Dao Lun (On Lao Zi, His book and His Doctrine of the Dao*). Wuhan: Hubei People's Press, 1982.

[10] Cf. Gu Di & Zhou Ying. *Lao Zi Tong* (*Complete Studies of Lao Zi*). Changchun: Jilin People's Press, Vol. 2, 1991; Chen Guying. *Lao Zhuang Xin Lun* (*New Essays on Lao Zi and Zhuang Zi*). Shanghai: Shanghai Classics Press, 1992.

[11] Cf. Zhang Dainian. "Lao Zi Zhe Xue Bian Wei" (An Investigation of Lao Zi's Philosophy), in *Zhong Guo Zhe Xue Shi Lun Wen Ji* (*Collected Essays on the History of Chinese Philosophy*). Jinan: Shandong People's Press, Vol. 1, 1979.

[12] A distinction is made between Daoism as a philosophy (*Dao Jia* or *Dao Xue*) and Daoism as a religion (*Dao Jiao*), according to Chinese philosophical tradition. Cf. Feng Youlan (Fung Yu-lan). "A Short History of Chinese Philosophy," in *Selected Philosophical Writings of Fung Yulan*. Beijing: Foreign Languages Press, 1991, pp. 193-198; also cf. Wang Ming. *Dao Jia Yu Dao Jiao Si Xiang Yan Jiu* (*Studies of Daoism as Philosophy and Religion*). Beijing: China

Social Sciences Press, 1987.

[13] Cf. Mencius. "Jin Xin Shang" (Chapter 7A), in *Meng Zi* (*The Book of Mencius*). Beijing: Zhong Hua Shu Ju, 1988.

[14] Cf. Dong Zhongshu. "Yin Yang Yi" (The Meaning of "Yin" and "Yang"), in *Chun Qiu Fan Lu* (*The Book of Dong Zhongshu*). Shanghai: Shanghai Gu Ji Press, 1990.

[15] Cf. Liu Shuxian. "You Tian Ren He Yi Xin Shi Kan Ren Yu Zi Ran Zhi Guan Xi" (The Relations Between Man and Nature in View of the Newly-Interpreted Heaven-Man Oneness), in *Ru Jia Si Xiang Yu Xian Dai Hua* (*Ideas of Confucianism and Modernization*). Beijing: China Broadcasting and Television Press, 1993.

[16] Cf. Wang Keping. "On the Social Development and the Rediscovery of the Doctrine of Nature-Man Oneness," in *Research Journal*, Beijing Second Foreign Languages Institute, No. 2, April, 1995. (Note: The article is based on a paper delivered at the 1994 Beijing International Symposium on Social Development and Oriental Culture.)

Part I The *Dao* as the Origin of All

Lao Zi was the first to coin the special concept of the *Dao*, which in turn serves as the keystone of his Daoism qua philosophy. Subtle and profound, the *Dao* is viewed as the origin of Heaven and earth, and the mother of all things. It thus features a principle of all individual principles, and a movement of dialectic characteristics. In addition, there is a distinction made between the *Dao* of Heaven (*tian dao*) and the *Dao* of Man (*ren dao*) that produce a highly enlightening interaction.

1 The Essence of the *Dao*

The exposition of the *Dao* reveals Lao Zi's doctrine of the origin and coming into being of the universe on the one hand, and his philosophy of "following the way of spontaneity" on the other. *You* (Being-within-form) and *Wu* (Being-without-form) are described as the two essential aspects of the *Dao* from which its subtlety, profundity and dynamic potency can be discerned and perceived accordingly. The nature of the *Dao* is a topic which runs throughout the text of the *Dao De Jing*, particularly in chapters 1, 4, 6 and 25 (DDJ).

1.1 (Chapter 1)

The *Dao*[1] that can be told is not the constant *Dao*.[2]
The Name[3] that can be named is not the constant Name.[4]
The Being-without-form[5] is the origin of Heaven and Earth;[6]
The Being-within-form[7] is the mother of the myriad things.[8]
Therefore it is always from the Being-without-form
That the subtlety of the *Dao* can be contemplated;[9]

Similarly it is always from the Being-within-form
That the manifestation[10] of the *Dao* can be perceived.[11]
These two have the same source but different names,[12]
They both may be called deep and profound.[13]
The Deepest and most profound
Is the doorway to all subtleties.[14]

Annotations:

[1] The Chinese concept of the *Dao* (*Tao*) literally means "way" or "road." Based on this primary meaning, it assumed in ancient times the metaphorical sense of the "Way of man," signifying human morality, conduct or truth, with its meaning confined to social and human affairs. Yet in Lao Zi's terminology it is found ascribed to certain metaphysically extended implications that vary with different contexts with regard to his doctrine of the origin of Heaven and earth (i.e. universe or nature as a whole), and to the general law of natural change, social development and ethical conduct as well.

As Han Fei Zi (c. 280-233 B.C.) defined it, the *Dao* is the total of all principles whereby all things are as they are. It is the basis of the countless individual principles. Principles (*li*) are the concrete rules that make each thing come into being, whereas the *Dao* is that whereby all things become complete. Therefore it is said that the *Dao* is what produces principles. With individual principles, one thing cannot be the other.... All things have their own different principles whilst the *Dao* brings the principles of all things into uniform agreement. (See "*Jie Lao*" [Explaining Lao Zi] in *Han Fei Zi*).

The characteristics of the *Dao* can be analysed as follows:

(1) The *Dao* is the natural law of all things, excluding all gods and heavenly impulses.

(2) The *Dao* is as eternal as the naturalness of the ever-existing physical world. It is thus infinite in time and space.

(3) The *Dao* is the essence of all things and manifests itself through its attribute *De* (*Te*). Hence the *Dao* cannot exist without all things existing.

(4) In terms of the *Dao* as the essence of all things, it is the

unity between the vital force (*qi*) as the world's physical base and the natural law of its changes.

(5) The *Dao* is the imperishable, essential in the physical world, and therefore all things are subordinate to the law of the Dao, which is powerful enough to clear all barriers from its path.

(6) The *Dao* functions in this manner: All things and phenomena are in constant motion and change, in the process of which they are transformed into their own opposites.

(7) All things and phenomena are involved in a kind of interrelationship which is accomplished via the unifying Dao.

(8) The *Dao* is neither visible nor tangible; it is beyond our sensory perception but yet cognitive by means of logical thinking. (see Yang Xingshun. *Zhongguo Gudai Zhexuejia Lao Zi Jiqi Xueshuo* [*Ancient Chinese Philosopher Lao Zi and His Doctrines*])

Following are more interpretations of the *Dao* offered for reference:

The word *Dao* is, according to Prof. Fung Yu-lan, one of the most important terms in Chinese philosophy. It has a primary meaning of "road" or "way." From this primary meaning it assumed already in ancient times a metaphorical significance, as the "way of man," that is, human morality, conduct or truth. During this time, its meaning was always restricted to human affairs, whereas when we come to the *Dao De Jing*, we find the word *Dao* being given a metaphysical meaning. That is to say, the assumption is made that for the universe to have come into being there must exist an all-embracing first principle, which is called *Dao* (see Fung Yu-lan. *A History of Chinese Philosophy*. p. 177).

The *Dao*, as a philosophical concept initially put forth by Lao Zi, carries two basic meanings: it sometimes indicates the substance of the physical world, that is, the noumenon of the universe, but in most cases it means the universal law that governs the motion and change of nature or reality. These two aspects tend to be so much entangled in Lao Zi's notion that the character of the law gets confused with its manifestation (see Zhang Songru. *Lao Zi Jiaodu* [*A Revised Reading of Lao Zi's Dao De Jing*]).

According to Tong Shuye, the idea of the *Dao* in *The Book of Lao Zi* is developed from the notion of *Ming* (Fate) in the pantheism prevailing since the Spring and Autumn Period (770-476 B.C.) in Chinese history. *Ming* was the negation of the concept of *Tian* (Heaven) and *Gui* (Ghost) available in the religious idealism of the past. As a result of denying the existence of God with will and personality and other deities, ghosts and spirits, there was no longer any master of the universe. Hence the ancient thinkers had to look beyond *Tian* and *Gui* for another universal master to govern the world in general and all human changes in particular. Thus emerged the theory of *Ming* as reflected in the pantheism. The notion of the *Dao* was thus based on the further abstraction of the theory of *Ming*, which can be seen as a natural product of the developmental process of thinking experienced by the ancient Chinese thinkers (see Tong Shuye. *Xianqin Lao Zi Sixiang Yanjiu* [*A Study of Lao Zi's Thought in Pre-Qin Dynasty Times*]). The *Dao* is also considered as the highest category of Lao Zi's philosophy. Reading the *Dao De Jing*, we find, according to Prof. Ren Jiyu, that the *Dao* has five distinct meanings: (1) It implies "the undifferentiated primitive state (chaos);" (2) It indicates "the motion of nature;" (3) It is "the proto-material;" (4) It is "invisible to man's eyes and imperceptible to the other sense organs;" and (5) It means "the law of all things." However, Lao Zi's *Dao* is "merely a preliminary supposition about the proto-material that forms all things, and Lao Zi himself had not yet the capacity to understand matter in general. Therefore, he puts forward the concept of undifferentiated (chaos) in his philosophical conception. The undifferentiated cannot be named: It is called 'the nameless' or 'simplicity'" (see *A Taoist Classic: The Book of Lao Zi*, pp. 4-5).

By means of substantial research into Lao Zi's way of thought and taking account of many other individual findings by Chinese scholars, Prof. Chen Guying has arrived at the conclusion that the *Dao* is characterized by several denotations to be apprehended accordingly in specific contexts. He consequently classifies the *Dao* as a metaphysically reality existent in some cases, as a type of universal law of things in other places, and lastly as an underlying rule or standard of human conduct and personal cultivation under certain circumstances. The *Dao* as presented in Chapter 1 implies a metaphysical character due to its being indescribable, unnameable and imperceivable by the senses, and having no definite form, even though it has a real existence and dynamically serves as the beginning of the universe (see Chen Guying. "Lao Zi Zhexue Xitong De Xingcheng" [The Development of Lao Zi's Philosophical System], in *Lao-Zhuang Xinlun* [*New Essays on Lao Zi and Zhuang Zi*]).

[2] In the original text the expression *chang dao* (constant *Dao*) is changed to be *heng dao* (eternal *Dao*) on the basis of the two copies of *The Book of Lao Zi* written on silk and unearthed in 1973 from an ancient tomb at Mawangdui, which dates back to the early Han Dynasty (c. 206 B.C.-180 B.C.). The tomb is located near Changsha, capital of Hunan Province. The relics found there contain two largely similar versions of the *Dao De Jing* which are considered by Chinese scholars as the earliest text of the book found so far. It is thought that the character *heng* was altered to *chang* simply to avoid the political taboo of repeating the name of Liu Heng, Emperor Wen of Han at the time the traditionally used text was written. However, both *chang* and *heng* mean the same in Chinese and they can therefore be translated into English as either "constant" or "eternal."

"Constant *Dao*" suggests such features of the *Dao* as eternity, indescribability, profundity, subtlety, irreplaceability and imperishability, etc. This is because the *Dao*, a universality of all changes, remains constant or eternal for ever, present in the myriad things as its manifestations move, change and generate along with the Heavenly way, natural law, or time and space.

[3] "The Name" is used by Lao Zi as another title for the *Dao*. The *Dao* he talks about differs from what was taken for granted, for example, the commonly-termed *Dao* as demonstrated by means of the system of rites and music (*li-yue*) in Confucianism. The *Dao* that Lao Zi advocates stays constant and universal. Correspondingly, the Name thus drawn from one's reflection and cognition of the Daoist *Dao* is distinct from the secular name for such social values as humanity and righteousness (*ren-yi*) advocated by Confucianism and others. The Name here is therefore

as constant or universal as the *Dao*. The relationship between the two (i.e. Name and *Dao*) and is allegorically identical to that between thinking and being—the former is the reflection of the latter.

[4] "Constant Name" is put in the same category as "constant *Dao*." That is, *chang ming* (constant Name) is identical with *heng ming* (eternal Name). The alteration of *heng* into *chang* was done for the reason cited in [2] above.

[5] Originally the *Dao De Jing* was not divided into two parts comprising 81 chapters. The division was done later, resulting in many variations of a minor nature in words and order. The punctuation of each chapter was done later as well. This has caused controversy among scholars. For instance, Wang Bi (226-249) punctuated the following sentence thus: *Wu ming, tian di zhi shi; you ming, wan wu zhi mu.* That is why some translations have "The Nameless is the origin of Heaven and Earth; the Named is the mother of the myriad things." Wang Bi explained that the Named comes from the Nameless; the beginning of the myriad things is the state of being formless and nameless. When it has form and name it helps to rear, develop, nurture and protect the myriad things. Hence it is called the mother of them. The *Dao* is formless and nameless, making all things become complete without knowing its doings. That is why it is regarded as the beginning of all beginnings (see Wang Bi. *Lao Zi Dao De Jing Zhu* [*Commentary on The Book of Lao Zi*]). But ever since Wang Anshi (1021-1086) many scholars have punctuated these two sentences thus: *Wu, ming tian di zhi shi; you, ming wan wu zhi mu.* They are accordingly translated as "The Being-without-form is the origin of Heaven and Earth; the Being-within-form is the mother of the myriad things." Neither *Wu* nor *You* has an equivalent in occidental languages. They are thus rendered here as "Being-without-form" and "Being-within-form." Some scholars are inclined to express them as "Non-being" (*Wu*) and "Being" (*You*). It is worth mentioning that "Non-being" in Lao Zi's terminology does not mean nothing or emptiness. It is actually in existence but without form, and therefore "vague and elusive" from sensory perception. Similarly, "Being" in Lao Zi's terminol-

ogy is of course different in meaning from the "Being" of Parmenides. In Daoism the term *You* as the actuality of the *Dao* which is antithetical to *Wu* as the potentiality of the *Dao* embodies antithesis of form and name. In other words, it is a material kind of being with changes, whereas in the views of Parmenides and Plato, it is an immaterial kind of being without changes. In order to avoid this misleading aspect of the terms, I prefer to translate *Wu* as "Being-without-form" and *You* as "Being-within-form."

I accept Wang Anshi's punctuation, as do many other scholars today such as Chen Guying and Sha Shaohai. To justify their argument they both cite Chapter 40 (DDJ): "The myriad things in the world come from Being-within-form. And Being-within-form comes from Being-without-form." Prof. Chen further argues that those who agree with Wang Bi's punctuation can also cite evidence in Chapter 32 (DDJ), that is, *Dao chang wu ming/ shi zhi you ming* (The *Dao* is constant and nameless/As soon as there was an established system there were names.) As luck would have it, *wu ming* (nameless) fits in the context as an interpretation of the character of the *Dao*, while *you ming* (there were names) does not, since it here involves the differentiation of social names or ranks, similar to social stratification. Names as such were a cardinal cause of conflicts or clashes and therefore could not be the root of all things (i.e. "the mother of the myriad things") as Lao Zi proclaimed.

It should be pointed out that *Wu* (Being-without-form) and *You* (Being-within-form) are two categories first formulated by Lao Zi, which in fact represent one of his key contributions to the development of Chinese philosophy before the Qin Dynasty (221-206 B.C.). In his book Lao Zi repeatedly emphasizes the distinction between the particular and the universal among all things, and equally the distinction between essence and appearance. Appearance is particular, while essence is universal. The particular emerges and vanishes, whereas the essential remains as it is for ever. From this point of view, Lao Zi's contemplation of *Wu* (Being-without-form) and *You* (Being-within-form) marks a great step forward in the history of human thinking and cognition.

Incidentally, *Wu* (Being-without-form) and *You* (Being-within-form) are two aspects contained in the *Dao*. The former can be regarded as a substitute related to the moment when Heaven and Earth were in chaos prior to their separation, while the latter can be regarded as a substitute related to the fundamental source of the myriad things. From Lao Zi's point of view, the world is oneness or unity, emerging from the movement of the *Dao*. In terms of the world's formation, the ancients believed that the separation of Heaven and Earth took place first, and the emergence of the myriad things came second; just as it was said: "There were Heaven and Earth, then the myriad things commenced to be" (see "Yizhuan Xugua" [Prelude of the Trigrams, A Commentary on the *Yi Jing* or *The Book of Changes*]). Therefore, Being-without-form and Being-within-form respectively stand for two stages in the engendering process of the world (see He Haokun & Huang Qiyue, *Cong Dao De Erchongxing Kan Lao Zi Zhexue Tixi De Tedian* [*Looking into the Features of Lao Zi's Philosophical System from the Perspective of the Duality of the Dao*]).

Being-without-form and Being-within-form operate as the dual character of the *Dao*, interrelated so closely as the two sides of a coin. Yet, these two aspects exemplify the dynamic course of the *Dao* moving from the invisible and universal to the visible and particular.

[6] The expression "Heaven and Earth" (*tian di*) is usually employed in Chinese to mean either nature or the universe as a whole.

[7] See [5] above.

[8] The Chinese word *wan* (ten thousand), when figuratively used, often means countless or innumerable, similar to "infinitely great or infinity" as a mathematical term. Therefore, "the ten thousand or myriad things" can be understood to mean "all things" or "everything."

[9] "Subtlety" is the English rendering of the Chinese term *miao*, which signifies, according to Wang Bi, "something extremely subtle." It is a fact that all things start with Being-without-form

and then come into Being-within-form, underlining subtlety as one of the *Dao*'s major characteristics.

[10] In Wang Bi's edition the word *jiao* is explained as "outcome." Literally it means "boundary." Some scholars extend this meaning to "clue" or "inkling." The Mawangdui silk copy of *The Book of Lao Zi*, the earliest edition so far discovered in China, uses another character pronounced *jiao* and meaning "shout," which seems obviously out of place in both the logical and contextual dimensions. It is possibly a mistake for another *jiao* which means "bright" or "clarity." Its extended meaning could be "show" or "manifestation," contextually corresponding to the preceding word, *miao* (subtlety). As has been observed, the *Dao* is delicate and subtle when it is functioning in its aspect of Being-without-form (*Wu*) as a potentiality, but clear and manifest when functioning in its aspect of Being-within-form (*You*) as an actuality (when it shows itself through the "myriad things").

[11] Heshang Gong (fl. 179-159 B.C.) and Wang Bi punctuated the sentences in this way: *Gu chang wu yu, yi guan qi miao*; *chang you yu, yi guan qi jiao* (Therefore those constantly without desires, by this means will perceive the subtlety of the *Dao*; those constantly with desires, by this means will see the boundary of the *Dao*). This seems to interrupt the stream of thought of the chapter on the one hand, and does not agree with Lao Zi's persistent stance against desires of all kinds on the other. For he was convinced that desires as such are the primary cause of human conflicts and social problems, and often plunge people into restlessness and anxiety. Thus Lao Zi frequently advises people to reduce or abandon their desires as much as possible in order to preserve their spirits and lives in one sense, and in another sense to perceive the subtlety and manifestation of the *Dao*. Hence I prefer the punctuation originated by Wang Anshi. That is: *Gu chang wu, yu yi guan qi miao*; *chang you, yu yi guan qi jiao*, which is then rendered as "Therefore it is always from (the perspective of) the Being-without-form that the subtlety of the *Dao* can be contemplated; it is always from (the perspective of) the Being-within-form that the manifestation of the *Dao* can be perceived." The justifications for this can be found in the

commentaries by many Chinese scholars today, such as Wang Huai, Yan Lingfeng, Chen Guying, Sha Shaohai, Gu Di, Zhou Ying, and others.

Some scholars (e.g. Gao Heng, Yi Shunding and Du Yushi) also adopt Wang Anshi's punctuation. Yet, they tend to paraphrase the sentences a bit differently by labeling *chang wu* (constant Being-without-form) and *chang you* (constant Being-within-form) as two interdependent concepts and facets integrated in the *Dao*. This viewpoint may well be taken for reference.

[12] "These two have the same source..." denotes the fact that both Being-without-form and Being-within-form derive from the same source—the *Dao*. Some scholars (e.g. Tong Shuye) have proposed that *Wu* (Being-without-form) and *You* (Being-within-form), *miao* (subtlety) and *jiao* (manifestation) all merge but have different names. In view of *tong* (togetherness) they appeared so inseparable that they were called *xuan* (deep and profound).

[13] The Chinese notion *xuan* is rendered here as "deep and profound," and Being-without-form and Being-within-form as two aspects of the *Dao* are characterized with such implications as inseparability due to their interrelationship, unpredictability due to their changeability and indescribability or unnameability due to their subtlety.

Chan Wing-tsit translates *xuan* as either "profound" or "mysterious." He holds that the word itself has a wide range of meanings, as have many other Chinese words. It means dark, abstruse, deep, profound, secret, mysterious, etc. In Daoist religious point of view, the aspect of mystery should be stressed, but in Daoist philosophy, the profound or metaphysical aspect is paramount. Thus *xuan-xue* should be translated as "metaphysical school," while *xuan de* should be translated as "profound and secret virtue." These expressions simply have to be understood in their contexts. *Xuan ming*, for example, is not just "profoundly dark," it also means noumenon (see Chan Wing-tsit. *A Source Book in Chinese Philosophy*. Princeton, 1973, p. 788).

[14] "The doorway to all subtleties" here refers to the *Dao* as an all-embracing principle of the myriad things and their endless

changes. Since the *Dao* is the unity of Being-without-form and Being-within-form, it operates at a deeper and more profound level, creating Heaven and Earth, and generating and transforming all things.

Commentary:

Talking about the *Dao*, Lao Zi proclaims first of all that language as an instrument for communication is rather limited in terms of its expressiveness. Thus he concludes that "the *Dao* that can be told is not the constant *Dao*." It is noteworthy that this observation could date back more than 2,500 years. Historically speaking, it has generated a continuous impact on the development of Chinese theories, experiences and artistic creation in general. This can be tesitified to, for instance, such conceptions as "It can be perceived but not communicated," "Words are forgotten when implications are obtained; implications are abandoned when imagery is realized," "All the significance and aura are achieved without writing down a single word," "Try to get hold of the inner spirit and go beyond the external shape," and so on. Hence the notion that any verbal language is limited in expression tends to influence the Chinese way of thinking in general, and that of contemplating artworks in particular. These hidden influences will be further clarified as our scrutiny and discussion of the *Dao De Jing* advance.

In spite of his assertion that "the *Dao* that can be told is not the constant *Dao*," Lao Zi still wrote more than 5,000 words in a poetic form to present his ponderings on and expounding of *Dao* as a key notion in his philosophy. In his book, the *Dao* has always to be understood in its specific context. It contains such categories of meanings as follows:

(1) The proto-material or substance which constitutes the universe;
(2) The potential driving force that creates all things;
(3) The underlying law related to the motion and development of all things; and
(4) The standard or code with which to measure human conduct.

The *Dao* discussed in this chapter has a double (i.e. both metaphysical and physical) significance. It is so subtle and profound that it is indescribable and unnameable in ready-made words or concepts. It functions as the ultimate beginning of Heaven and Earth, and as the original source of all that exists. Thus it enjoys infinite potential and creativity. As a matter of fact, the flourishing and transforming of everything between Heaven and earth merely manifest the continuous working of the *Dao*'s potential.

Being-without-form (*Wu*) and Being-within-form (*You*) signify two aspects of the *Dao* in Lao Zi's conception. They are employed to demonstrate a dynamic process of the *Dao* from its invisible state toward its visible state. The interrelationship between these two facets of the *Dao* seems analogically identical to that between name and object or thinking and being.

Some scholars tend to use such terms as "Non-being" for the Daoist concept of *Wu* and "Being" for *You*. However, it is imperative to point out that this "Non-being" in Lao Zi's thought does not mean "nothing." It is something real both in existence and in effect. It reflects the invisible or hidden character of the *Dao* as a kind of potentiality beyond our sensory perception. We assume that the concept *Wu* is used by Lao Zi to describe the state of the *Dao* before it achieves its actuality or manifestation—*You*. It is also worth stressing that the Daoist concept of "Being" is far different in meaning from the "Being" as expounded and articulated by Parmenides and Plato. This is just because the former, as the manifestation of the *Dao*, can be concrete and many, whereas the latter, owing to its transcendental trait, remains abstract and one. In short, the former is said to be a material kind of being, while the latter is an immaterial kind of being.

According to Chen Guying, the *Wu* as such is full of inexhaustible and yet invisible vitality; and correspondingly it contains endless and numerous *You*. The interaction between *Wu* and *You* exemplifies the dynamic process of the metaphysical *Dao* engendering Heaven, earth and the myriad things. As a consequence of this process, this seemingly transcendental *Dao* comes into close contact with the concrete or phenomenal world, thus making the *Dao* anything but a hanging-in-the-air or empty concept. That is why the *Dao* is deemed to feature a "double character" which is somewhat metaphysical on the one hand, and physical on the other.

As has been observed, this chapter attempts to expalin the *Dao* as something beyond verbal expression and conceptualization, and that it is the origin of Heaven, earth and all things. Many people are under the impression that Lao Zi's statement is deliberately mystifying when he calls the *Dao* "deeper and more profound." In fact what Lao Zi is stressing here is that the *Dao*, as the fountain-head of the myriad things, lies in the deep and profound origin of the universe. Although Lao Zi proclaimed that the *Dao* can not be named or told, he actually offers certain ideas about the *Dao*, for instance, its indescribability and unnameability. Later in Chapter 25 (DDJ) Lao Zi further explains the essence of the *Dao* by admitting that something existed prior to Heaven and earth, but whatever it was, it was in a state of chaos. As there was no name available for it, he called it the *Dao* for the sake of convenience. According to scholars of the *Dao De Jing*, Lao Zi made use of many terms from the empirical world to interpret the *Dao*, but then discarded them one after another. This indicates that empirical terms are inadequate for defining the *Dao*, and underlines the subtlety of the *Dao*.

It should be mentioned in passing that the concept of the *Dao* as fashioned by Lao Zi may have been derived from two pre-existing terms known as *tian dao* (the *Dao* of Heaven) and *tian ming* (Heavenly destiny or fate), which seem to be associated with primitive shamanism. Lao Zi's concept of the *Dao* may have been a substitution for a supernatural being or God used worshiped by the ancient Chinese. This may explain why religion in the sense of a supernaturally sanctioned order has been virtually absent from the Chinese cultural context ever since.

A sound comprehension of the *Dao*, as we may claim, can hardly be attained without examining the writings of another notable Daoist, Zhuang Zi (Chuang Tzu). Unlike his predecessor Lao Zi, who expressed his vision of the *Dao* in a highly condensed poetic and aphoristic style, Zhuang Zi strove to explain the *Dao* along with its characteristics by means of metaphoric prose. For instance, he comments on the nature of the *Dao* through the voice of a person he names *wu shi* (meaning "no beginning"). In Knowledge Wandered North (i.e. Chapter 22, "Zhi Bei You," in *The Book of Zhuang Zi*), he says, "The *Dao* cannot be heard; if heard, it is not the *Dao*. The *Dao* cannot be seen; if seen, it is not the *Dao*. The *Dao* cannot be described; if described, it is not the *Dao*. That which gives form to the formed is itself formless. Can you understand that? There is no name that fits the *Dao*." This is obviously an extended explication of the *Dao* as it appears in Chapter 14 (DDJ). Then, the subsequent remarks made by Zhuang Zi can be counted as a further explanation. That is, "He who, when asked about the *Dao*, gives an answer does not understand the *Dao*. And he who asks about the *Dao* has not really heard the *Dao* explained. The *Dao* is not to be asked about, and even if it is asked about, there can be no answer. To ask about what cannot be asked about is to ask for the sky (meaning to try to measure the immeasurable, such as the sky). To answer what cannot be answered is to try to split hairs. If the hair-splitter waits for the sky-asker, they neither will ever perceive the time and space that surround them on the outside, or understand the Great Beginning that is within. Such men can never trek across the Kunlun Mountains, (the most formidable range of mountains known to the ancient Chinese and often cited metaphorically to suggest something sublime or extremely difficult), can never wander in the Great Void (meaning here the universe)" (see Burton Watson. *The Complete Works of Chuang Tzu*, pp. 243-244). This obviously stresses the subtlety, profundity and indescribability of the *Dao*. However, it goes to extremes by absolutizing and mystifying these features of the *Dao*. If the above is the case, how could it be possible for Lao Zi to write more than 5,000 words about it? And correspondingly, how could it be possible for Daoism as a school of thought to have lodged itself permanently as a quintessential part of Chinese philosophy? Many philosophers, both Chinese and non-Chinese, have ever since endeavored to comprehend the nature and character of the *Dao*. It is intriguing to notice that another answer to the question as to what the nature of the *Dao* is offered in Zhuang Zi's work (Chapter 23, "*Geng-sang Chu*"). It goes like this: "It (the Dao) comes from no source; it goes back in through no aperture. It has reality, yet there is no place where it resides. It has duration, yet no beginning or end. Something emerges, though through no aperture—this refers to the fact that it has reality. It has reality, yet there is no place where it resides—this refers to the dimension of space. It has duration, but no beginning or end—this refers to the dimension of time. There is life, there is death, there is a coming out, there is a going back in—yet in the coming out and going back its form is never seen. This is called the Heavenly Gate (*tian men*). The Heavenly Gate is non-being. The myriad things come forth from non-being. Being cannot create being out of being; inevitably it must come forth from non-being. Non-being is absolute non-being, and it is here that the sage hides himself" (see Burton Watson, Ibid., pp. 256-257). The term Heavenly Gate (*tian men*) means similar to the version "doorway to all subtleties" in Chapter 1 (DDJ). The "sage" mentioned in this context appears somewhat like a god, yet a humanized god similar to a divine person. Additionally, the English rendering of *You* as "being" should be "Being-within-form," and that of *Wu* as "non-being" should be "Being-without-form." For Zhuang Zi's consideration of the two categories corresponds to Lao Zi's in this context.

1.2 (Chapter 4)

The *Dao* is empty (like a bowl),[1]
Its usefulness can never be exhausted.[2]
The *Dao* is bottomless (like a valley),
Perhaps the ancestor of all things.[3]
Invisible or formless, it appears non-existing
But actually it exists.[4]
I don't know whose child it is at all.[5]
It seems to have even preceded the Lord.[6]

Annotations:

[1] The original expression dao chong is rendered in English as "The *Dao* is empty." Being empty, as one of the essential

features of the *Dao*, can be said to have a twofold implication: Firstly, it signifies the essence or substance of the *Dao* as being indescribable and profound; Secondly, it means the subtle way the *Dao* functions inexhaustibly in itself. In chapters 5 and 11 Lao Zi goes on to offer a series of concrete examples to illustrate the functioning of the *Dao*.

[2] The Chinese term *bu ying* is rendered in English as "being inexhaustible." As has been discerned already, the *Dao* is the origin of all things, and the principle of all principles. Dynamic and productive, the *Dao* is the fountain head of the world and all its contents. Hence it is used without being exhausted, and functions without stopping.

[3] The Chinese phrase *wan wu zhi zong* is rendered in English as "the ancestor of all things." This implies that the *Dao* as an all-principle is powerful enough to produce and determine all things.

[4] The expression *zhan xi* literally means "what depth or profundity!" It is employed here to suggest the nature of the *Dao*. In plain words, it describes the *Dao* metaphorically as something hidden, potential and submerged.

[5] The rhetorical question *shui zhi zi* (whose child?) indicates the existence of the *Dao* which does know any ancestor or anything preceding itself. This tells us that the *Dao* is the initiator of all.

[6] The conclusion *xiang di zhi xian* (The *Dao* seems to have existed before the Lord) marks a very important concept in Lao Zi's philosophy. The Chinese word di refers to the Lord or God of Heaven, who would then be supposed to create and dominate all things under the sky. As far as natural religion is concerned, both primitive and ancient men used to believe that all their surroundings and all phenomena were derived from the magic power of the Lord of Heaven. In other words, the Lord of Heaven was the ancestor of all things. Nevertheless, Lao Zi's concept of the *Dao* is of something prior to the Lord of Heaven. This conclusion turns out to be incorporated in the description of the *Dao* in Chapter 1 (DDJ).

Commentary:

The *Dao* is depicted in this chapter as being empty. The state of being empty as such reflects the quality and substance of the *Dao*. Needless to say, the empty form which the *Dao* features does not mean that there is nothing inside it. The *Dao* actually embodies a dynamic potentiality and creative agency, which produces innumerable things and functions as such inexhaustably.

Though being empty and above form, the *Dao* is seen in Lao Zi's mind's eye to be far more essential and fundamental than the Lord of Heaven, who had previously been respected as the ancestor of all things in the universe. According to Lao Zi, the *Dao*, instead of the Lord, remains the origin of heaven and earth or the mother of the myriad things.

It is interesting to notice that in Christian culture the Lord or God has been all along worshiped as the creator of all things. This was also true of the natural religion of ancient China. That is to say, primitive men were convinced that everything was invented and controlled by a supernatural being, which was simply due to the fact that they were unable to understand or explain the natural elements and phenomena which they confronted. Their acquired knowledge of the external world was at a very low level. Hence they tended to ascribe whatever happened beyond their understanding to the divine power of the supernatural being they imagined to exist. There were therefore the notions of *di* (Lord), *shen* (deity), and *gui* (spirits). As time went by, people became skeptical about those notions, and in the era directly preceding Lao Zi's, the philosopher Zi Chan once remarked that "The Heavenly Way is remote while the human Way is close by." This sounds like a skeptical stance on the fancied existence of the Lord of Heaven. It seems to recommend a kind of not-to-bother attitude toward the Lord who was supposed to govern the Heavenly Way, and it reminds us of what Confucius said later about *gui* (spirits) and *shen* (divine beings) in a widely-quoted statement as follows: "We should respect but keep aloof from the spirits and divine beings."

According to Prof. Ren Jiyu, there is no negation or denial of the existence of the Lord to be found in such Chinese classics as

The Book of Poetry (*Shi Jing*), *The Book of Zuo Zhuan* (*Zuo Zhuan*), and *Conversations of the States* (*Guo Yu*). In fact, nobody dared then to underestimate the supreme position of the Lord, despite a few complaints about injustice in the aspects of reward and punishment which were believed to be blindly exercised by the Lord. It was rather paradoxical that they would hate and curse the Lord of Heaven in view of the injustice they encountered, and still confess to Him when wronged or ill-treated or harried into natural disasters, etc. In striking contrast, Lao Zi's perception of the *Dao* instead of the Lord turns out to be overarching, for it works as the ancestor of all things. The uniqueness of his philosophy also lies in his perspective that Heaven and earth in his terminology represent the sky and the ground.

1.3 (Chapter 6)

The spirit of the valley is immortal.[1]
 It is called the subtle and profound female.[2]
The gate of the subtle and profound female
 Is the root of Heaven and Earth.
It is continuous and everlasting,
 With a utility never exhausted.

Annotations:

[1] The Chinese expression *gu shen* (the spirit of the valley) is rather ambiguous. Some Lao Zi scholars (e.g. Yan Fu and Chen Guying) assume that *gu* signifies a state of emptiness or virtuousness, and *shen* endless and unpredictable changes. Some other scholars (e.g. Ai Qi) think that *gu shen* refers to a deity in an empty or virtuous state. I personally agree with Mr. Sha Shaohai, who believes that *gu shen* implies another name for the *Dao* itself. In the above context, the lines "The spirit of the valley (*gu shen*) is immortal. It is called the subtle and profound female" suggest the metaphorical characteristics of the eternal *Dao*. Such an interpretation appears to correspond to Lao Zi's system of thought as a whole.

[2] The term *xuan pin* (subtle and profound female) indicates in its concrete sense the female sex organ as a metaphor for the *Dao*, which is subtle, deep and mysteriously productive. It is

worth noting that people in ancient times used to revere what they thought was the magic power contained inside the female organ. This kind of reverence or worship is clearly reflected and expressed in primitive rock paintings and carvings. Nowadays people would probably laugh or jeer at a primitive painting or sculpture portraying the female sex organ in an exaggerated fashion. But we should put ourselves in the position of our ancestors in terms of their primitive cognitive dimension, for that kind of exaggerated manifestation in art denotes some form of natural religious feeling and significance.

Commentary:

This chapter again describes the magical productivity of the *Dao*. It is noticeable that Lao Zi uses the term *shen* (spirits) in a casual manner and in a pantheistic sense. In contrast, the notion of *shen* (divine beings) carries somewhat of a religious meaning in both Confucianism and Moism. It should be kept in mind that *gu shen* (valley spirit) has, as it were, nothing to do with any form of spiritual or divine beings in the above context. It factually refers to the most wonderful *Dao* featuring vacuity or emptiness, subtlety and constancy.

In addition, the metaphor *xuan pin* (subtle and profound female organ) for the *Dao* is employed several times in the *Dao De Jing*. It symbolizes the invisible power or potentiality of the *Dao* that produces all beings. The metaphor as such is largely derived from the worship of the female organ for its productiveness and mysteriousness by people in antiquity. The expression, "The gate of the subtle and profound female is the root of heaven and earth," is obviously identical in meaning to that describing the *Dao* as follows: "Being-without-form is the beginning of Heaven and earth," and as "Being-within-form is the mother of all things."

1.4 (Chapter 25)

There was something undifferentiated and all-embracing,[1]
Which existed before Heaven and Earth.[2]
Soundless and formless,[3] it depends on nothing external
And stays inexhaustible.[4]

It operates with a circular motion
  And remains inextinguishable.[5]
It may be considered the mother of all things under Heaven.[6]
I do not know its name, and hence call it the *Dao* far-fetchedly.[7]
If forced to give it another name, I shall call it the Great.[8]
The Great is boundless and thus functioning everywhere.
It is functioning everywhere and thus becoming far-reaching.[9]
It is becoming far-reaching and thus returning to the original point.[10]
Therefore the *Dao* is great.
Heaven is great.
Earth is great.
And Man is also great.
There are four great things in the universe,[11]
  And Man is one of them.[12]

Man follows the way of Earth.[13]
Earth follows the way of Heaven.[14]
Heaven follows the way of the *Dao*.[15]
And the *Dao* follows the way of spontaneity.[16]

Annotations:

[1] This "something undifferentiated and all-embracing" means the *Dao* in its original and somewhat chaotic state, in which all things were undiscriminating and encompassed as a whole.

[2] The most fundamental aspect of the *Dao* lies in Lao Zi's preoccupation with the *Dao* as preceding Heaven and earth and all things as well. This notion as such is repeated in the chapters that have been discussed previously.

[3] He Shanggong renders *ji* as "soundless" and *liao* as "formless," implying "incorporeal." These characteristics of the *Dao* are also explicated in such chapters as 14 and 35 (DDJ).

[4] This quality of the *Dao* indicates its independence and

everlastingness. The *Dao* itself serves as something equivalent to the Western concept of the absolute and eternity, provided that the religious sense of the latter is excluded.

[5] As for the Chinese expression *zhou xing* in this context there are two representative interpretations: One says that the *Dao* functions everywhere and permeates or internally determines everything, according to Heshang Gong and Wang Bi; the other assumes that *Dao* is always on the move, as though operating in a circular motion, and hence it never stops or vanishes. When taking into account the movement of the *Dao* (i.e. "becoming far-reaching and thus returning to the original point," and "Reversion is the movement of *Dao*," see Ch. 40, DDJ), we are inclined to agree with the second explanation.

[6] Lao Zi was preoccupied with the idea that the *Dao* is creative, productive and the originator of the whole universe. His preferred employment of "mother" (*mu*) as a metaphor for the *Dao* well confirms his stress on the feminine or Yin aspect of Chinese culture in general.

[7] Lao Zi himself could hardly think of an available or exact term to represent what he was pondering in his mind. However, he really desired to introduce a new concept of his own in order to break down the theistic conventionalism characterized by the imagined pre-existence of a personified Lord of Heaven as the creator of all things. Hence he offered a series of tentative alternatives along with further relevant descriptions.

[8] The concept of "Great" (*da*) is used here to emphasize the all-powerfulness and all-embracingness of the *Dao* as the origin of all things.

[9] These descriptions of the *Dao* that functions everywhere and becomes far-reaching are intended to demonstrate the greatness, powerfulness and potentiality, as well as the perpetual movement of the *Dao*.

[10] The word *fan* here is an ambiguous term which seems to contain two key meanings: becoming the opposite, and returning to its root or original point. Lao zi uses it to denote both, forming a dialectical interrelationship between the things involved. See our later discussion of the movement of the *Dao*, especially

Chapter 40 (DDJ).

[11] It is proclaimed in the *Yi Zhuan* (*Commentary on The Book of Changes*) that there are three great things in the universe —including Heaven, earth and man. Yet there is one more great thing according to Lao Zi, that is, the *Dao*, which is considered to be the origin of all things.

[12] It is historically significant to rank man as one of the four great things in the universe. By so doing, man is placed in a position to make a proper use of the other three and even all things. As a matter of fact, the values of all other things would be reduced to nil if not for the existence of man.

[13] The earth is tranquil and selfless, serving as an inexhaustible source of life. Man lives on the earth, where he can get what he needs to keep himself alive providing he works in harmony with its underlying law. Therefore, Wang Bi believes that man can be secured and assured so long as he acts upon the law of the earth.

[14] The Heaven (i.e. the sky) is high, endless and boundless. It may do favors to all things below without asking for anything in return. The earth does the same, but this is only possible when it follows the way of Heaven.

[15] This statement means that Heaven can maintain its completeness and fulfil its accomplishments only if it bases itself on the law of the *Dao*.

[16] Some Lao Zi scholars misinterpret *dao fa zi ran* as "The *Dao* follows Nature." The *Dao* is essentially natural and originally the mother of Heaven and earth, as another name for nature. When observing the working and essence of the *Dao* as a whole throughout this book, we tend to conclude that *zi ran* signifies "spontaneity" or "naturalness" in the context concerned. We therefore have rendered it thus: "The *Dao* follows the way of spontaneity" (of the way of naturalness). The way of spontaneity refers to *Dao* itself in practice.

Commentary:

This chapter attempts to expound, first of all, the existence of the *Dao*, featuring independence, ever-lastingness, pre-existence, absoluteness, etc. It is, in short, the master producer of all things in the universe, and the ultimate law to be followed.

Secondly, it exposes some fundamental qualities of the *Dao* —soundlessness, formlessness, greatness and boundlessness... All these imply that the *Dao* embraces and affects all things, even though it is not directly observable or tangible.

Thirdly, it illustrates the dynamic character of the *Dao* and its law of movement. The dialectic between its becoming its opposite and returning to its original point is highly enlightening and instructive with regard to the development and transition of world affairs in general and social matters in particular. As for this aspect, a detailed formulation will be supplied later, when we come to Chapter 40.

Last but not least, it highlights the *Dao* as the way of spontaneity or naturalness, and as the ultimate law to be followed by Heaven, earth and man. The *Dao* can be regarded as the hidden measure or determinant of all things in the world.

2 The Features of the *Dao*

Lao Zi's concept of the *Dao* serves as the keystone for his philosophy in general, and the starting point for his doctrine of the origin of the universe in particular. With high awareness of the duality of the *Dao*, known as Being-without-form (*wu*) and Being-within-form (*you*), Lao Zi exposes such general features as the *Dao*'s imagelessness, soundlessness, formlessness, vagueness and elusiveness with regard to "the inseparable One" (i.e. the *Dao*) and their interactions with their counterparts. In this section we concentrate on chapters 14, 35, 21 and 5 (DDJ).

2.1 (Chapter 14)

You look at it but can not see it;
  It is called the imageless.[1]
You listen to it but can not hear it;
  It is called the soundless.[2]
You touch it but can not find it;
  It is called the formless.[3]

These three cannot be further inquired into
For they are the inseparable One.[4]
The One is not bright when it is up,
And not dark when it is down.[5]
Infinite and indistinct, it cannot be named,
Thus reverting to a state of non-thingness.[6]

This is called shape without shape,
Or image without image.
It is also called the Vague and the Elusive.[7]
When meeting it, you cannot see its head,
When following it, you cannot see its back.[8]
Hold on to the *Dao* of old,[9]
In order to harness present things.
From this you may know the primeval beginning.
This is called the law of the *Dao*.[10]

Annotations:

[1], [2] and [3] The three features of the *Dao*—"the imageless," "the soundless" and "the formless"—all reflect the subtlety of the *Dao* that goes beyond sensory perception.

[4] "The inseparable One" stands for the *Dao* itself. Similar terms are used in other contexts, for instance, in chapters 22 and 39 (DDJ).

[5] The *Dao* is not manifest or visible when it is without form; it becomes clear and perceivable when it is within form as a result of its transformation into *De*. These two aspects of the *Dao*, like the two sides of one coin, turn out to be identical to Being-without-form and Being-within-form, as discussed previously with regard to the nature of the *Dao* (see Part I, 1.1).

[6] The term "non-thingness" (*wu*) does not mean that there is nothing at all. Instead it denotes a state of being without shape. In other words, it refers to the existence of the *Dao* as the origin of all things, remaining unavailable to the senses.

[7] The Chinese concept *hu huang* is translated as "the Vague and Elusive," as two essential characteristics of the *Dao*. They themselves are compatible with the indescribable and unname-

able features of the *Dao* (see Part I, 2.3).

[8] This illustrates the greatness of the *Dao* as it exists everywhere or embraces all things as a whole.

[9]"The *Dao* of old" (gu zhi dao) indicates that the existence of the *Dao* precedes those of all things in the world.

[10] Apart from this interpretation, rendered as "the law of the *Dao*," the original expression *dao ji* is also explained by some Lao Zi scholars as "the foundation of the *Dao*."

Commentary:

As depicted in this chapter, the general features of the *Dao* appear to be multi-dimensional. They can be generalized as imagelessness, soundlessness, formlessness, shapelessness, vagueness, elusiveness and namelessness. They are also described as invisibility, intangibility, indescribability and infinity. Yet, by scrutinizing them we may tentatively conclude that the *Dao* as such is characterized by these two fundamental aspects: firstly, the non-observable aspect as implied in "it is not bright when it is up;" that is to say, the *Dao* is invisible and indistinct when it is above form. It simply transcends the empirical and corporeal things as well as physical perception. Secondly, the observable aspect as suggested in "it is not dark when it is down." This means that the *Dao* becomes clear and manifest when it is within form, or, in other words, when it is transformed into *De*. These two aspects, non-observable and observable, could be likened somewhat to the metaphysical and physical concepts of occidental philosophy.

The greatness or infinite nature of the *Dao* is revealed in the passage, "When meeting it, you cannot see its head; when following it, you cannot see its back." This seems at the first sight to be somewhat mystic. However, with regard to the non-observable aspect of the *Dao*, this shows that the *Dao* is omnipotential.

The significance of the expression "the *Dao* of old" lies in its efficacy in "harnessing present things." This indicates that the *Dao* in the abstract stays potentially in power for ever. When followed by man, it helps him to tackle social issues, and govern a state or even the whole world in the most effective and peaceful manner. That is why Lao Zi strongly recommends people to "hold on to it." It is worth mentioning that such characteristics of the *Dao* (or the inseparable One) described as "the Vague and Elusive" (*hu huang*) happen to be rather perplexing to many readers of Lao Zi because they are so nebulous. Nevertheless, those who have a sound knowledge of Chinese *qigong* would be most likely to understand the wording employed by Lao Zi. *Qigong* is known as a system of exercises involving deep breathing, with the purpose of spiritual nourishment and personal cultivation. It has been practiced in China since ancient times. Similar to meditation, it attempts to purify the mind and free it from inner tensions and desires, and even external temptations. Lao Zi advocates getting rid of selfishness and desires in order to return to the primeval state of simplicity and tranquility. Thus I assume that the practical approach to doing so is implicitly associated with *qigong*.

2.2 (Chapter 35)

If you hold fast to the great image,[1]
  All the people under Heaven will come to you.[2]
They will come and do no harm to each other,
  But will all enjoy comfort, peace and health.
Music and dainties can make passers-by tarry,[3]
  While the *Dao*, if spoken out, is insipid and tasteless.
Being looked at, it is imperceptible.
Being listened to, it is inaudible.
Being utilized, it is inexhaustible.

Annotations:

[1] The term *da xiang* (great image) refers to "the image without image," according to Lin Xiyi's annotation. It is in fact used for the *Dao* or the manifestation of the *Dao* which functions as the guiding principle for a successful ruler in a social sense.

[2] The expression that "All the people...will come to you" is meant to demonstrate people's willingness to become citizens of a state under the leadership of a ruler who has embraced the *Dao*.

[3] "Music and dainties" (*yue yu er*) are apparently as appealing to the senses and desires of the people as the notions of

"humanity and the rites" advocated by Confucianism in Lao Zi's time.

Commentary:

This chapter intends to exemplify the engaging power of the *Dao* in a social sense. A wise ruler who grasps the *Dao* is likely to win the hearts of all the people under Heaven; he will be then in a position to bring peace and order to the whole world, and accordingly make people feel secure, protected and happy. Unlike tangible and attractive things, for instance, "music and dainties" or "humanity and the rites" as fine-sounding promises, the *Dao* is insipid and tasteless, imperceptible and inaudible as well as inexhaustible. Nevertheless, it is capable of making the world peaceful and its people content.

2.3 (Chapter 21)

The character of the great *De*[1]
Follows from the *Dao* alone.[2]
What is called the *Dao*
Appears elusive and vague.[3]
Vague and elusive as it is,
There is the image in it.
Elusive and vague as it is,
There is the real in it.
Profound and obscure as it is,
There is the essence in it.[4]
The essence is very concrete
And contains the proof inside itself.[5]
From the present back to the past[6]
Its name continues to ever last,
By which alone we may know the beginning of all things.[7]
How do I know their beginning as such?
Only through this.[8]

Annotations:

[1] The original term *kong de* is translated into "the great De" and is regarded as the manifestation of the *Dao*. Its quality is

all-embracing, operating in everything and everywhere.

[2] *De* works in conformity with the *Dao* simply because the former is the manifestation of the latter. Since they are interrelated, one must bear in mind the fact that the *Dao* is something like an omni-principle underlying all things, whereas *De* exhibits the power of the *Dao* through observable functions.

[3] Such characteristics of the *Dao* as those of being "vague and elusive" correspond to its indescribability and intangibility, and therein lies the wellspring of the "coming-into-being" of all things.

[4] In the *Inner Chapters of the Guang Zi* (*Guang Zi Nei Pian*) *jing* is interpreted as *qi*, and regarded as the origin of energy. It is rendered here in English as "the essence," according to Yan Ling-feng and Chan Wing-tsit, who annotates that "The word *ching* (the Chinese pronunciation of which is *jing*) also means intelligence, spirit or life force. "The essence" may be supposed to imply "the essential *qi* as the origin of vital energy or the life force."

[5] "The proof" refers to the fact that "the essence" as the vital *qi* or energy is working constantly, even though it is invisible.

[6] A number of the *Dao De Jing* versions (e.g. those of Heshang Gong and Wang Bi) present the expression *zi jin ji gu* (from the present back to the past) the other way round as *zi gu ji jin* (from the past till the present). My correction follows the Mawangdui version of the *Dao De Jing*. In addition, another reason is that the Chinese word gu rhymes with *fu* at the end of the subsequent expression *yi yue zhong fu* (we may know the beginning of all things).

[7] The word *fu* can be literally identified with the word for father in the ancient Chinese language. It is actually used here to denote *shi* (beginning). "The beginning of all things" is equivalent to "the origin of the universe."

[8] Here "this" stands for the *Dao* or "the nature of the *Dao*."

Commentary:

Depicted in this chapter are the basic characteristics of the *Dao*, which is incorporeal and invisible, but exists and functions in reality. Hence it is out of the *Dao*'s state of being "vague and elusive" that the myriad things are created and produced. Simply put, the *Dao* is the originator of the universe and the myriad things in it. This interpretation allows us an overview of how things come into being. During this process "the real" (as things) may be traced back to "the image." And "the image" may be traced back to "the essence"—and "the essence" can then be traced back to the *Dao* as a state of being "vague and elusive."

In addition, this chapter exposes the character of *De* as the manifestation of the *Dao*. The former represents in a tangible mode the latter as an omni-principle or omni-determinant underlying all things. The concept of *De* is manifold: It can be the attributes of things in the physical world; it can be the functions of affairs in the human society; and, above all, it can be the virtue of a person in the course of the cultivation of his or her personality. The interrelationship between the *Dao* and *De* is interdependent to the extent that the former, as the source of creation, is shown or made known through the latter. It is unlike the relationship between the Platonic "Idea" (eidos) of a bed and "the bed" itself, for the simple reason that the former is absolute while the latter is the mimesis or shadow of the former. There is obviously a kind of ranking involved here in the sense of different values.

It should be pointed out that the historical development of Chinese artistic theory finds a permanent and permeable influence originating in the following statements: "Elusive and vague as it is, there is the image in it. Vague and elusive as it is, there is the real in it. Profound and obscure as it is, there is the essence in it." The *Dao* of Chinese art is said to lie in the ideal and achievement of *yi jing* (the highest reach of the artistic spirit), which is largely determined by *xiang wai zhi xiang* (image beyond form) and *yun wai zhi zhi* (significance beyond charm), among other characteristics. Take Chinese landscape painting (freehand brushwork painting in particular) for example: It always places the stress on the realization of *yi jing* and *shen si* (spirit-alikeness). Thus the Chinese artist tends to care far less than his occidental counterpart for perspective as a technique to produce three-dimensionality and life likeness as a result of elaborate imitation; rather, he pays much more attention to creating a vivid touch to convey the spirit, meanwhile using form to show the spirit as well. That is why Chinese freehand brush-work painting is often characterized by spontaneous expression and bold outline instead of an authentically identifiable form or object. It would be relevant and instructive to make a reference to the following reference in Chapter 14: "It is called shape without shape or image without object. It is also called a state of being vague and elusive."

2.4 (Chapter 5)

Heaven and Earth are not humane.[1]
They regard all things as straw dogs.[2]
The sage is not humane.[3]
He regards all people as straw dogs.
The space between Heaven and Earth is like a bellows, isn't it?[4]
While vacuous, it is never exhaustible.
When active, it turns out even more.
(To talk too much will surely lead to a quick demise.[5]
Hence, it is better to keep to tranquility.)[6]

Annotations:

[1] Heaven and earth appear as physical and natural existences. They follow the way of spontaneity inasmuch as they have no preferences for anything in the world. They let all things be what they are or let them go through a natural cycle, for instance, the change and replacement of the four seasons, the life and death of human beings, the appearance and disappearance of plants, the shift of day and night, so on and so forth. By this statement Lao Zi attempts to explain the fact that Heaven and earth have no such feelings, emotions, affections, likes or dislikes as human beings do.

[2] The Chinese term *chu gou* (straw dogs) refers to straw images of dogs used as sacrificial offerings at ceremonies such as those for worshiping Heaven or praying for rain. After the ceremonies they were discarded as worthless. "Straw dogs" serves as a metaphor, suggesting that Heaven and earth show no sympa-

thy for anything or anybody. They themselves stick to the way of nature, and also let all others hold to the way of naturalness so as to preserve their respective selves or egos. This obviously corresponds to Lao Zi's conception that "Man follows the way of earth; earth follows the way of Heaven; Heaven follows the way of the *Dao*; and the *Dao* follows the way of spontaneity."

[3] "The sage is not humane." This is equal to saying that the sage, alike Heaven and earth, has no preference for or benevolence toward anything or anybody, but simply follows the way of naturalness without being pretentious or imposing. This type of sage is the Daoist (Taoist) sage, different from the Confucianist sage and pursuing great humanity for all instead of limited humanity for a few. He seems to be equivalent to the "man that follows the way of earth" as recommended by Lao Zi.

[4] Talking about the universe, Lao Zi exhibits his individual insight and striking imagination. As a result, he likens the vast space between Heaven and earth to a bellows, which is characterized with such features as emptiness, productiveness and inexhaustibility. The image itself is fresh, individual and impressive, well exemplifying the style of Lao Zi as a poetic philosopher or philosophical poet.

[5] By "To talk too much" (*duo yan*) is meant too many political orders, monarchical decrees, secular moral lessons, etc. The Chinese word *shu* can be understood as *su*, rendered in English as "soon" or "quickly." The sentence means that if a state coerces its subjects, perhaps by issuing too many orders or instructions, it will surely find itself running counter to its goals and speed up its demise. As a matter of fact, an efficient government does not have to issue a plethora of rules, regulations or laws. It has been proved historically that the more the official orders that emanate from the government, the less effective they are and the swifter the decline of the prestige of the government. Such a situation leads to a government that only has the ability to issue political orders, and lacks the ability to carry them out.

[6] Contained in many editions of the *Dao De Jing* is the expression *bu ru shou zhong*, which has been translated into English as "holding on to the mean" by Mr. Robert G. Henricks,

or rendered literally as "keep to the center" by Prof. Chan Wing-tsit. These renditions are rather misleading because they tend to make the reader conceive this notion from a Confucianist standpoint. Lao Zi scholars such as Yan Lingfeng and Chen Guying assume that the Chinese word *zhong* (center or the mean) may be a printing error or misspelling of *chong* (empty or vacuous). Other scholars tend to agree that the term *zhong* (center) might stand for the center of a bellows, which is empty or void inside. In addition, scholars like Ma Shulun and Gao Heng proclaim that the last two lines ("To talk too much will surely lead to a quick demise. Hence it is better to keep to tranquility.") do not fit into the context at all. That is why Prof. Gu Ji inserts them in the original Chapter 9 (DDJ). No matter which is the case, we reckon that the concept of *zhong* is characterized by such features as emptiness and inexhaustibility, having nothing to do with the doctrine of the mean as conceived Confucianist terminology.

Commentary:

In this chapter Lao Zi seems to focus on discussing the inhumanity of Heaven, earth and the sage, and the character of the *Dao*. Yet, by reading between the lines one can discover that Lao Zi's philosophy of take-no-action is part and parcel of his whole exposition. The inhumanity of and emptiness between Heaven and earth can well be seen as the extension of his principal idea of take-no-action. Heaven and earth follow the way of naturalness without taking arbitrary action. Yet, they incessantly generate one thing after another. Similarly, the sage conforms to the way of naturalness without taking action, yet he enables people to maintain their genuine selves and become what they should be. The counterpart of "take-no-action" is "take-action," of which "too much talk" (i.e. too many political orders or decrees) is a concrete example in the aspect of government. Then what would happen in the end if "take-action" of this kind were taken? It would be nothing but a quickened failure or death. Therefore Lao Zi reckons that "It is better to keep to tranquility," which is offered as conclusive advice.

It is noteworthy that Zhuang Zi recommends a kind of great or perfect humanity in contrast to inhumanity in general. He holds that Heaven and earth that possess Great Beauty remain silent (*tian di you da mei er bu yan*). The Chinese character *mei* can mean both "beauty" in an aesthetic sense and "good" in an ethical sense. When it is employed to suggest the latter, it is equivalent in meaning to "humanity." Hence a statement of Zhuang Zi implies that Heaven and earth have Great Humanity but never show it off. As a consequence of following the way of Heaven and earth, "the (Daoist) sage, in his conduct of war, might destroy a country without losing the hearts of the people. His benefits might extend to ten thousand generations without being a lover of man" (Cf. "The Great and Venerable Teacher" in *The Book of Zhuang Zi*). This is simply because Zhuang Zi maintains that "he who purposely manifests affection is not a man of humanity" (Ibid.) since "great humanity is not purposely affectionate" and "does not accomplish its object" if "constantly exercised" (Cf. "On Making All Things Equal" in *The Book of Zhuang Zi*). It is due to this belief that the Daoist sage "tears all things into pieces, yet he is not righteous. His blessing reaches all generations, yet he is not humane. He is more ancient than the highest antiquity, yet he is not old. He covers Heaven, supports earth and fashions the various forms of all things, yet he is not skillful. In him I make an excursion" (Cf. "The Great and Venerable Teacher"). The "excursion" is definitely of a free and easy type aimed at nourishing one's spiritual life and developing one's personal independence. It is through this "excursion," according to Zhuang Zi, that one would be able to realize that great humanity which is free from both affection and manifestation. It is at this stage that one would be close to the attainment of the *Dao*.

As for the simile 'bellows' (*tuo yue*) used by Lao Zi for the space between Heaven and earth, it can be viewed as a symbol of the *Dao* in terms of its characteristics, such as emptiness and inexhaustibility. It is noteworthy that Zhuang Zi employs the metaphor "the store of nature" (*tian fu*) to suggest the potentiality of the *Dao*. "The store," he proclaims, "when things are put in it, is not full; when things are taken out, it is not empty" (Cf. "On Making All Things Equal"). The function of "the store" easily reminds us of "the valley" as described by Lao Zi. It is deep and bottomless, serving as the source of all things. What is inside can never be used up precisely because it is able to accommodate as well as generate everything.

3 The Movement of the *Dao*

The motion of the *Dao* is reckoned as having a dialectical character that reflects the growth, change and decline of all things in a developmental cycle. The idea associated with "reversion" (*fan*), if not absolutized as it is by Lao Zi, can still have a valid message even judged from a modern perspective. Here we focus on Chapter 40 (DDJ).

3.1 (Chapter 40)

Reversion is the movement of the *Dao*.[1]
Weakness is the function of the *Dao*.[2]
All things under Heaven come from Being-within-form.[3]
And Being-within-form comes from Being-without-form.[4]

Annotations:

[1] The concept of *fan* (reversion) contains a similar meaning in this context as it does in Chapter 25 (*da yue shi*, *shi yue yuan*, *yuan yue fan*—The great is boundless and thus functioning everywhere. It is functioning everywhere and thus becoming far-reaching. It is becoming far-reaching and thus returning to the original point). In addition, it is used here to signify a dynamic and circular movement of the *Dao* according to such contemporary Lao Zi scholars as Gao Heng and Chen Guying.

[2] The term *ruo* (weakness) is ambiguous as well. There are so far a number of interpretations of this, of which we cite three key ones as follows: firstly, it is supposed to denote the function of the *Dao* that exemplifies itself through the soft and weak; secondly, the function of the *Dao* lies in helping all things grow and become complete naturally without any imposing force or

pressure; and finally, the function of the *Dao* displays itself by the dialectical fact that the soft and weak are to overcome the hard and strong as is expressed by Lao Zi in *rou rou sheng gang qiang*. I am inclined to agree with the third interpretation since it corresponds to Lao Zi's philosophy of *shou rou* (keep to the soft and weak) as a whole.

[3] The Chinese character *you* is rendered here as Being-within-form identical in meaning with the same concept figuratively described as "the mother of all things" (*wan wu zhi mu*) in Chapter 1 (DDJ).

[4] The notion of *wu* (Being-without-form) means the same as it does in Chapter 1. It implies the original state of the *Dao*, which is characterized by invisibility and yet with initiative potentiality.

Commentary:

Brief and concise as it is, this chapter is strikingly rich in connotations. It is generally concluded that Lao Zi exposes his dialectical concept of the *Dao* in terms of its movement and function, which in turn comes to be a law of change and transformation from one side to its opposite.

According to observations by Che Zai, Chen Guying and others, "reversion" (*fan*) refers to a kind of interrelation between opposites in one sense, and in another sense, a kind of return to the root known as the unity of opposites. The former conveys the meaning of being opposite while the latter, the meaning of transformation and change. We think that the movement of the *Dao* in such a manner of "reversion," may be well symbolized by the tai ji, in which the two forces known as *Yin* and *Yang* are always in motion, interdepending and interacting at the same time. The generalization that "reversion is the movement of the *Dao*" can be seen as a refined version of what is said about the *Dao* in Chapter 25 (see Annotations [1] above). It is noticeable throughout human history that things (i.e. a nation, culture, economic strength, political power etc.) are doomed to roll downhill once they reach their acme. This indicates that they tend to reverse to their opposites in an ever-changing process. If we give due consideration to our surroundings, for example, the changes detected in plants and the stages experienced in the life cycle, we may collect sufficient evidence to justify the dialectical movement of the *Dao*. It is schematically interesting to quote a well-known Chinese saying from *The Book of the Hou Han Period* (*Hou Han Shu*: Huang Qiong Zhuan): "Things that are too high fall down easily; things that are too white stain easily; songs that are too pretentious have few listeners; reputations that are too lofty often fall short of reality" (Cf. *Chinese Maxims*, p. 129). All these possibilities seem to be in conformity with the Chinese conception of "Inevitable reversal of the extreme" (*wu ji bi fan*).

It is worth pointing out that Lao Zi, even though emphasizing the opposing interrelationship between things and the significant role of their transaction or transformation, ultimately focuses on the idea of returning to the root as the final destination for all things. For it is right there in his ideal that absolute stillness, tranquility or state of take-no-action will be realized and actualized, and accordingly all the conflicts and antitheses in the world will draw to an end.

The statement, "Weakness is the function of the *Dao*" is in fact a further justification of the foregoing assertion that "Reversion is the movement of the *Dao*." Lao Zi's philosophy features a preference for "cleaving to the soft and weak" (*shou ruo*). He often uses *shui* (water) as an image when illustrating the overwhelming power of "the soft and weak." It is helpful for gaining a better understanding of this notion if we approach it with reference to his discussion in Chapter 78 (*tian xia zhi ruo mo guo yu shui, er gong jian qiang zhe mo zhi neng xian*....—Nothing under Heaven is softer and weaker than water, and yet nothing can compare with it in attacking the hard and strong....).

However, one should be aware of the problematic aspect of Lao Zi's confirmation that the soft and weak is bound to conquer the hard and strong. This is largely due to his absolutization of the former by cutting it off from actual and varying circumstances or conditions in both subjective and objective dimensions.

Also offered in this chapter is a generalized explication of how all things "under-the-sky" come into being. It is here once again that Lao Zi traces the origin of the universe. Both Being-within-form and Being-without-form are different names for the *Dao*, and are likened to the two sides of the same coin. In short, the expression in this context is a modified as well as a condensed one of the ideas presented in Chapter 1 (see Part I, 1.1).

4 The *Dao* and the Myriad Things

Lao Zi holds the view that the *Dao* is the omni-principle of all individual principles. Thus the *Dao* produces all things; and likewise all things develop from the *Dao*. The interactions and interrelations between the *Dao* and the myriad things are in fact the extension of his theory about the ultimate origin and coming into being of the universe, the process of which is historically significant due to its connection with the way of thought and world view of the ancient Chinese. And the function of the *Dao* in general can still find its traces and influences deep in the psycho-cultural structure of the Chinese people today. To be chiefly discussed in this section are chapters 42, 32, 34, and 39 (DDJ).

4.1 (Chapter 42)

The *Dao* produces the One.[1]
The One turns into the Two.[2]
The Two give rise to the Three.[3]
The Three bring forth the myriad of things.
The myriad things contain Yin and Yang as vital forces,
Which achieve harmony through their interactions.[4]

Annotations:

[1] "The One" here stands for the Whole as the Ultimate Origin of Heaven and Earth. It is allegorically perceived as the chaos of the universe where everything stayed in an original state of entirety or without discrimination in between. It can be said to be another name for the *Dao* as the beginning of all things. It is thus used repeatedly by Lao Zi in chapters 10, 22 and 39, etc. In Chinese language "the One" also features absolute uniqueness and unity as well, which are in turn aspects of the *Dao*.

[2] "The Two" refer to two vital forces known as *Yin* and *Yang*. A further rendering of *Yin* and *Yang may* be as two essential kinds of *qi* (variously described as matter, energy, vital breath, power, etc.) that oppose and complement each other. The ancient Chinese people in general and thinkers in particular believed that all things were produced as a result of their interactions or complementary interrelations. The concepts of *Yin* and *Yang* carry a much wider sense in different contexts.

[3] "The Three" are usually supposed to be a well-balanced type of *qi* which results from the interactions between *Yin* and *Yang*. "The three" are interpreted as three types of *qi* owing to the interactions of *Yin* and *Yang*: In the first type the *Yin qi* overwhelms the *Yang qi* (*yin sheng zhi qi*), whereas in the second type the opposite happens and the *Yang qi* overwhelms the *Yin qi* (*yang sheng zhi qi*); and the third type then is what is above-described as well-balanced—both the *Yin qi* and *Yang qi* form into a harmonious realm.

This description seems to me to correspond to the general-characteristics of all things in reality that may well be illustrated via a continuum; that is, some go to extremes while others are slotted into places between the two ends of the continuum.

[4] The Chinese word *chong* is used here as a verb, meaning the interacting and dynamic relationship between the *Yin qi* and *Yang qi*, which then lead to the harmony of the substances. But Fung Yu-lan assumes that *chong qi* is another kind of *qi* encompassing the *Yin qi* and *Yang qi* within itself. It is similar to "the One" or the *Dao* in this context.

Commentary:

This chapter discusses the originality of the *Dao* and the coming into being of the world. The concepts of "the One," "the Two" and "the Three" are symbolically employed to explicate the process of how the *Dao* produces the myriad things. This process is characterized with a transition or evolution from the simple to the complex, which happens to reflect the development of all creation. In short, this discourse of Lao Zi is typical of his doctrine concerning the origin and coming into being of the universe which all trace back to *Dao*.

4.2 (Chapter 32)

The *Dao* is eternal and has no name.[1]
Though it is simple and seems minute,[2]
Nothing under Heaven can subordinate it.
If kings and lords were able to maintain it,
All people would submit to them spontaneously.[3]
Heaven and Earth unite to drip sweet dew,
Without the command of men, it drips evenly over all.[4]
Once a system comes into being,
Names are instituted.[5]
Once names are instituted,
One has to know where and when to stop.
It is by knowing where and when to stop
That one can be free from danger.
Everything under Heaven is embraced by the *Dao*,
Just like every river or stream running into the sea.[6]

Annotations:

[1] This proposition is, with regard to the eternity and unnameability as basic features of the *Dao*, first put forth by Lao Zi in Chapter 1 (see Part I, 1.1) and then repeated in other chapters, such as 37 and 41 apart from this one.

[2] The Chinese word *pu* means "simple" or "simplicity," which is characteristic of the *Dao*, according to Lao Zi. The word *xiao* literally means "minute" but actually implies the ability of the *Dao* to permeate everything. Lao Zi describes the *Dao* as both *da* (great) and *xiao* (minute):

The former refers to the all-embracing and omnipotence of the *Dao* (see chapters 25, 14, in Part I, 1.4 and 2.1), and the latter to the all-permeating capacity of the *Dao* as presented in this context. A relevant interpretation is found in Zhuang Zi's remark that "the *Dao* is great without an outside and minute without an inside."

[3] This exemplifies the appealing gravity of the *Dao* that makes people willing to be the subjects of the kings and lords who have applied the *Dao* to their government.

[4] The Chinese expression *gan lu* sometimes means "sweet dew" and sometimes "rainfall." It falls upon all things alike without preference precisely because of the action of the *Dao*.

[5] Historically speaking, once *zhi* (social system) was formulated and established, the naming and ranking of the people and things were launched. This resulted in a variety of names, titles, roles and positions.

[6] The *Dao* is figuratively likened to "the sea" because of its vastness and boundlessness, which can accommodate "every river or stream." In other words, the *Dao* itself can be boundless enough to accommodate all under Heaven.

Commentary:

Lao Zi makes simplicity a characteristic of the *Dao*, which in turn reflects the primitiveness of the *Dao*. This notion in fact signifies the way of spontaneity (i.e. naturalness) and take-no-action. If a leader can hold on to it and put it into social practice, they are sure to win the people over and govern the country in peace.

Da (great) and *xiao* (minute) are obviously antithetic in common sense, but implicitly interrelated in the functioning of the *Dao*, somewhat similar to *you* (being-within-form) and *wu* (being-without-form) as two complementary aspects of the *Dao*. Both *da* and *xiao* are abstract terms. The former suggests that the *Dao* embraces and covers all to the extent that "when meeting it, you cannot see its head; while following it, you cannot see its back." This implies that the *Dao* is invisible and formless to the extent that it permeates and determines everything everywhere.

The "sweet dew" as a product of the *Dao* "drips evenly over all." This demonstrates that the *Dao* treats all things alike, as though it embodies a spirit of equality. Modest and accommodating, the *Dao* receives all things in the way the sea conceives every river and stream. Hence it becomes boundless and inexhaustible. Even so, it does not claim any glory for itself but lets things be what they are. The parabolic depiction of the *Dao* through the image of the sea also carries the message that the *Dao* renews itself due to its receptiveness. It is something that remains open to all for ever. This is compatibly true of Lao Zi's philosophical system that always produces new and instructive findings whenever it is read and reread.

As mentioned in this chapter, Lao Zi reminds people of the importance of knowing where and when to stop once names were assigned. This in fact advises people to bridle their desires and to be contented with what they have. Otherwise they may get into trouble in the course of their hot and blind pursuit of external temptations.

4.3 (Chapter 34)

The great *Dao* flows everywhere.[1]
It may go left, it may go right.
All things rely on it for existence,
  And never does it turn away from them.[2]
When it accomplishes its work,
  It does not claim credit for itself.[3]
It preserves and nourishes all things,
  But it does not claim to be master over them.[4]
Thus it may be called the minute.[5]
All things come to it as to their home,
  Yet it does not act as their master.
Hence it may be called the great.[6]
This is always the case with the sage
  Who is able to achieve his greatness
  Just because he himself never strives to be great.

Annotations:

[1] The original line reads *da dao si xi*. The word *si* used to represent one of the water systems called *Si Shui* in ancient China which were located in present-day Henan Province. It is utilized in this context to mean the flowing of a river with rich water resources. This implies that the *Dao* goes everywhere and exists in everything.

[2], [3] and [4] These features represent the nature of the *Dao*, which works so naturally without any purpose.

[5] and [6] See the discussion of *da* (great) and *xiao* (minute) in the foregoing chapter.

Commentary:

This chapter exposes the function of the *Dao* related to the development of all things. The function as such lies in "following spontaneity" and features a kind of selflessness. According to Lao Zi, the *Dao* is the mother or creator of all things in the world. However, what it does is help them grow and become what they are, never claiming the accomplishments for itself and never attempting to dominate anything at all. Therefore the *Dao* appears as a generous giver or nurturer in respect of all its surroundings.

The sage lauded above is always the Daoist type. He follows the *Dao* as the ultimate example and approaches it through his action upon it. The reason why he is "able to achieve his greatness" can be multi-fold. Since "he never strives himself to be great," he makes no distinction between "the great" (*da*) and "the minute" (*xiao*). Since he makes no distinction between "the great" and "the minute," he acts without any preference or calculation in favor of this or that. This approach is in the long run positive in the accumulation of achievements on the one hand, and on the other, it serves to free him from being a "tall poppy" that is liable to be cut down in a competitive world.

4.4 (Chapter 39)

Of those in the past that obtained the One:[1]
Heaven obtained the One and became clear;
The earth obtained the One and became tranquil;
The Gods obtained the One and became divine;
The Valleys obtained the One and became full;
All things obtained the One, and became alive and kept growing;
Kings and lords obtained the One and the world became peaceful.

Taking this to its logical conclusion we may say:
If Heaven had not thus become clear,
It would soon have cracked;
If the earth had not thus become tranquil,

It would soon have broken apart;
If the Gods had not thus become divine,
They would soon have perished;
If the valleys had not thus become full,
They would soon have dried up;
If all things had not thus become alive and kept growing,
They would soon have become extinct;
If kings and lords had not thus become honorable and noble,
They would soon have toppled and fallen.[2]

It is always the case[3]
That the noble takes the humble as its root
And the high takes the low as its base.
Hence kings and lords call themselves
The orphaned, the solitary or the unworthy.
This is regarding the humble as the root of the noble,
Is it not?
People disdain the "orphaned," "solitary" or "unworthy."
And yet kings and lords call themselves by these terms.
Therefore the highest honor needs no flattering.
Thus with everything—
Sometimes it may increase when decreased,
And sometimes it may decrease when increased.[4]
For this reason—
They desire not to dazzle and glitter like jade,
But to remain firm and plain like stone.[5]

Annotations:

[1] "The One" is again used as a substitute for the *Dao*.

[2] This is a good-natured warning offered to leaders in general. According to Lao Zi, rulers are likely to be overthrown and discarded if they fail to conduct state affairs by means of reliable policies and a noble spirit. Or, in modern terms, a government of whatever kind is apt to deteriorate if it happens to grow power-oriented instead of people-oriented.

[3] The last stanza seems to be contextually disassociated from the first two stanzas since it noticeably deals with the virtue of

modesty on the part of nobles and leaders.

[4] This idea reflects the dialectic aspect of Lao Zi's philosophy as rgards decrease and increase. Subjectively speaking, when one is modest enough to lower himself as if decreasing his self-esteem, he is liable to be easily accepted by others and win their respect and thus enjoys a kind of increase of his self-esteem, and vice versa. Objectively speaking, things may well suffer from a decrease when they are meant to be increased; they are likely to have an increase when they are deliberately to be decreased. it seems that Lao Zi intends to encourage people in general and rulers in particular to be modest and humble in one sense, and expect things to develop in a natural way in another sense.

[5] By this statement is meant that the sage ruler in Lao Zi's mind should remain modest, plain and simple instead of being arrogant, self-important or showy. Otherwise his self-image as well as authority will be subject to decrease rather than increase.

Commentary:

In this chapter one may well observe that gods even became divine with the help of the One, as another term for the *Dao* in Lao Zi's philosophical discourse. It is also noticeable in the context that gods appear to be liable to the same fate as the other things cited if they fail to attain the One (i.e. the *Dao*). In addition, gods are ranked (possibly in chronological order) after Heaven and earth. This may indicate that Heaven and earth precede gods in Lao Zi's perspective (see Chapter 4 for an identical case in which the Lord or God is filed after the *Dao*). Nevertheless, they are all in the same boat by virtue of the fact that they are likely to vanish if unable to grasp the *Dao*. In plain language, no matter what they may be (e.g. Heaven, earth, gods, valleys, the myriad things, kings, marquises, etc.), they are doomed to failure or extinction if they betray the *Dao*, or in other words, if they deviate from the *Dao*. This is precisely because the *Dao* in Lao Zi's mind functions as the source of all energies and the origin of all things. It does not merely generate everything, but determines everything. Hence it seems to work as a frame of reference for all. In comparing the *Dao* with gods, the former stays primary and original, whereas the latter are secondary and derivative.

The Chinese concept of *yi* is rendered into English as the capitalised "One." It can be detected in Lao Zi book that this term usually carries a two-fold sense as follows: Firstly, it stands for the *Dao* as an omni-potent power that produces as well as underlies all things in the world; secondly, it refers to *qi* known as the vital force in chaos or the primitive matter coming out of the *Dao*.

With regard to the relationship between the *Dao* and all things, as explicated by Lao Zi, his absolutization of the *Dao* turns out to be rather problematic and arbitrary. He dogmatically asserts that the destiny of all things lies in the palm of the *Dao* without any exception or condition. This seems to be somewhat misleading because it leaves no room for the initiatives and variables in existence.

According to Prof. Ren Jiyu, "This chapter begins with mention of the universality and importance of the *Dao* from which Heaven, earth, spirits, valleys, rulers and the myriad things come. It goes on to argue that without the *Dao*, or going contrary to it, all things from Heaven and earth to kings and princes will exist no more.

Epithets such as *gu* (the orphaned), *gua* (the solitary) and *bu gu* (the unworthy) by which rulers used to refer to themselves in the olden days are by no means flattering terms, but through such derogatory names they could actually make their majesty and nobility obvious and salient. Lao Zi preaches that one should not be at the front, nor be the last, so that one can be free from danger. (see Ren Jiyu. *A Taoist Classic*: *The Book of Lao Zi*, p. 58.)

5 The *Dao* of Heaven and the *Dao* of Man

The distinction between the *Dao* of Heaven and the *Dao* of man is set out in striking contrast. The former demonstrates itself as a symbol of naturalness, selflessness and equality in a virtuous sense, according to Lao Zi. It is therefore viewed as a measurement or frame of reference for the latter. The respective services and differences of the two are basically reflected in chapters 77 and 79 (DDJ).

5.1 (Chapter 77)

Does not the *Dao* of Heaven resemble the drawing of a bow?[1]
When the string is taut, press it down.
When it is low, raise it up.
When it is excessive, reduce it.
When it is insufficient, supplement it.
The *Dao* of Heaven reduces whatever is excessive
And supplements whatever is insufficient.[2]
The *Dao* of man does the opposite.
It reduces the insufficient
And adds more to the excessive.[3]
Who is able to have a surplus to offer to the world?
Only the one who has the *Dao*.[4]
The sage does not accumulate for himself.
The more he shares with others, the more he possesses.[5]
The more he gives to others, the richer he becomes.[6]
The *Dao* of Heaven benefits all things and causes no harm.
The *Dao* of the sage acts for others but never competes with them.[7]

Annotations:

[1] By "the drawing of a bow" is allegorically meant the process of drawing a bow while aiming an arrow at a target, which requires some form of corresponding adjustment described subsequently by Lao Zi as an illustration of how the *Dao* of Heaven works.

[2] Lao Zi arrives at this conclusion from his intuitive as well as empirical observation of natural phenomena. In his eyes, such phenomena as the transition from day to night, the succession of the four seasons, the life and death of all beings, etc., appear to feature paradoxically antithesis and identity, in addition to equality and unity. Viewed from an immediate perspective, they all seem to be naturally or spontaneously what they are instead of

being forced or dominated by an external power. Hence Lao Zi generalizes this situation as the *Dao* of Heaven for it corresponds to his philosophy of "following the way of spontaneity" and "take-no-action."

[3] This depiction intends to show in contrast how the *Dao* of man as a social law or code of human conduct functions and differs from the *Dao* of Heaven. This can be traced back to the historical background of the Spring and Autumn Period (722-481 B.C.) in ancient China, when conflicts and clashes were of frequent occurrence, actually stirred up by desires for more land, power and property. Therefore, Lao Zi reveals the *Dao* of man from a critical viewpoint.

[4] In many Chinese versions of the *Dao De Jing*, the rest of the text from this line onward is included in Chapter 81. We rearrange it here according to a contextual analysis and with regard to possible misplacement of the separable bamboo slips on which the original texts were inscribed in Lao Zi's day (also see Gu Di and Zhou Ying. *Lao Zi Tong*, pp. 594-604). The "*Dao*" (in quotes) refers to the *Dao* of Heaven as advocated by Lao Zi.

[5] and [6] These are the virtues of a man in harmony with the *Dao* or a Daoist sage. They could be relevantly comprehended from the actual effects of moral education and universal love.

[7] "The *Dao* of the sage" is a contextual rendering of the Chinese term *sheng ren zhi dao* in the original text.

Commentary:

From his intuitive and empirical observation of natural phenomena, such as transition and change, motion and replacement, growth and decline, rise and fall, and life and death of all beings in the world, Lao Zi comes to the conclusion that there is such a thing as the *Dao* of Heaven, which, in its fuction as the law of nature, lets all things be what they can be and become what they can become without imposing, dominating or taking any action. The *Dao* of Heaven is the heart of the universe that keeps all things in balance.

Then, based on his observation of the reality of that chaotic competitive and harsh age in which he lived, rent by repeated clashes and wars between the kingdoms, Lao Zi delineates the *Dao* of man as a general social law or code of human conduct similar to the "law of the jungle." He postulates rapacity and possessiveness as fundamental characteristics of the *Dao* of man.

According to Lao Zi's thought as a whole, the *Dao* of man itself, if practiced and worshiped, will surely excite insatiable greed and desires for more possessions; this will inevitably lead to exploitation of man by man and class discrimination, and then to inter-personal clashes and struggles, and eventually to social disorder and suffering.... In a word, it is conducive to a vicious circle. That is why it must be condemned and abandoned.

In respect of the negative aspects of the *Dao* of man, Lao Zi recommends the *Dao* of Heaven not only as a counterbalance to the former, but also as an ultimate criterien or frame of reference owing to its great virtues such as the universal heart of selflessness and the noble spirit of balancing all things under the sky. That is to say, the *Dao* of Heaven must be imitated, followed and acted upon by man. This is merely Lao Zi's ideal as a result of his deep concern and sympathy for the tragic human condition in his era. However, good-intentioned as it may be, this recommendation is after all wishful thinking, in striking contrast with hard reality. But this does not necessarily mean that his wish and hope have no instructive message with regard to the keenly competitive and frustratingly problematic society in which we live nowadays.

It is worth mentioning in passing that the *Dao* of Heaven is also reflected in Lao Zi's remark that "Heaven and earth unite to drop sweet dew which falls evenly over all things without being forced." All this could be seen as the source of the notion of egalitarianism or equal division of property which is deeply rooted in the mentality of the Chinese people. Hence, when its merit is appreciated from a sociological perspective (i.e. social stability), its demerits should not be neglected in an economic sense (i.e. economic development). The Chinese are fairly sensitive and highly conscious of the painstaking efforts made so far to break up the "iron rice bowl" (i.e. "equal pay for unequal work") in the course of China's current program of social and economic reform.

The sage is "the only one who has the *Dao*" (i.e. the *Dao* of Heaven) and is characterized by such virtues as universal love and generosity, as usually embodied in an absolute giver. The *Dao* of the sage is the realization or extension of the *Dao* of Heaven in society or human praxis, according to Lao Zi. All men alike are encouraged not simply to admire the virtues of the Daoist sage, but to model their personal development upon him via practical activities. Only by so doing, according to Lao Zi, can society be at peace and people enjoy harmonious relations.

5.2 (Chapter 79)

To reconcile two sides in deep hatred
  Is surely to leave some hatred behind.
If one returns good for evil,[1]
  How can this be taken as a proper solution?[2]
Therefore the sage keeps the counterfoil of the tally,[3]
  Yet he does not demand payment of the debt.
The virtuous man is as kind and generous as the tally keeper
  While the non-virtuous is as harsh and calculating as a tax collector.
The *Dao* of Heaven has no preference.[4]
It is constantly with the good man.[5]

Annotations:

[1] This expression has been transposed here from Chapter 63 (DDJ) upon the recomendation of Yan Lingfeng and Gu Di, as a result of their textual analyses and philological studies.

[2] This "solution" refers to the situation implied in the first two lines. Lao Zi holds that its efficacy is so limited that it can not clear away all the hatred involved. He therefore proposes that one returns good for evil so as to make it impossible for hatred to recur.

[3] The Chinese term *zuo qi* is translated as "the counterfoil of the tally." The latter was something like a modern contract. It used to be inscribed on a piece of wood and cut into two parts held respectively by the two parties concerned. They would be produced later as proof or evidence concerning the contract.

[4] "The *Dao* of Heaven has no preference" (*tian dao wu qin*)

is close in meaning to "Heaven and earth are not humane"—They both suggest the essence of the *Dao* which treats all things alike.

[5] "The good man" (*shan ren*) here stands for the virtuous man who has achieved the *Dao* and its potency (*De*). In the final analysis, he can be identified as the Daoist sage.

Commentary:

That "one should return good for evil" is well-noted as Lao Zi's idealized solution to hatred. It is offered to the people in general and the ruler in particular. In a totalitarian country the government tends to be power-oriented and property-hungry. Thus it is apt to apply policies of heavy taxation and severe punishments. This brings about an accumulation of complaints and growth of hatred which may some day explode as suddenly as a dormant volcano. The history of China is full of instances of revolts and rebellions caused by such policies.

The *Dao* of Heaven that "has no preferences" is clearly personified by Lao Zi. It serves as a mirror of Daoist naturalism in contrast to the *Dao* of man, which has preferences. The former is positive while the latter is negative; likewise, he (e.g. a ruler) who practices the former is "kind and generous" to the extent that he will be supported and beloved, whereas he (e.g. a ruler) who adopts the latter is "harsh and calculating" to the extent that he will be cursed and overthrown. This is moral lesson still valid for leaders nowadays.

Part II *De* as the Manifestation of the *Dao*

In Lao Zi's mind, both the *Dao* and *De* exist and function everywhere. Generally speaking, one is invisible while the other is observable. The interaction between the two can be likened to that between Being-without-form (*wu*) and Being-within-form (*you*). As a matter of fact, *De* is seen as the manifestation or concretization of the *Dao*. That is why they are analogically said to be the two sides of one coin. The transformation from the *Dao* into *De* is highly necessary, for it (the *Dao*) would be otherwise a disembodied idea and possibly lose its existential rationale. The qualities of *De* actually embody the potentiality or potency of the *Dao* itself.

6 From the *Dao* into *De*

Both the *Dao* and *De* have a variety of interpretations, which are presented in pairs. They include, for example, the Way and its Power, the Way and its Potency, the Way and the Walk on the Way, the all-embracing first principle for all things and the principle underlying each individual thing, the omni-determinant of all beings and its manifestation, etc. No matter what they may be, there is an interaction between them and a transformation from one into the other. This topic is explored with particular reference to chapters 51 and 38 (DDJ).

6.1 (Chapter 51)

The *Dao* begets all beings,
  And *De* fosters them.[1]
Substance gives them physical forms,
  And the environment completes them.[2]
Therefore all beings venerate the *Dao* and honor *De*.

As for the veneration of the *Dao* and the honoring of *De*,
It is not out of obedience to any orders;
It comes spontaneously due to their naturalness.[3]
Hence the *Dao* begets all beings,
And *De* fosters them, rears them and develops them,
Matures them and makes them bear fruit,
Protects them and helps them breed.
To produce them without taking possession of them,
To raise them without vaunting this as its own merit,
And to nourish them without controlling them,
This is called Profound *De*.[4]

Annotations:

[1] This marks out the respective sphere of the *Dao* and *De* in view of the origin and becoming of all things.

[2] "Environment" is a translation of the Chinese word *shi*, and connotes chiefly living, geographical, regional and climatic conditions. It is also interpreted as the natural force derived from the change of the seasons (according to Heshang Gong), the potential power underlying each individual thing, or the dynamic state lying in opposites like *Yin* and *Yang* and their interaction in all beings.

[3] This implies that everything develops naturally and becomes what it is without being imposed by any external force. The *Dao* and *De* are there to help them in the way of doing nothing, or to just let them be what they can be.

[4] The lines (which start with "To produce them without taking possession of them...") were misplaced in Chapter 10 in some versions of the *Dao De Jing*. The original term *xuan de* is rendered as "Profound *De*" suggesting the depth, profundity, selflessness and transcendence of *De* as such. It in fact exhibits the function and potency of the *Dao*.

Commentary:

Lao Zi maintains consistently that the *Dao* is the origin of all things with regard to their coming into being and development. This helps to round out Lao Zi's notion that the *Dao* came into being first of all, and accordingly features a sharp contrast with the Christian culture which is grounded on the personification of God as the Creator of the universe.

This chapter reconfirms Lao Zi's idea that the *Dao* begets all beings alike without being observed since it works in the way of "taking-no-action." Then *De* as its potency and manifestation fosters all beings through observable means such as "substance," "environment," "sweet dew," selfless protection, etc. By scrutinising the text one can discern that the growth of all beings undergoes such a process as generalized as follows: The *Dao* produces them all first, and then it stays inherent in them and transforms itself into *De* as the principle of each individual being; in accordance with this *De* all beings develop with individual characteristics; finally they grow mature or become what they are with the help of their surroundings or environment (see Chen Guying. *Lao Zi Zhuyi Ji Pingjie*, p. 246). During this process as a whole, the *Dao* is venerated and *De* honored for they both follow the way of spontaneity or naturalness when begetting and fostering all beings. In other words, they are free from any imposing action or force such that they let things be what they can be, or become what they can become. They themselves serve as natural laws allowing all things to develop without any consciousness or purposefulness. Thus they are characterized by great virtue in giving birth and freedom, and offering help and protection selflessly to all beings. In the end they do not claim any merit for what they have done, through which the existence and development of all creation is rendered possible.

The "Profound *De*" as the manifestation of the *Dao* can well be termed the "Great Virtue" which transcends mundane values entangled with desires, conflicts, competitions, gains and losses, etc. This "Profound *De*" can be looked upon as a special part of the nature of the *Dao*, and a general spirit embodied in Lao Zi's philosophizing. In addition, it is, explicitly or implicitly, advocated and advised to be adopted and conducted by mankind as a solution to the crisis of the human condition. If we review Lao Zi's thought in respect of the problems which we confront nowadays, we may find it still instructive to a great extent.

6.2 (Chapter 38)

The man of superior *De* is not conscious of his *De*,[1]
And in this way he really possesses *De*.
The man of inferior *De* never loses sight of his *De*,[2]
And in this way he has no true *De*.
The man of superior *De* takes no action
And thus nothing will be left undone.[3]
The man of inferior *De* takes action
And thus something will be left undone.[4]
The man of superior humanity takes action
And so acts without purpose.[5]
The man of superior righteousness takes action
And so acts on purpose.[6]
The man of superior propriety takes action,
And when people do not respond to it,
He will stretch out his arms and force them to comply.[7]

Therefore, only when the *Dao* is lost does *De* disappear.[8]
Only when *De* is lost does humanity appear.
Only when humanity is lost does righteousness appear.
Only when righteousness is lost does propriety appear.

Now propriety is a superficial expression of loyalty and faithfulness,
And the beginning of disorder.
The man of foreknowledge has but the flower of the *Dao*[9]
And this is the beginning of ignorance.
Hence the great man dwells in the thick instead of the thin.[10]
He dwells in the fruit instead of the flower.[11]
Therefore he rejects the latter and accepts the former.[12]

Annotations:

[1] The word *De* generally means "virtue" in both an ethical and social sense. It also denotes the realization and acquisition of the *Dao*. The cultivation of *De* varies in degree from person to person. "The man of superior *De*" follows the way of spontaneity

and never displays his *De* in any pretentious form. That is why he is "not conscious of his *De*" but "really possesses *De*."

[2] "The man of inferior *De*," on the contrary, tends to hold a superficial attitude toward the *Dao*. He therefore keeps to the exhibitionist form of *De*. That is why he "never loses sight of his *De*" (i.e. so-called *De* in the eyes of Lao Zi) but has "no true *De*."

[3] This rendering is made according to the Chinese phrase *shang de wu wei er wu bu wei* (see Gu Di and Zhou Ying. *Lao Zi Tong*, pp. 269-274) instead of *shang de wu wei er wu yi wei* ("The man of superior *De* takes no action and so acts without purpose.") in other versions of the *Dao De Jing*.

[4] Since "the man of inferior *De*" takes action on purpose, he is apt to encounter the probabilities of either success or failure in fulfilling his objectives.

[5] The expression "without purpose" means "without the purpose of exhibiting humanity or of extracting from others any responses or favors in return."

[6] The expression "on purpose" means "action(s) deliberately taken to exhibit righteousness and expect in return something favorable."

[7] The statement implies how the advocators of propriety act against the principle of take-no-action or the way of naturalness by imposing their value systems upon others. Lao Zi's critique of this "action" is discernably sarcastic.

[8] This version is based on the rearranged line gu shi dao er shi de according to the philological studies done by Gu Di and Zhou Ying (see *Lao Zi Tong*, pp. 278-279). This is based on the fact that the *Dao* and *De* are inseparable, like the two sides of the same coin. The interrelation between the *Dao* and *De* as such threads through Lao Zi's philosophical system. Yet, in some editions of the *Dao De Jing* the line goes: *gu shi dao er hou de* ("Only when the *Dao* is lost does *De* arise"), which seems to make a distinction between the *Dao* and *De* in the sense of time sequence on the one hand, and treats *De* as a value paradigm independent of the *Dao* on the other. This seems to be logically problematic with regard to the entirety of Lao Zi's doctrine.

[9] The phrase *dao zhi hua* can be translated literally as "the

flower of the *Dao*" and figuratively as "the ornament of the *Dao*," suggesting the appealing surface or superficial appearance of the *Dao*. It is still far away from "the fruit," i.e. the substantial truth of the *Dao*.

[10] "The great man" stands for the Daoist sage. "The thick" is explained by Heshang Gong as meaning "simplicity, honesty and sincerity." I think "the thick" in this context refers to what is adequate, like the "superior *De*," while "the thin" refers to what is inadequate, like "propriety" (*li*, which also means "rite," "ceremony," "ritual," or "code" as well as "norms" of conduct).

[11] As mentioned above, "the fruit" is figuratively used for the substantial truth of the *Dao*, whereas "the flower" is used for appealing appearance of the *Dao* as is reflected in "superior humanity" (*shang ren*), "superior righteousness" (*shang yi*), etc.

[12] Lao Zi encourages people to approach the "superior *De*" as the truth of the *Dao* rather than the "inferior *De*" as the appearance of the *Dao* involving humanity (*ren*), righteousness (*yi*) and propriety (*li*) all together.

Commentary:

In this chapter Lao Zi presents his hierarchy of values comprising the "superior *De*" and the "inferior *De*" as its two broad categories. The former is highly recommended as the manifestation of the *Dao*. It is characterized by its adhesion to the principle of "take-no-action" or the way of spontaneity. Likewise "the man of superior *De*" is, according to Lao Zi, an ideal personality to be imitated by all walks of life, for he is the one who has attained the genuine *Dao*.

In view of the latter, its elements go downward from "superior humanity," through "superior righteousness" to "superior propriety" which were officially appreciated by the ruling class then and persistently advocated by the *Ru Jia* (which was later developed into "the school of Confucianism") ever since. If considered from Lao Zi's perspective, they all tend to deviate from the way of naturalness and the principle of take-no-action no matter whether or not they aim at self-exhibition and favorable returns. Hence they may show inadequacy in doing this, and weakness in doing that; or worse still, they may be reduced to mere pretentious protocols which restricts their behavior and puts them in mental straitjackets. History has shown that it would be employed, more often than not, by self-seeking people.

Lao Zi expresses his preference for the "superior *De*" for being symbolic of simplicity and sincerity in one sense, and corresponding to his philosophy of taking no imposing action in the other sense. At the same time, he tenders his critique of the "inferior *De*" since it works the other way round. This also reflects his nostalgia for Daoist innocence and plainness, and his anxiety derived from his observation that social instability results from damage to and desertion of the *Dao*, and meanwhile from the propagation and application of other low-brow values such as "humanity" (*ren*), "righteousness" (*yi*), and "propriety" (*li*), etc.

Incidentally, the "fruit" of the *Dao* is plain, true and associated with the "superior *De*," whilst the "flower" of the *Dao* is dazzling, false and connected with the "inferior *De*" as has been described above.

7 The Qualities of *De*

De functions in various domains due to its diversity of qualities. Similarly, it is cultivated and manifested in different ways, which all accord with the criteria of the *Dao*. The figurative depiction of the profundity of *De* as an innocent infant is a rich contribution to one's understanding of the effects of *De*. In this regard, chapters 54 and 55 (DDJ) deserve attention.

7.1 (Chapter 54)

He who is good at building cannot be shaken.[1]
He who is good at holding can lose nothing.[2]
Thus his ancestral sacrifice can pass down
From generation to generation.[3]
When cultivated and exercised in the person,
De will become pure and genuine.
When cultivated and exercised in the family,
De will become full and overflowing.

When cultivated and exercised in the community,
De will become constant and everlasting.
When cultivated and exercised nationwide,
De will become powerful and abundant.
When cultivated and exercised worldwide,
De will become universal and widespread.

Therefore, (by taking it as a standard should we)
Use this person to examine other persons,
Use this family to examine other families,
Use this community to examine other communities,
Use this country to examine other countries,
And use this world to examine other worlds.[4]
How do I know the situation of all things under Heaven?
Precisely by the method above-mentioned.

Annotations:

[1] This is possible (according to Lao Zi), for he builds in terms of the *Dao*.

[2] The same case as with [1].

[3] This indicates the advantage of adhering to *De* as a code of conduct outwardly and as the demonstration of the *Dao* in essence. If people are conscious of its significance when it comes to building and holding things, they will encounter no failure, loss or frustration. Instead, they will enjoy continuity of a positive and constructive kind.

[4] "This world" means the world where *De* as the manifestation of the *Dao* is cultivated and exercised, while "the other world" is the world where *De* is not cultivated or exercised yet. Similarly with "this person" and "other persons," "this family" and "other families," "this community" and "other communities," and "this country" and "other countries" in this context.

Commentary:

This chapter can be understood as a moral teaching Lao Zi offers chiefly to the lords, aristocrats and ruling class in general. They will benefit a great deal providing they act upon the *Dao* themselves and apply it to their conduct of affairs.

De is conceptualized as the manifestation and function of the *Dao*. When fostered and carried out in accordance with the *Dao*, *De* features a wide variety of advantages in myriad realms. Judged respectively from the ethical and social perspectives, for instance, *De* plays a significant part in the virtuous cultivation of the personality, proper regulation of the family, effective organization of the community, stable government of the country and peaceful environment of the world.

It is worth pointing out that some Chinese scholars (e.g. Ren Jiyu) assert that Lao Zi is preoccupied with the interests of the nobility instead of those of the populace. Accordingly, the benefits and advantages provided by *De* are confined to a handful of rulers and aristocrats, since ordinary people in his day could not enjoy the sacrifices of their posterity. This is true to some degree. Yet, a scrutiny of the text in question impresses us that Lao Zi's aim is to radiate the *Dao* and *De* from person to person, from family to family, from community to community, and from country to country, and finally all over the world. Only by so doing can the world be free from disorder, and its people from suffering.

7.2 (Chapter 55)

He who possesses *De* in abundance
  Can be compared to a newborn infant.
Poisonous insects will not sting him.
Fierce brutes will not injure him.
Birds of prey will not attack him.
His bones are weak and his sinews tender,
  But his grasp is firm.
He does not yet know about the intercourse of male and female,
  But his organ is aroused
  For his physical essence is at its height.
He may cry all day without becoming hoarse,
  For his innate harmony is simply perfect.
The essence and harmony as such are natural and constant.
To know this is called being wise.[1]

The desire to multiply life's enjoyments means ill omen.[2]
The mind to employ *qi* excessively suffers fatal stiffness.[3]
Things that have grown strong commence to become old.
This is called "being contrary to the *Dao*."
Whatever is contrary to the *Dao* will soon perish.

Annotations:

[1] Contextual studies inform us that Lao Zi's concept of *ming* (which can be translated literally as "light") means "wise" or "wisdom," while *zhi* means "knowledge" or "learning." This is testified by Lao Zi's notions such as *zhi ren zhe zhi, zi zhi zhe ming* ("He who knows others is learned; he who knows himself is wise." See Chapter 33, DDJ), *shi wei wei ming* ("This is called subtle wisdom." See Chapter 36, Ibid.), etc.

[2] From a Daoist viewpoint, any desire to increase life's enjoyments in a pleasure-seeking manner will surely harm and injure life itself. It is disastrous to add more to life's enjoyments as well as being against the way of spontaneity or naturalness in Lao Zi's thinking.

[3] The Chinese term *qi* here means the physically vital force or energy which preserves life. The excessive use of *qi* will inevitably lead to over-exhaustion and disharmony between Yin and Yang as two kinds of essential and complementary *qi* in the body. The expression "fatal stiffness" implies lack of vitality or physical decline leading to death. This is in line with Lao Zi's conviction that "the hard and stiff are companions of death" (see Ch. 76, DDJ).

Commentary:

In this chapter, as has been observed by Ren Jiyu, "Lao Zi preaches the philosophy of nonaction as an attitude toward life, and teaches people to return to a state of primitive ignorance. He advocates being like an innocent child without desires. This accords with the criteria of the *Dao*, and one can avoid disasters by remaining weak, soft and ignorant, otherwise he will soon perish owing to his opposition to the principle of the *Dao*" (see *A Taoist Classic: The Book of Lao Zi*, p. 75).

Moreover, we assume that Lao Zi figuratively describes his

philosophy of self-preservation in a twofold sense: social and physical. As for the former, it is reflected in the quotation cited above. If viewed from a social dimension, a newborn baby, weak and tender as it is, is free from attack by "poisonous insects," "fierce brutes" and "birds of prey," which are symbolic of evil-natured and cold-blooded savages in society, always ready to cut down those who become prominent. If a person were as ignorant and innocent as an infant without desires, he would exist without threatening the interests of anyone else. Therefore he could avoid jealousy, hatred, and danger; or in other words, he could defend, passively or otherwise, and preserve himself. This well responds to the saying that "ignorance is bliss."

With regard to self-preservation in a physical sense, the fact that a newborn infant is taken as a model by Lao Zi is largely due to the fact that it is filled with vitality and has not lost a single grain of its essential *qi*, or life-force. An innocent child usually lives a natural life, different from adults, who have strong desire and high life-consciousness. Lao Zi believes that "the tender and soft are companions of life," and so is the child. Hence, he who wants to preserve his physical life should follow the living state of infancy. In the final analysis, this state of being embodies the way of naturalness and freedom from desires.

With regard to the material and bodily pleasure-seeking phenomena and related problems that we encounter nowadays, we can profit from Lao Zi's instruction: "The desire to multiply life's enjoyments means ill omen; the mind to employ *qi* excessively suffers fatal stiffness."

Part III The Human Condition in Perspective

Lao Zi lived at a time of frequent warfare, power struggles, greed-ridden materialism, changing values, and so on. Protesting such tragic social reality, he never failed to gain insights into the problems of the human condition and the miseries from which people suffered in his day. Problems and miseries actually come from both outside (the environment) and inside (the ego). Sharp observation allowed Lao Zi to offer solutions to such problems, and many of his ideas are still relevant to the problems people contend with nowadays.

8 On Have-Substance and Have-No-Substance

Distinct from "Being-within-form" and "Being-without-form," as defined in Chapter 1 of the *Dao De Jing* (see Part I, 1.1), "Have-substance" and "Have-no-substance" as a pair of concepts reflect Lao Zi's dialectical thinking in terms of their interaction and complementary relations. Lao Zi seems to infuse more importance into "Have-no-substance" (which means here "the empty space" or "nonexistence" in a physical sense such as the vacancy inside a room, the space inside a utensil or the holes between the spokes of a wheel, etc.) since he believes it is more decisive in the aspects of utility and function. This is consistent with his general principle that "Being-within-form comes from Being-without-form" on the one hand, and his idea of "vacuity" (*xu*) for its receptivity and accommodability on the other. A textual analysis of Chapter 11 serves to illustrate the interrelations between "Have-substance" and "Have-no-substance."

8.1 (Chapter 11)

Thirty spokes are united around the hub to make a wheel,
But it is on the central hole for the axle[1]
That the utility of the chariot depends.
Clay is kneaded to mold a utensil,
But it is on the empty space inside it[2]
That the utility of the utensil depends.
Doors and windows are cut out to form a room,
But it is on the interior vacancy[3]
That the utility of the room depends.
Therefore, Have-substance brings advantage[4]
While Have-no-substance creates utility.[5]

Annotations:

[1], [2] and [3] "The central hole," "the empty space" and "the interior vacancy" are concrete examples used to illustrate the concept of "Have-no-substance" (*wu*). This is often the case with Lao Zi's expression of abstract ideas.

[4] "Have-substance" is the English rendering of Lao Zi's notion of *you* which is in this context different from the concept of 'Being-within-form' (*you*) as presented in Chapter 1 of the *Dao De Jing* (see Part I, 1.1). Although the same Chinese word (*you*) is used, its connotations are far apart. The former carries a physical sense tied to the phenomenal world, whereas the latter has a metaphysical sense related to the production and general principle of all things.

[5] "Have-no-substance" is the English version for Lao Zi's idea of *wu*, which is also distinct from the concept of Being-without-form (*wu*) as has been analyzed in Chapter 1 of the *Dao De Jing* (see Part I, 1.1). The primary discrepancy between them is determined by the fact that the former is something blank or empty in contrast with something concrete around it, while the latter features the essence of the *Dao* that is invisible and intangible to sensory perception. In other words, "Have-no-substance" is what can be approached from a spacial and phenomenal perspective, while Being-without-form is what can be conceived from an abstract or a metaphysical perspective. Under certain circum-

stances, Have-no-substance can be rendered as Have-vacuity.

Commentary:

This chapter intends to demonstrate the dialectical interrelationship between Have-substance and Have-no-substance, or advantage and utility. Lao Zi maintains that these two aspects are seemingly opposite. However, being counterparts, they help complete each other, and therefore remain inseparable and interdependent on each other. Yet, Lao Zi emphasizes the importance of Have-no-substance which he thinks is the more decisive correlative. In view of this tendency, we should be aware of the fact that it is right for Lao Zi to underline the dialectical unity of Have-substance and Have-no-substance with regard to the advantage and utility of a chariot, utensil and room, but wrong (or logically problematic at least) for him to elevate Have-no-substance as an absolute opposite to Have-substance. After all, according to Prof. Fung Yu-lan, Have-no-substance as an empty space in a bowl, cup or house comes into effect as a consequence of the concrete Have-substance.

In most cases we are inclined to focus on the concrete dimension of things, while neglecting or ignoring their discrete aspect. But Lao Zi is observant enough to bring out the hidden utility or functionability of the latter, which often seems to be useless in appearance. His thought-way contains a kind of everlasting significance which may help us to develop an all-sided view on the one hand, and creative thinking on the other.

It is noteworthy that Lao Zi, as a thinker, enjoys sharp observation. He is therefore adept at using specific and familiar examples to illustrate theoretically abstract ideas, thus making his arguments both comprehensible and convincing. A wheel and its central hole, a bow and its empty space, and a room and its interior vacancy are all set side by side in contrast, justifying the interaction between Have-substance and Have-no-substance. This seems to denote a kind of metaphorical sense which helps the reader obtain a better understanding of the function of the *Dao* and its two aspects: Being-within-form and Being-without-form.

Incidentally, the idea that "Have-substance brings advantage while Have-no-substance creates utility" (*you zhi yi wei li*, *wu zhi yi wei yong*) is also influential in other domains, such as Chinese arts. Have-substance (*you*) and Have-no-substance (*wu*) as two different but inseparable categories are closely associated with another pair known as "concretization" (*shi*) and "abstraction" (*xu*), which, it can be assumed, are actually derived from the former. "The mutual production between abstraction and concretization" (*xu shi xiang sheng*) is applied as a general principle to the creation of art genres, including Chinese traditional painting, calligraphy, opera, architecture and horticulture, and even poetry. Further discussion is offered later in Part III, 12.

9 On Take-Action and Take-no-Action

Take-no-action is one of the essential features of the *Dao*. It is virtually a substitute expression for "follow spontaneity" or "the way of naturalness." It is therefore recommended by Lao Zi as the ideal for political and governmental praxis since it facilitates the proper outcome of everything. Conversely, take-action, as an opposite solution, can be misleading and hindering owing to its imposition of purposefulness and limited capacity, as has been discussed previously (see Part II, 6.2). In this connection we will look into chapters 37 and 29 (DDJ).

9.1 (Chapter 37)

The *Dao* invariably takes no action,[1]
And yet there is nothing left undone.
If kings and lords are able to maintain it,[2]
All things will submit to them due to self-transformation.[3]
If, after submission, they have resurging desires to act,
I should subdue them by the nameless simplicity.[4]
When they are subdued by the nameless simplicity,
They will be free of desires.
Being free of desires, they will be tranquil,
And the world will of itself be rectified.

Annotations:

[1] According to Heshang Gong, that "the *Dao* invariably takes no action" is a general principle of the *Dao* itself. The expression "takes no action" is an English rendering of Lao Zi's term *wu wei*, which implies "the way of following spontaneity" (*shun zi ran ye*), according to Wang Bi. It finds its equivalent in the expression "doing nothing" in some versions of the *Dao De Jing*. Yet, one must remember not to approach its meaning from a purely practical dimension. In plain terms it should be understood as "doing nothing of a forceful nature" or "taking no unnecessary or blind action." Hence Chan Wing-tsit explains that "non-action (*wu-wei*) does not literally mean 'inactivity' but rather 'taking no action that is contrary to Nature,' in other words, letting Nature take its own course" (see Chan Wing-tsit. *A Source Book in Chinese Philosophy*, p. 136.).

[2] The pronoun "it" here refers to the *Dao* that "takes no action" and yet there is nothing left undone.

[3] The original phrase *zi hua* is rendered as "self-transformation" indicating that all things come naturally into being and develop spontaneously into what they are due to the role of the *Dao*.

[4] "Nameless simplicity" (*wu ming zhi pu*) is another expression for the *Dao*.

Commentary:

Lao Zi is preoccupied with the human condition with a view to bringing about social stability and peace. Living in a chaotic as well as changing age, he has seen enough of the problems and sufferings caused by political reforms and administrative actions (e.g. decrees aimed at ensuring social order, taxation requirements, and repeated advocacy of such norms as "humanity," "righteousness," and "propriety," etc.) introduced by rulers during his time. Lao Zi opposes all political reforms and governmental actions since they tend to make things worse rather than better. Hence he advises the ruling class to act upon his supreme principle of "take-no-action." In fact, he blames all problems and sufferings on the ruling class, who are filled with desires and ambitions (i.e. power-hungry and achievement-oriented). Such desires and ambitions are to Lao Zi the source of all evils and ills in society. Thus they should be subdued by means of the *Dao*, depicted as the "nameless simplicity." Only by so doing can the ruling class become tranquil; only when they have become tranquil and realized the significance of "take-no-action" will they desist from political intrigue and turbulence. Accordingly, Lao Zi envisages the diminution of all troubles once and for all, and consequently, government will be conducted in the right orbit, and peace and stability will be restored to the world. This idea finds similar expression in chapters 2 and 45 (see Part III, 12.1, 15.5).

The basic components of "take-no-action" as the ultimate solution to all troubles encompass "simplicity," "tranquility" and above all "elimination of desires." These are all meant to encourage the ruling class to create a plain and simple living style for the whole of society, and remain free from any pursuit of personal gain (e.g. power, property, luxury, etc.) or expansion of selfish wants. By acting upon these principles the rulers will benefit, as they will live a peaceful life themselves and meanwhile make it possible for the ruled to live in the same fashion.

Another piece of advice offered to the ruling class lies in the principle of "self-transformation" on the part of the populace in general. That is, the commoners should be left free to develop individually in their own way precisely because anything forced upon them would go astray in the opinion of Lao Zi.

This point is worth emphasizing and clarifying further. That is, by "take-no-action" (*wu wei*) is meant that man should act and react as naturally as possible upon objective principles instead of imposing his subjective judgment or wishful thinking onto other people or external things. So natural are such phenomena, for instance, as the growing of plants in the fields, the swimming of fish in the water, the sprouting of leaves on the willows, the flying of birds in the sky, and the blossoming of flowers in the garden or elsewhere, that man cannot do much about them. He should not bother them or interfere in their way of life. If he tries to "pull the plants to make them grow faster," or to "take fish from the water to the land," what would become of them then? In short, "take-no-action" implies that man should do things in accordance with their individual natures and let them be what they can be. This reminds us of Zhuang Zi, who continues this line of thought by means of illustrative examples. The duck's legs are short, for instance, but if man tries to lengthen them, the duck will feel pain. And similarly, the crane's legs are long, but if man tries to cut off a portion of them, the crane also will feel pain. Therefore, man should not shorten what is by nature long nor lengthen what is by nature short, because any modification of nature through externally forced action is unexceptionably the cause of pain and suffering. It is of frequent occurrence in this world that man takes actions to change or modify the existing nature of things. He may assure himself of his good intentions, and yet, what he considers to be good may not be considered good by others. As a result, the actions one takes may violate the natural law and lead to something negative. It may be enlightening to consider one of Zhuang Zi's parables: "The emperor of the South Sea was called Shu; the emperor of the North Sea was called Hu; and the emperor of the Central Region was called Hundun. Shu and Hu from time to time came together for a meeting in the territory of Hundun, who always treated his two guests very generously. Shu and Hu discussed how they could repay his kindness. 'All men,' said they, 'have seven holes for seeing, hearing, eating, and breathing. But Hundun alone has none of them. Let us try to bore some for him.' So every day they bored one hole; but on the seventh day Hundun died" (see "Ying Di Wang" in *A Taoist Classic: Chuang-Tzu*, tr. Fung Yu-lan, p. 113). The Chinese names of the three characters are virtually symbolic. Shu could mean "change" or "haste," Hu could mean "sudden" or "speed," and Hundun could mean "chaos," "primitivity" or "simplicity." Shu and Hu could symbolize "take-action," whereas Hundun could symbolize "take-no-action." The message is more than suggestive.

Nevertheless, the notion of "take-no-action" (*wu wei*) has its negative impact owing to its literal interpretation and misconception. To be exact, when it is superficially interpreted as "inactivity" or "doing nothing at all," it militates against human initiative; when it is mistaken as a way of waiting for one's turn or luck, it seems to encourage patience, passiveness, and tolerance; when it is practically adopted as an approach to self-defence, it seems to call for irresponsibility or escapism from social commitment... As a consequence, "take-no-action" in the distorted sense of this term is somewhat rooted as an element in the psychology of some Chinese people. Hence they tend to be rather tolerant of and shrink from difficulties, hardships, rebuffs, failures, challenges, and even foreign invasions. That is the main reason why Lu Xun, China's leading 20th century writer, severely attacked the doctrines of Lao Zi and Zhuang Zi by labelling them as poisonous doses prescribed for passive and defensive "patients."

It is worth mentioning the conclusion made by Lao Zi in chapter 48 (DDJ) that "if one likes to do anything arbitrary, he is not qualified to govern all under Heaven." By the expression "do anything arbitrary" (*you shi*) is meant "take-action" (*you wei*) in Lao Zi's terminology. It is considered to be negative and disadvantageous in the long run, contrasting sharply with "doing nothing" or "take-no-action." It should be made clear that "doing nothing" or "take-no-action" means doing whatever is not aimed at disturbing other people or going against the natural law in the view of Lao Zi. However, he tends to absolutize the advantages of his favorite principle. That is why it is taken more often than not as meaning something extremely passive.

9.2 (Chapter 29)

I think that one will not succeed
　When he desires to govern the state and act upon it.[1]
The state as a sacred vessel should not be acted upon,
　Nor should it be held on to.[2]
He who acts upon it will harm it.
He who holds on to it will lose it.
Thus the sage takes no action, and therefore fails in nothing;
　He holds on to nothing and therefore loses nothing.

Of all the creatures some lead and some follow;

Some breathe and some blow;
Some are strong and some are weak;
Some rise up and some fall down.
Hence the sage discards the extreme,
The extravagant and the excessive.[3]

Meanwhile, he desires to have no desires[4].
He does not value rare treasures.
He learns what is unlearned.[5]
He returns to what is missed.[6]
Thus he helps all things in natural development,
But does not dare to take any action.[7]

Annotations:

[1] The reason why "he will not succeed" lies in his taking (arbitrary) action against the principle of the *Dao* ("take-no-action").

[2] "The state" is a translation of *tian xia*, which can be rendered literally as "under Heaven." It refers not only to a specific social institution or political system, but also to the people involved. Hence, the ruler cannot govern and control "the state" according to his will alone.

[3] There exist individual differences and various needs. The sage should treat them accordingly and naturally by means of the *Dao* that "follows the way of spontaneity."

[4] From this line downward are sentences transposed from Chapter 62 of other versions, following Gu Di's philological research. (see Gu Di and Zhou Ying. *Lao Zi Tong*, pp. 312-314). "He desires to have no desires" means the willingness to eschew selfishness and return to simplicity.

[5] and [6] By "what is unlearned" and "what is missed" are meant the same principle of the *Dao*.

[7] This shows the *De* of the sage, who is always ready to help things but never dares to take arbitrary or willful actions.

Commentary:

This chapter introduces Lao Zi's warning the ruling class. He postulates that all things and people in the world have individual differences and distinct needs, even though they have something in common. They are characteristically independent so that they can hardly be governed by drastic measures that are introduced arbitrarily, nor can they be controlled by patternizing their conduct and ideology as the ruler wishes or hopes. Thus leadership of whatever kind cannot endure long if it fails to understand the above-mentioned situation. For this reason, Lao Zi subsequently offers his advice in terms of the supreme principle of "following the way of spontaneity" and "take-no-(arbitrary)-action." Meanwhile, he expects the rulers to lead the people or govern the country by adroitly guiding actions according to circumstances (*yin shi li dao*).

10 On Pleasure-Snobbery and Acquisitiveness

It seems to be paradoxical that the progression of civilization tends to bring forth advantages and disadvantages at the same time. The situation was more or less the same in the past. Lao Zi persistently focuses on the negative aspects of civilization in view of social ills. Based on his observation and anatomy of problematic reality in his time, his exposure of pleasure-snobbery and acquisitiveness sheds much light on the human condition even today. To be discussed here are chapters 12, 53 and 67 (DDJ).

10.1 (Chapter 12)

The five colors make one's eyes blind.[1]
The five tones make one's ears deaf.[2]
The five flavors dull one's palate.[3]
Racing and hunting unhinge one's mind.[4]
Goods that are hard to get tempt people to rob and steal.[5]
Hence, the sage cares for the belly instead of the eyes;[6]
And he rejects the latter but accepts the former.

Annotations:

[1] "The five colors" are yellow, green, red, white and black. Here the expression means a rich variety of colors which appear sensuously dazzling.

[2] "The five tones" of ancient Chinese music were known as *gong*, *shang*, *jue*, *zhi* and *yu*—the five notes of the ancient Chinese five-tone scale. They correspond somewhat to 1, 2, 3, 5 and 6 in numbered musical notation. Here the expression means enjoyable and exciting music.

[3] "The five flavors" are sweet, sour, bitter, pungent and salty. Here the expression means sensuous delicacies.

[4] "Racing and hunting" implies passionate or unbridled indulgence in entertainment.

[5] "Goods that are hard to get" indicates treasures or valuables in particular, and wealth or property in general.

[6] "The belly" signifies the possibility of easy contentment with what one has, while "the eyes" stand for the insatiable desire for sensuous enjoyment. Lin Yutang renders "the belly" (*fu*) as "the inner self."

Commentary:

With penetrating insight into materialistic civilization in general and sharp observation of the easy access the rich have to a luxurious way of life in particular, Lao Zi levels criticism at pleasure-snobbery and wealth-oriented acquisitiveness as two overwhelming social problems encountered in his time. Things included in the categories of "the five colors," "the five tones," "the five flavors," "hard-to-obtain goods" and "racing and hunting" are the major sources of pleasure and targets of acquisition. They are so tantalizing that those engrossed in them may fall into over-indulgence. This will then lead to such detrimental consequences as distorted perception (i.e. dazzled eyes, deaf ears and spoiled palate), mental inbalance (i.e. desire- and passion-riddenness) and aberrant behavior (i.e. robbery and theft). Hence, Lao Zi warns people (especially the rich) to rein in their pleasure-seeking and wealth-acquisition urges by caring for "the belly instead of the eyes."

To "care for the belly" means, as Chen Guying put it, "to regulate the inner life so that it remains tranquil, simple and unruffled. To care for the eyes means to pursue a kind of outer life driven by greedy desires. The more one indulges in the latter, the more one gets engrossed in it and attached to it; accordingly the more one will suffer from self-estrangement, and the more empty one's soul will become. Therefore, Lao Zi reminds people to get rid of external temptations, and instead concentrate on peace of mind as well as inherent simplicity" (see Chen Guying. *Lao Zi Zhuyi Ji Pingjie*, p. 108).

Reconsidering these old ideas of Lao Zi, we can still feel their relevance to reality today, and possibly sigh with regret at materialistic society given over to the pursuit of pleasure, wealth and commodities. The rapid development of commercial markets, for instance, can be attributed to acquisitiveness: The more you drink Coca-Cola—because "you cannot beat the taste"—the more thirsty you will become because you want more; and likewise, as the rapid advance of the culture industry produces a growing variety of objects as dazzling and momentary as 'fire-crackers' in Adorno's terms, the further you pursue them, the further your taste will decline.

Incidentally, it must be stressed that Lao Zi is not simply anti-art or anti-culture, as some scholars maintain. He virtuously condemns the lavish way of life sought after by the rich on the one hand, and the potential dangers stirred up by acquisitive motives on the other. This intention can be proved by his advocacy of simplicity and freedom from desires.

10.2 (Chapter 53)

If I have a little wisdom,[1]
  I will walk along a broad way
  And fear nothing but going astray.
The broad way is very even,
  But the powerful delight in by-paths.[2]
The courts are exceedingly corrupt,[3]
  Whereas the fields are exceedingly weedy
  And the granaries are exceedingly empty.
They are wearing elegant clothes,[4]
  Carrying sharp swords,
  Enjoying exquisite food and drink,
  And owning abundant wealth and treasures.

They can be called robber chieftains.
This is surely against the *Dao*.

Annotations:

[1] "I" stands for the Daoist sage or wise ruler.

[2] "The broad way" (*da dao*) denotes the right approach to either personal cultivation or state leadership which follows the *Dao*; "by-paths" indicate the wrong or misleading approach which goes against the *Dao*. "The powerful" signifies the rich and noble.

[3] "The courts" here stands for government in general.

[4] By "they" here is meant the powerful (officials), the rich and the nobility as a whole.

Commentary:

In this chapter Lao Zi openly attacks the powerful for their corruption of government, indulgence in excessive enjoyment, lavish vanity-snobbery, indifference to the common people and, above all, exploitation of the people. Thus he expresses his indignation by calling them "robber chieftains."

According to Lao Zi, they live self-centered lives dominated by pleasure-seeking, and acquisitiveness due to the sheer fact that they refuse to "walk along the broad way" but "delight in by-paths." That is to say, they prefer to take actions contrary to the supreme principle of the *Dao*. This is a fatal error, for such transgressors not only lose what they once enjoyed, but also plunge their very selves into jeopardy. We can collect more than sufficient evidence from history to show that corrupt governments and unjust property divisions tend to stir up uprisings or rebellions in all nations and at all times.

10.3 (Chapter 67)

I have three treasures
 Which I grasp and keep.[1]
The first is "kindness."
The second is "frugality."
The third is "to dare not be ahead of the world."[2]

With kindness, one can become courageous.[3]

With frugality, one can become generous.[4]
With not daring to be ahead of the world,
One can become the leader of the world.[5]

Now it is a fatal mistake[6]
To seek courage by abandoning kindness,
To seek generosity by abandoning frugality,
And to seek precedence by abandoning retreat.
With kindness, one can be victorious in the case of attack,
And remain firm in the case of defence.
Heaven will help and protect such a one through kindness.

Annotations:

[1] In most versions of the *Dao De Jing* there are in Chapter 67 these lines: *tian xia jie wei wu dao da bu xiao*; *fu wei da, gu si bu xiao*; *ruo xiao, jiu yi qi xi ye fu* (All the world says that my *Dao* is great and does not resemble anything concrete; just because it is great, it does not resemble anything concrete; if it did resemble anything concrete, it would have been for long very insignificant). We have placed them in Chapter 70 for they fit the context there according to Gu Di's philological justification. (see Gu Di & Zhou Ying. *Lao Zi Tong*, pp. 615-618.).

[2] This implies Lao Zi's ideal of "non-competition," "non-struggle" and "retreat," of which he considered that there was a great shortage in his chaotic times.

[3] "Kindness" is a rendering of *ci*, which also means love, affection, compassion and even tolerance. "Courageous" is a rendering of *yong*, which also means brave or bravery. In this context, according to Jiang Xichang, that "one can become courageous" means that one is liable "to be modest, to compromise and to defend instead of competing, offending or invading."

[4] Han Fei Zi interprets this idea by remarking that "the wise man who uses his property frugally will have a well-off family; the sage who treasures his spirit will be full of energy...." Because of frugality, one will not be lavish with one's wealth and will accordingly save up more; then he will be able to offer some to others. The fact of the matter is that "frugality" as a kind of

virtue has been recommended throughout Chinese history, as an approach to developing a well-off family or country.

[5] According to Gu Di, the ancient Chinese term *cheng qi* means *da qi* (great vessel) or *shen qi* (divine vessel), both of which are symbolic of a supreme power to order the lords of all the kingdoms under Heaven. That is why *cheng qi zhang* is rendered as "the leader of the world."

[6] The original expression is *ze bi si yi*, which can be literally translated as "Thus it will surely end in death." "Fatal mistake" is employed here to mean the same thing, and the word "now" to suggest the existing crisis resulting from the rich and powerful remaining so self-centered as to disregard the three treasures advocated by Lao Zi.

Commentary:

Ren Jiyu assumes that "this chapter specifically applies the principle of the *Dao* to politics and military affairs. Lao Zi introduces the so-called three precious things...and maintains that only the ability to fall back is bravery, the ability to shrink is to stretch, and that avoiding prominence and precedence makes one come first. Breach of the three principles will bring complete failure" (see A Taoist Classic: *The Book of Lao Zi*, p. 88).

Sha Shaohao criticizes Lao Zi for setting forth such three treasures as "kindness," "frugality" and "not daring to be ahead of the world," and seeming to have them all absolutized. Thus "retreat" or "defense" turns into an unalterable and supreme principle, and accordingly "courage," "generosity" and "precedence," symbolic of "advance," are neglected. The latter (precedence or daring to be ahead of the world) plays virtually a leading role in the process of development. This proves that Lao Zi deviates here from his normal dialectical approach.

Apart from the above-mentioned observations, it can be said that Lao Zi offers his three treasures in respect of the social problems of his time—rampant pleasure-snobbery, insatiable acquisitiveness and harsh competition among the people in general, and the rich and powerful in particular. He warns them in no uncertain terms that those who go against the three treasures as an interrelated code of conduct are doomed to failure and disaster. With regard to the three treasures, the last two seem to be largely directed toward self-preservation and self-defence, while the first (i.e. kindness), toward spiritual nourishment. In addition, it seems to be of universal significance, for kindness as such can never be enough in the competitive world we happen to live in, now as then.

11 On the Hard and the Soft

It seems to be a universal rule that the strong conquer the weak, and that the hard overwhelm the soft. However, Lao Zi thinks in reverse—from a dynamic and dialectical perspective. He grounds his philosophy of keeping to the soft and tender upon his empirical observation of natural changes. Plain and simplistic as his thinking may be, his method of reverse speculation remains fairly instructive even today. Chapters 43, 76 and 78 (DDJ) are the focus of this.

11.1 (Chapter 43)

The softest thing in the world
  Runs in and out of the hardest thing.[1]
The invisible force penetrates any creviceless being.[2]
Thereby I come to know the advantage of take-no-action.[3]
Few in the world can realize the merits of wordless teaching
  And the benefits of do-nothing.[4]

Annotations:

[1] The Chinese expression *chi cheng* literally means the free fashion of galloping horses. It is here rendered as "runs in and out," implying the overwhelming power of the softest thing over the hardest thing. The old Chinese saying that "Constantly dripping water wears holes even in stone" (*di shui chuan shi*) can adequately serve as a metaphor for the potential of the soft that is able to overcome the hard.

[2] The Chinese term *wu you* is translated as "the invisible force," which is derived from water for example. It is also

rendered as "that-which-is-without-form." "The creviceless being" stands for *wu jian*, meaning all things that have no seams in their appearance.

[3] and [4] Both "take-no-action" and "do-nothing" are English renderings that can be used interchangeably for Lao Zi's concept of wu wei, as has been explained previously (see Part III, 9).

Commentary:

It is noticeable that Lao Zi propounds in this chapter the view that the soft and weak overcome the hard and strong in one sense, and the advantages that come from "take-no-action" in another. Meanwhile, he proposes his philosophy of compromising for the sake of gaining more, and of retreating for the sake of advancing further.

This could also be taken as advice to the strong and powerful for they tend to be short-sightedly arrogant or self-important. It is well to keep in mind the fact that things are always on the move, developing into their opposites and replacing one another naturally. Therefore, historically sedimented in the Chinese psychology is a distinct understanding of the interactions between "the strong and the soft," "the firm and the yielding," "advance and retreat" and "contract and expand." In *The Great Treatise on The Book of Changes* (*Yi Jing Xi Ci Zhuan*), one may read with enlightenment the following: "Therefore, the eight trigrams (*ba gua*) succeed one another by turns, as the firm (*gang*—also meaning the strong) and the yielding (*rou*—also meaning the soft or the tender) displace each other...When the sun goes, the moon comes; when the moon goes, the sun comes. The sun and the moon alternate, and thus light comes into existence. When cold goes, heat comes; when heat goes, cold comes. Cold and heat alternate, and thus the year completes itself. The past contracts; the future expands. Contraction and expansion act upon each other; hereby arises that which furthers. The inchworm draws itself together when it wants to stretch out. Dragons and snakes hibernate in order to preserve life...." Quite ostensibly, the movement of the inchworm is symbolic of the interaction between retreat (drawing itself together) and advance (stretching out);

and similarly, the habits of dragons and snakes are symbolic of the interaction between tranquility (hibernating in a static sense) and motion (preserving life in a dynamic sense).

11.2 (Chapter 76)

When alive, man is soft and tender.[1]
After death, he is hard and stiff.[2]
All things like grass and trees are soft and tender when alive,
Whereas they become withered and dried when dead.
Therefore, the hard and stiff are companions of death
Whereas the soft and tender are companions of life.
Hence an army will be shattered when it becomes strong.[3]
A tree will be broken when it grows huge.[4]
The hard and strong fall in the inferior position;
The soft and tender stay in the superior position.

"The violent and strong do not die natural deaths."[5]
I shall take this principle as the father of my teaching.[6]

Annotations:

[1] By "soft and tender" is here meant the actual condition of the human body.

[2] By "hard and stiff" is here meant the literal state of the human corpse.

[3] This implies that when an army becomes strong it tends to be aggressive and apt to show off its strength by attacking others. By so doing it runs the risk of weakening itself and finally being destroyed.

[4] A fully grown tree is likely to be felled for it is buffetted by more wind in a storm, or it is cut down for timber owing to its usefulness.

[5] Like a strong army that tends to display its power, the violent and strong will soon meet their doom instead of a natural end.

[6] "The father of my teaching" indicates the root, foundation, beginning or general principle of Lao Zi's teaching.

Commentary:

In this chapter, Lao Zi cites a number of handy and approachable examples drawn from natural phenomena and military affairs. He employs them to reinforce his notion that the soft and tender are the most potential and powerful, whereas the hard and strong are the most fragile and teeter on the brink of termination or destruction. This demonstrates the fact that Lao Zi tends to view things in respect of their intrinsic development and changes. In effect, his dialectical thinking features insight into the dynamic interaction between the opposite facets of all things, which is already implied by the well-known generalization presented in Chapter 40 that "Reversion is the movement of the *Dao*. Weakness is the function of the *Dao*" (see Part I, 3).

It is also discernable that Lao Zi clings to a skeptical perspective all the way through. He reverses against all certainties with regard to the positive values overwhelmingly celebrated in the society of his time. Hence his ideas appear to be antithetical to either well-established norms or accepted logic. However, one should never fail to neglect the absolutization of the conviction that the soft and tender are bound to conquer the hard and strong, which threads through Lao Zi's doctrine. Such absolutization cuts "the soft and tender" off from any other variables or possible influences, thus making a certainty out of the negation of other certainties or values positively socialized and appreciated during that period.

11.3 (Chapter 78)

Nothing in the world is softer and weaker than water,[1]
 But no force can compare with it in attacking the hard and strong.
For this reason there is no substitute for it.
Everyone in the world knows
 That the soft can overcome the hard,
 And the weak can overcome the strong,
 But none can put it into practice.
Therefore the sage says:
"He who shoulders the disgrace for his nation
 Can be the sovereign of the country;
 He who bears the misfortune of his nation
 Can be the king of the world."

Positive words seem to be their opposite.[2]

Annotations:

[1] The image of water is figuratively used by Lao Zi to illustrate his notion that the soft and weak can overcome the hard and strong.

[2] This is a rendering of *zheng yan ruo fan* as one of the essential concepts propounded in the *Dao De Jing*. According to an annotation made by Heshang Gong, "positive words" (*zheng yan*) means upright words that tell the truth. Yet, they cannot be rightly conceived or understood by ordinary people as they are mistaken for something negative, wrong or absurd. Relevant instances are easily found in the *Dao De Jing*, such as "The soft can overcome the hard, and the weak can overcome the strong" (Ch. 78); "An army will be shattered when it becomes strong, and a tree will be broken when it grows huge" (Ch. 76); "What is most full seems to be empty...The most straight seems to be crooked; the greatest skill seems to be clumsy; the greatest eloquence seems to be stammering" (Ch. 45); "The *Dao* that is bright seems to be dark; the *Dao* that goes forward seems to retreat; the *Dao* that is level seems to be uneven; the lofty *De* looks like a humble valley; the greatest glory looks like a disgrace...." (Ch. 41), etc.

Commentary:

As has been detected by many readers and Lao Zi scholars, this chapter highlights once again the character of water. Water appears soft and weak, but it can bring down hard and strong things alike. From this natural phenomenon Lao Zi infers that softness, weakness and humbleness are conducive to gains instead of losses. A wise ruler should apparently keep to himself all humiliation or disgrace by being as humble as water itself. Thus he seems to be in the lowest place, but in fact he stays in a high position above the others in view of the potential power concerned.

It is noticeable that Lao Zi recommends the functions of water which is metaphorically used to schematize the characteristics of the *Dao* and *De* in his terminology. Water seems to enjoy such positive features as follows: first and foremost, it is beneficial to the growth of all things in the world; secondly, it is not competitive with others; thirdly, it goes down to the lower places and tends to keep an appearance of humbleness; finally, being a symbol of the soft and weak, it has such great potential power that it can well defeat the hard and strong. And this potential power is largely determined by the perseverance or persistent character of water itself. Viewing the *Dao De Jing* as a whole, we can safely conclude that Lao Zi's depiction of water in terms of its functions and features as such reflects his recommended philosophy of "sticking to the soft and tender" on the one hand, and on the other, accords with his primary principle that "Weakness is the function of the *Dao*."

It is worth mentioning that the image of water is also positively and figuratively used by Sun Zi, a contemporary of Lao Zi. In his well-known book titled *The Art of War* (*Sun Zi Bing Fa*), he writes that "the laws of military operations are like water; the tendency of water is to flow from heights to lowlands. The law of successful operations is to avoid the enemy's strength and strike his weakness. Water changes its course in accordance with the contours of the land. The soldier works out his victory in accordance with the situation of the enemy. Hence, just as water retains no constant shape, so in war there are no constant conditions. He who can modify his tactics in accordance with the enemy situation and thereby succeeds in winning may be said to be divine" (see Sun Zi. *The Art of War*, pp. 41-42).

12 On the Beautiful and the Ugly

As regards the distinction between the beautiful and the ugly, Lao Zi's treatise is characterized by relativity and mutualism. This is seen to be based on his observation that there are always two opposites in everything under the sky. These two opposites contrast and complete each other. Thus one cannot do without the other due to their mutuality and, likewise, one cannot exist without the other either. Here we make particular reference to Chapter 2 (DDJ).

12.1 (Chapter 2)

When the people of the world know the beautiful as beauty,
There arises the recognition of the ugly.
When they know the good as good,
There arises the recognition of the evil.[1]

This is the reason why
Have-substance and have-no-substance produce each other;
Difficult and easy complete each other;
Long and short contrast with each other;
High and low are distinguished from each other;
Sound and voice harmonize with each other;
Front and back follow each other.[2]

Thus, the sage conducts affairs through take-no-action;[3]
He spreads his doctrines through wordless teaching;[4]
He lets all things grow without his initiation;
He nurtures all things but takes possession of nothing;
He promotes all things but lays no claim to his ability;
He accomplishes his work but takes no credit for his contribution.[5]
It is because he takes no credit
That his accomplishment stays with him for ever.

Annotations:

[1] The beautiful and the ugly, the good and the evil are contrasted with each other. As antithetical categories associated with judgment, they come into being in pairs and in mutual contrast. In plain terms, what is considered beautiful is so because of the contrast with what is considered ugly, and vice versa. It is the same with the good and the evil.

[2] These lines are meant to exemplify Lao Zi's conviction that concepts are usually brought forth and manifested by virtue of bilateral opposition and mutual accomplishment (*xiang fan xiang cheng*).

[3] "The sage" is the Daoist sage as an ideal personality who

follows the way of spontaneity without taking any action contrary to Nature or the natural law.

[4] "Wordless teaching" (*bu yan zhi jiao*) implies in this context that the education of the people in general should be carried out without formal rules, regulations or compulsory supervision, but instead, through imperceptible guidance and influence. In addition, "wordless teaching" may, in Lao Zi's mind, suggest both a discouragement of governmental administration that resorts to a train of orders, and a negation of the national education that relies on a kind of ideology.

[5] Taking possession of nothing" (*fu you*), "laying no claim to his ability" (*fu shi*), and "taking no credit for his contribution" (*fu ju*) are the essential virtues of the Daoist sage. These qualities are meant to encourage people in general to do, create and give what they can. At the same time people are advised to reduce their desire for possessing things, exhibiting their abilities, and glorifying their achievements. This is precisely because all social conflicts, man-to-man clashes and even warfare are, in the eyes of Lao Zi, derived from personal (i.e. among the ruling class in particular) desires and ambitions in the aspects of demonstrating one's competence, enlarging one's property and expanding one's territory. Needless to say, these desires and ambitions will lead naturally to contests, competition and even military action and counteraction.

Commentary:

This chapter streses that everything features a unity of two opposites. The fact of the matter is that if we try to approach and evaluate conceptually what surrounds us, we often find a tendency to classify almost all things in terms of their respective values and contradictive dimensions. Thus there emerge antithetical concepts in pairs, such as beautiful and ugly, good and evil, have-substance and have-no-substance, difficult and easy, long and short, high and low, front and back, etc. Their interactions can be largely boiled down to the characteristics of bilateral opposition and paradoxically mutual production as exist in the phenomenological world. In other words, they come into being in a relative, contrasting and, above all, interdependent mode.

In view of the beautiful and the ugly as two different categories in particular, Lao Zi was the first thinker in Chinese history who did not make a black-and-white distinction between them. From his dialectical perspective he observes that the beautiful and the ugly are brought into being in the process of value judgment through comparison and contrast. That is to say, they are different but not absolutely antithetical to or incompatible with each other. They seem to have no positive hiatus between them. They are in effect interlinked to the extent that they co-exist or set off each other. This argument can be well justified by a statement in Chapter 20 (DDJ): "How much difference is there between the beautiful and the ugly?" (*mei zhi yu e, xiang qu ruo he*). This sentence is also rendered as "How much difference is there between good and evil?" for "beautiful" (*mei*) and "good" (*shan*), "ugly" (*e*) and "evil" (*e*) were used interchangeably as ethical terms in ancient China. Contrary to other philosophers like Confucius, who tends to make a clear-cut discrimination between beautiful and ugly, Lao Zi develops an insight into the relativity and changeability of the two categories, such that he refuses to absolutize the apparent opposition between them. As further evidence we can cite a quotation from Chapter 58 (DDJ) as follows: "The normal can suddenly turn into the abnormal; good can suddenly turn into evil" (*zheng fu wei qi, shan fu wei yiao*).

After all, Lao Zi's dialectical stance toward the beautiful and the ugly is of a negative kind, often leading to relativism. According to Li Zehou and Liu Gangji, this relativism does not lie in the fact that the two categories concerned form a contrast, but instead in the intention to erase the discrepancy between them. In each circumstances people can become easily adaptable to the confusing reality and hold on to an attitude to life which goes beyond the distinction between what is regarded as beautiful and what is regarded as ugly. This attitude is notably reflected in Chapter 20 (DDJ): "Common folks are so brilliant; I alone seem to be in the dark. Common folks see differences and are clear-cut; I alone see no distinctions." Thus, compared to the Confucianists' persistent pursuit of the beautiful (good) and battle against the ugly (evil) even at the expense of life, Lao Zi's position is relatively negative and therefore less recommendable (see Li Zehou and Liu Gangji. *Zhongguo Meixue Shi* [*A History of Chinese Aesthetics*], p. 213).

On the other hand, it is an over-simplification to assert that Lao Zi attempts to completely deny and eliminate the distinction between the beautiful and the ugly. It seems more accurate to say that he advocates a rather indifferent attitude to such a distinction, even though he is highly conscious of its existence. The main reason for this lies in the hard fact that Lao Zi himself could not do anything about it during that harsh time when power and wealth spoke far more loudly than anything else. Hence, he deliberately ignores the distinction even though the populace cling to it in most cases.

However self-deceiving and self-contained his stance may be, Lao Zi never gives up in practice the search for the beautiful in the genuine sense of this term. In his conception what is really beautiful is characterized by simplicity, naivety, plainness, quietude, tranquility, purposelessness, etc. It is, in a word, equal to and identified with his concept of the *Dao*. One is able to get into the perfect realm of real beauty only when he has ridded himself of enslavement by external things and obtained authentic freedom of the spirit. That is to say, he has realized the essential significance of the *Dao* at this stage. In addition, Lao Zi takes a skeptical view of the mundane discrimination between the beautiful and the ugly. Take his criticism of the rich and powerful for example. They lived lavishly and abandoned themselves to the "five colors," "five tones" and "five flavors" (see Ch. 12, DDJ), which were seen in their eyes as something sensuously beautiful and enjoyable. But Lao Zi looks upon them as something destructive and detrimental to the health. Furthermore, "wearing elegant clothes, carrying sharp swords, enjoying exquisite food and drink..." (see Ch. 53, DDJ) were considered beautiful by the nobility, but appeared to Lao Zi as something dangerous and pernicious. Therefore he indignantly calls the self-indulgent possessors of those things "robber chieftains."

In the final analysis, Lao Zi, judging from either a skeptical or relativistic perspective, tends to maintain that what is taken as beautiful or the ugly by the multitude turns out to be insignificant or valueless on the one hand, and sheerly relative and contrastive on the other hand. They can be interchangeable or reducible to one another, and those who dote on them are deviating from the *Dao*, which is the one and only source of what is really beautiful in Lao Zi's view.

13 On Beauty, Truth and Goodness

Lao Zi's exposition of beauty, truth and goodness features his dialectical thinking and skeptical perspective. His insight into the contradictions among the three values is penetrating, and his critique of the pretentiousness and artificiality is still enlightening even today. The unity of the three values seems to Lao Zi to be only possible in the *Dao* and not in a society imbued with craftiness and deception. Let us examine chapters 81 and 62 (DDJ).

13.1 (Chapter 81)[1]

True words are not beautiful;
  Beautiful words are not true.[2]
A good man is not an eloquent arguer;
  An eloquent arguer is not a good man.[3]
He who knows does not show off his extensive learning;
  He who shows off his extensive learning does not know.[4]

Annotationss:

[1] In accordance with the philological research done by Ma Shulun and Gu Di, we have transposed to Chapter 77 (DDJ) the second stanza of this text, that usually begins with "The sage does not accumulate for himself...." (see Part I, 5.1)

[2] "True words" (*xin yan*) are so plain, sincere and straightforward that they do not allow any rhetorical polishing or adorning. Therefore, they often appear to be flat and displeasing. Conversely, "beautiful words" (*mei yan*) are so carefully chosen and modified that they are generally fine-sounding and inviting.

However, they are usually meant to either cover up what is true or mix up the true, the false and even the mendacious.

[3] "A good man" (*shan zhe*) is fairly close in meaning to a Daoist sage. He is supposed to pursue and embrace the truth alone (the *Dao*). Having attained it by chance, he will maintain it without arguing about what it is or how it is possible. For the attainment of the *Dao* is a personal experience and perception rather than a verbal description. This mode of conduct and attitude toward the *Dao* is strikingly distinct from that of "an eloquent arguer" (*bian zhe*), because the latter tends to be an exhibitionist who pretends to know when he does not really know (the *Dao*).

[4] These two lines serve as supportive statements for the distinction that is made previously between "a good man" (*shan zhe*) and "an eloquent arguer" (*bian zhe*). "He who knows" (*zhi zhe*), in Lao Zi's view, is a man of truth and wisdom. He is most likely to forget words and reluctant to learn such things as orthodox ideas, conventional rites and historical records, as advocated by Confucianists. "He who shows off his extensive learning" (*bo zhe*) is regarded by Lao Zi as a name-dropper deviating from the pursuit of truth, or the *Dao*. He is learned in appearance but superficial and pretentious in reality from the Daoist outlook.

Commentary:

It is, first of all, noteworthy that in Chinese culture "words" (*yan*) include sayings, speeches, discourses and writings in general. They are seen to be a reflection not only of a style, but also of a personality. This naturally corresponds to the firm and traditional conviction that "one's literary works can be intrinsically identified with one's personality (*wen ru qi ren*)." Hence, the discussion of beauty, truth and goodness in this context contains both a rhetorical and ethical sense. Of these values truth is implicitly the most crucial and decisive as it derives from the *Dao* on the one hand, and on the other, Lao Zi himself firmly opposes whatever is false and pretentious.

Lao Zi's ideas of beauty, truth and goodness could be misleading to the extent that the reader may hurry to conclude that Lao

Zi wrongly opposes the unity of the three values. The fact of the matter is that his ideas are an extension of his skeptical view of the relativity between the beautiful and the ugly. He grounds his observation and generalization on his critical and somewhat cynical stance vis a vis civilization as a whole, because civilization, in the eyes of Lao Zi, "rejects the great *Dao*" and thus "the doctrines of *Ren* and *Yi* arise;" likewise, "knowledge and craftiness appear" and thus "great hypocrisy emerges" (see Ch. 18, DDJ). As a consequence of such a social climate, luxury-acquisitiveness and pleasure-snobbery squeeze out simplicity and genuineness; similarly, beautiful or sweet words are coined to conceal evil-natured intentions or motives, and eloquence is held in esteem at the cost of the pursuit of supreme truth and wisdom related to the *Dao*. In short, the significance of Lao Zi's critique of civilization lies in the antithetical relationship between beauty and truth as well as beauty and goodness.

Lao Zi points out that the three categories of beauty, truth and goodness can never become unified into one due to the problems arising from civilization and the human condition. However, they can become inseparable if they are identified with the *Dao*. This is, according to Lao Zi, only possible in his ideal society free from all the problems mankind has always confronted throughout his history. Thus we may go further and assert that Lao Zi talks about beauty, truth and goodness based on fundamental principle of the *Dao*. His criticism of "beautiful words," "eloquent arguer," and "he who shows off his extensive learning" is largely directed at the pretentious and hypocritical aspects of what are commonly termed humanity, benevolence, righteousness, etc. The possibility of the unity of beauty, truth and goodness merely relies on the insightful perception and achievement of the *Dao*. The *Dao De Jing*, a book of over 5,000 words, is in effect composed of really "beautiful words" employed by the author to describe the *Dao*. Liu Xie (c. 465-532) comments, "Lao Zi dislikes falsehood, and therefore cries out that 'beautiful words are not true ones.' But his book of 5,000 excellent words is proof that he does not completely discard beauty and grace" (see "The Section of Qing Cai", in *Wenxin Diaolong*).

However, Lao Zi is again found to have absolutized the opposition between beauty and truth as well as beauty and goodness. This shows the intuitive, simplistic and also lop-sided aspect of his dialectics. It is definitely arbitrary to oversimplify in such a manner the diversity of things in the world and complicated social phenomena. Generalizations are not to lead one to become mired in mechanical metaphysics rather than active dialectics, thus arriving at such dogmatic conclusions as "true words are not beautiful," "beautiful words are not true," "a good man is not an eloquent arguer," "an eloquent arguer is not a good man," "he who knows does not show off his learning" and "he who shows off his learning does not really know,"...so on and so forth.

13.2 (Chapter 62)

The *Dao* is the storehouse of all things.
It is treasured by the good man,
And also preserved by the bad man.[1]

Honored words can gain respect from others.[2]
Fine deeds can have an impact on others.[3]
Even if a man is bad,
Why should he be ever rejected?
Therefore the sage is always good at saving men,
And consequently nobody is rejected.[4]
He is always good at saving things,
And consequently nothing is rejected.
This is called the hidden light.[5]
Therefore, the good man is the teacher of the bad.
And the bad is the material from which the good may learn.[6]
He who does not value the teacher
Or care for the material,
Will still be greatly deluded
Though he thinks himself clever.
Such is called the significant subtlety of the *Dao*.[7]

Therefore, on the occasion of enthroning an emperor
Or installing the three ministers,[8]
It is better to offer the *Dao* as a present
Though there are grand ceremonies of saluting them
With the round jadeware, followed by the four-horse chariot.
Why did the ancients value this *Dao* so much?
Did they not say, "Those who seek shall attain and
Those who sin shall be freed?"[9]
For this reason it is valued by all under Heaven.[10]

Annotations:

[1] This suggests that the *Dao* does not discriminate between people. Instead, it treats all men alike and offers protection to them all.

[2] The expression "honored words" is a rendering of *mei yan*, which literally means beautiful words. In this context "honored words" are true words uttered by the Daoist sage.

[3] "Fine deeds" is used to translate *mei xing*, which literally means beautiful deeds. They are supposed to be performed by the Daoist sage.

[4] The Daoist sage acts upon the *Dao* as the supreme principle without rejecting anybody or anything in the world. That is why the *Dao* deserves to be called the "great and all-embracing (*Dao*)."

The lines from "Therefore, the sage is always good..." to "such is called the significant subtlety of the *Dao*" are transposed into this text from Chapter 27 (DDJ), following Gu Di (see Gu Di and Zhou Ying. *Lao Zi Tong*, pp. 496-509). They are meant to interpret the idea that "Even if a man is bad, why should he be ever rejected?" Lao Zi is obviously idealistic in respect of human education and behavioral modification. This notion later became mingled with the principles of Chinese *Chan* (*Zen*) Buddhism: "Try to forgive and save all living creatures," "Remember to be always kind and charitable to all beings," etc. Hence there arose subsequently a popular Chinese saying that "A murderer can be transformed into a Buddha as soon as he puts down his knife."

[5] "Hidden light" (*xi ming*) implies the preserved wisdom

capable of understanding the *Dao*. It is also interpreted as the act of following the *Dao* with reference to the concept of "light" (*ming*) as expounded in chapters 16 and 55 (DDJ).

[6] "The bad" serve as negative examples from which one draws instructive and valuable lessons.

[7] "The significant subtlety" (*yao miao*) is attributed to the *Dao*, denoting a subtle and profound truth within.

[8] "Three ministers" (*san gong*) refers to the three top court officials during the Zhou dynasty (111-249 B.C.). They are known in Chinese as Tai-shi, Tai-fu and Tai-bao, respectively.

[9] The saying "those who seek shall attain and those who sin shall be freed" indicates again the all-embracing nature of the *Dao*, which rejects nobody. To be exact, the first part is also meant to explain that *Dao* is easily available and attainable, provided that it is sincerely pursued; the second part contains a hidden message that the *Dao* is able to help the misguided or sinners to go straight or turn over a new leaf.

[10] The pronoun "it" in this line stands for the *Dao*.

Commentary:

Lao Zi assumes that "The *Dao* is the storehouse of all things." That is to say, the *Dao* is the source of beauty, truth, good and everything else. It is treasured by both good and bad people precisely because it functions as an all-embracing principle and helpful guidance, such that it treats all men alike and offers protection to them all without any reservation or condition. Hence, the *Dao* can be widely recognized and valued if it is clarified and promoted by "honored words" and "fine deeds."

The latter are what the Daoist sage performs in accordance with the *Dao*. They are highly positive concepts symbolic respectively of beauty and goodness between which there is no conflict at all in this context. This is a result of their assumed unity or identity with the *Dao*. In striking contrast, beauty, goodness and truth as well would remain subject to doubts and contradictions in civilized society, as Lao Zi believes.

It is interesting to notice that Lao Zi and Confucius do not see eye to eye on this point. Lao Zi insists on a negative attitude;

as a rebel against civilized society, he plays down such human values as truth, beauty and goodness, and meanwhile denies any ray of hope for their practical unity. On the contrary, Confucius persists in a positive attitude; as a defender of civilized society, he tries by every means to affirm and advocate the possible unity of the human values in current consideration. In short, "Lao Zi looks at the problems of beauty, truth and goodness from a critical perspective of social civilization... His negative remarks about these social values are not purely inactive and ephemeral. They actually lay bare the historical fact that the clashes and incompatibilities between values are universally and chronically in existence in civilized society. By definition, they demonstrate Lao Zi's individual insight into the problematic kernel of the society of his time, as well as his critical spirit with regard to its dark side." (see Li Zehou & Liu Gangji. *Zhongguo Meixue Shi*, Vol. I, p. 217)

14 On Modesty and Retreat

Modesty as a virtue has all along been appreciated and recommended in the history of Chinese thought and ethics. It is not only practically desirable in social life for the sake of human relations, but also spiritually indispensable with regard to self-cultivation and self-preservation. As for the doctrine of retreat as contrasted with advance, it does not encourage people to withdraw from society, as is often misconceived. Instead, it advises people not to flaunt intelligence and successes, as this will surely bring about disaster. These themes are notably presented in chapters 8, 9, 24 and 45 (DDJ).

14.1 (Chapter 8)

The supreme good is like water.[1]
Water is good at benefiting all things
  And yet it does not compete with them.
It dwells in places that people detest,
  And thus it is so close to the *Dao*.[2]

In dwelling, (the best man) loves where it is low.[3]
In the mind, he loves what is profound.[4]
In dealing with others, he loves sincerity.
In speaking, he loves faithfulness.
In governing, he loves order.
In handling affairs, he loves competence.
In his activities, he loves timeliness.
Since he does not compete,
He is free from any fault.[5]

Annotations:

[1] By "the supreme good" is meant the best man with the qualities of water, as described subsequently.

[2] The water as such embodies the best man who is close to the *Dao*.

[3] The best man stays modest and low like water.

[4] This implies that he loves the depth and tranquility characteristic of the *Dao*.

[5] He who does not compete usually takes no (arbitrary) action. As a result, he will hardly commit errors or faults.

Commentary:

Lao Zi is fond of using the image of water to suggest such virtues as modesty, selflessness, non-competition, etc. Water appears humble, always flowing down to and dwelling in the low places. It remains selfless, always benefiting all things without competing with them. However, it is potentially powerful enough to overcome whatever is hard and strong. According to Lao Zi, nothing in the world is softer and weaker than water, but no force can compare with it in attacking the hard and strong. For this reason there is no substitute for it (DDJ, Ch. 78, also see Part III, 11.3). Hence the ideal personality is expected to embody these qualities of water. As has been observed in reality, only those who take up what others are reluctant to do are most likely to succeed either in their careers or personal development.

14.2 (Chapter 9)

To talk too much will lead to a quick demise.

Hence, it is better to keep to tranquility.[1]
To keep what is full from overflowing
Is not as good as to let it be.[2]
If a sword-edge is sharpened to its sharpest,
It will not be able to last long.[3]
When your rooms are filled with gold and jade,
You will not be able to keep them safe.
If you become arrogant because of honor and wealth,
It will bring upon you misfortune.
Retreat as soon as the work is done.
Such is the *Dao* of Heaven.[4]

Annotations:

[1] These are lines are transposed from Chapter 5 of the *Dao De Jing* in accordance with Gu Di's philological research. Relevant annotations are offered for reference in Part I, 2.4.

[2] This indicates that one should handle things naturally or spontaneously.

[3] By "sword-edge..." is meant show-offs in general.

[4] "The *Dao* of Heaven" of "the Heaven's Way" benefits all things by helping them grow and develop. But it never claims this as its own achievement. Thus it is considered by Lao Zi as the model for the *Dao* of man to follow.

Commentary:

This chapter reflects a moderate attitude toward social life, external things and personal cultivation in general. It encourages people to become modest instead of showy and arrogant, to be contented instead of greedy and demanding, and to retreat in a timely fashion instead of advancing blindly. Otherwise, one will be liable to get into trouble and lose what he has already gained.

By "retreat" is not meant withdrawal from society and retiring into the mountains as a hermit. Its implication lies in *De*, which does not allow one to show off what he has accomplished in one sense, and not claim to be a higher achiever than others in another. For it is in Lao Zi's mind that any self-importance or self-expansion as a result of personal success will turn out to be a cause of failure or destruction in the end.

14.3 (Chapter 24)

He who stands on tiptoe is not steady.[1]
He who doubles his stride cannot go far.[2]
He who displays himself is not wise.[3]
He who justifies himself is not prominent.[4]
He who boasts of himself is not given any credit.
He who feels self-important is not fit for leadership.
From the perspective of the *Dao*,
These are like remnants of food and tumors of the body,
So disgusting that the one with the *Dao* stays away from them.
Likewise the sage knows himself but does not display himself.[5]
He loves himself but does not feel self-important.
Hence he rejects that and accepts this.[6]

Annotations:

[1] This suggests that he who is eager to stand out will go the opposite way.

[2] This idea is close in meaning to the proverb "More haste, less speed."

[3] and [4] Lao Zi believes that self-display (of one's intelligence or achievements) as well as self-justification (of one's position or arguments) are largely derived from egoism, which hinders people from gaining an all-round view of things concerned.

[5] The sentences from this downward are transposed from Chapter 72 of other versions, in accordance with Gu Di's (see Gu Di & Zhou Ying. *Lao Zi Tong*, pp. 235-236).

[6] "That" refers to "display himself" (self-display) and "feel self-important" (self-importance) while by "this" is meant "knows himself" (self-knowledge) and "loves himself" (self-love in the sense of self-preservation of body and spirit). This conclusion is bolstered by reference to Chapter 38, at the end of which Lao Zi remarks, "The man of foreknowledge has but the flower of the *Dao* and is at the beginning of ignorance. Hence the great man dwells in the thick instead of the thin. He dwells in the fruit instead of the flower. Therefore he rejects the latter and accepts

the former" (see Part II, 6.2).

Commentary:

This chapter features a figurative expression of the demerits of self-display, self-opinion, self-exaggeration and self-importance, which are likened to "the remnants of food and tumors of the body" by Lao Zi. It is noticeable that Lao Zi strongly detests arrogance and exhibitionism, as contrasted strikingly with modesty as an important virtue of human conduct and a possibility of realizing the *Dao*.

Regarding the first two lines: "He who stands on tiptoe is not steady. He who doubles his stride cannot go far," we find that the former serves as advice to those who are so vain as to try to stand out from others while neglecting both objective and subjective conditions; the latter warns those who are eager for quick success and instant benefit. In addition, they also imply Lao Zi's dialectical viewpoint that one should remain modest in order to establish oneself, and should retreat in order to advance. It is often proved in practice that there is some truth in what Lao Zi says.

14.4 (Chapter 45)

What is most perfect seems to be incomplete,
  But its utility cannot be impaired.
What is most full seems to be empty,
  But its utility cannot be exhausted.
The most straight seems to be crooked.
The greatest skill seems to be clumsy.
The greatest eloquence seems to stutter.
The tranquil overcomes the hasty.[1]
The cold overcomes the hot.[2]
By remaining quiet and tranquil,
  One can become a model for all the people.[3]

Annotations:

[1] In many other versions of the *Dao De Jing* this line goes like this—*zao sheng han*—which is then rendered as "Rapid walking overcomes cold." We agree with Jiang Xichang, Yan Lingfeng and Chen Guying, who change it to *jing sheng zao*, for

this is more fitting to the context on the one hand, and for Lao Zi's entire system on the other. It is thus translated as "The tranquil overcomes the hasty." The same idea is also expressed in Chapter 26 (DDJ) by the statement, "The tranquil is the lord of the hasty" (*jing wei zao jun*). Wang Bi explains that "the hasty is conducive to trouble, while the tranquil is conducive to complete genuineness."

[2] Similarly, this line goes *jing sheng re* in many other versions of the *Dao De Jing*. It is here rendered as *han sheng re*, according to the contextual rvision made by the three above-mentioned Lao Zi scholars. It is then translated as "The cold overcomes the hot." "The cold" is a figurative expression for "the tranquil," whereas "the hot" stands for "the hasty."

[3] Some Lao Zi scholars translate *qing jing ke yi wei tian xia zheng* as "By remaining quiet and tranquil one can become the ruler of the world" or "the chief of all under Heaven." This is mentioned here for reference only.

Commentary:

The first part of the text reveals some essential aspects of the ideal personality in Lao Zi's mind. They appear considerably different from what they really are. This observation reflects Lao Zi's dialectical thought on the one hand, and his recommended way of personal cultivation on the other. As has been noticed, the actualization of the idealized personality is first of all dependent on the *De* of modesty and the philosophy of retreat.

The second part of the chapter is mainly associated with the dialectical interactions between "the tranquil" and "the hasty." The former can overcome the latter because tranquility leads to calmness, sharp observation, good reasoning and, above all, wisdom. The notion of tranquility and its advantages advocated by Lao Zi are linked to his principle of "take-no-(arbitrary)-action" in view of its deep structure.

15 On Knowledge and Wisdom

Lao Zi makes a distinction between general knowledge and

true wisdom. He holds a negative stance on the former, as he thinks it could be possibly superficial and even pretentious. But he gives much credit to the latter since he believes that it is closely associated with the *Dao* as the origin of all things. It is observable that the approach to wisdom proposed by Lao Zi features honesty, modesty, purity, sincerity, "self-knowledge" and simplicity. To be scrutinised with regard to this theme are chapters 33, 47, 52, 56 and 71 (DDJ).

15.1 (Chapter 33)

He who knows others is knowledgeable.[1]
He who knows himself is wise.[2]
He who conquers others is physically strong.
He who conquers himself is really mighty.[3]
He who is contented is rich.
He who acts with persistence has a will.
He who does not lose his root will endure.[4]
He who dies but is not forgotten enjoys longevity.[5]

Annotations:

[1] The Chinese word *zhi* (*zhi shi*, *ji zhi*) used to mean in ancient times "knowledgeable" or "knowledge," "intelligent" or "intelligence," or "wise" or "wisdom." I am inclined to render it as "knowledgeable," in accordance with the context in which Lao Zi implicitly distinguishes between knowledge and wisdom: the former is seemingly inferior to the latter in view of their respective value and significance.

[2] The Chinese word *ming* (as in *gao ming* and *ming zhi*) has such connotations as "brilliant" or "brilliance," "wise" or "wisdom," or "enlightened" or "enlightenment." It is translated as "wise" here with respect to the context.

[3] What he conquers in himself usually refers to his weaknesses or shortcomings. By so doing can he become really mighty without being pretentious.

[4] The term "root" is often employed by Lao Zi to signify the all-principle of the *Dao*.

[5] If a person is remembered after death by subsequent generations for what he has done during his lifetime, he is

thought to be still alive in their hearts or to "enjoy longevity." This is typical of the Chinese notion of immortality or eternity in a sense of this-worldliness.

Commentary:

This chapter is a characteristic generalization of Lao Zi's philosophy of human existence. The ideas are presented in the form of contrast and comparison. It is rather difficult, due to the complexity of social interactions and experiences, to develop a sound knowledge of other people's strengths and weaknesses, even though credit has all along been given to mutual understanding and intersubjective social communication. This is compatible with self-defence, self-concealment, etc. At the same time, it is more difficult to know and identify one's own demerits or shortcomings, for almost everyone tends to be self-centered and self-opinionated. One is liable to justify and glorify one's words and deeds, and so self-criticism and self-knowledge are both recommended and encouraged as twin ideals for personal cultivation and self-development.

The catchphrase, "the most precious of all human qualities is genuine self-knowledge" (*ren gui you zi zhi zhi ming*), is widely appreciated among the Chinese people. It originates in the *Dao De Jing* and has been internalized in the psychology of the Chinese nation as a whole. The attainment of these ideals oriented to individual understanding or self-cultivation is largely determined by the degree of one's adherence to the *Dao* as the fountainhead of wisdom. With enough wisdom of this kind, one can be in a position to recognize one's own weaknesses and thereby bolster one's will to overcome them. It is by virtue of so doing that one grows wise and mighty in the pure senses of these terms.

Lao Zi's exposure of the importance of self-knowledge and self-conquest in respect of personal weaknesses is noticeably profound and dialectical. This observation is significant and positive from the viewpoint of either epistemology or individual mental cultivation. However, there is always a limit to one's cognitive power in this aspect due to the tendency of self-justification, self-glorification, self-centeredness and self-defensiveness, as mentioned above. In practice, the so-called "wisdom of self-knowledge" is mostly grounded on an open and receptive attitude toward relevant criticisms and opinions offered by other social members.

15.2 (Chapter 47)

Without going out of the door
  One may know all-under-the-sky.[1]
Without looking through the window
  One may see the *Dao* of Heaven.[2]
The further one goes,
  The less one knows.
Therefore the sage knows without going about,
  Understands without seeing,
  And accomplishes without taking action.

Annotations:

[1] "All-under-the-sky" is the English rendering of the Chinese term *tian xia*, which is used here to signify everything in the world.

[2] The concept *tian Dao* (the *Dao* of Heaven) refers to the law of development and change as it exists in the universe. Its objective nature can not be altered by means of human will or expectation. Thus it remains far more powerful than the *Dao* of man.

Commentary:

In this chapter Lao Zi denies the value of practical experience or learning on the one hand, and on the other, he advises a contemplative approach to the true knowledge of all things and the *Dao* of Heaven as well. However, knowledge as such does not mean an accumulated amount of cognition or a vast range of information of the phenomenological world. It implies, in fact, the most essential insight into the nature of all things. In short, it is true knowledge or genuine wisdom in Lao Zi's terminology.

For a long time this idea was conceived of as something idealistically false, if not humbug. Yet, with more and more people practicing *qigong* (traditional Chinese breathing exercises with stylized movements) as a means of spiritual meditation, and as the effects of *qigong* come to be more and more appreciated, some scholars have started to realize the implications of what Lao Zi recommends here. Prof. Xu Xihua of Yunnan University has testified to this after having practiced *qigong* for over three years (see *Chinese Qigong Journal*, 1988, 5-6, 1989, 2).

What Lao Zi describes here may remind the reader of the experience of Sakyamuni, the founder of Buddhism, who once sat under a tree in meditation for 48 days and nights. It was on the evening of the 49th day that he finally gained an insight into truth and causality for over three generations ahead. In other words, he had attained the supreme wisdom or enlightenment necessary for attaining Buddhahood. Since then such notions as *hui yan tong* or *tian yan tong* (i.e. inner or heavenly enlightenment for attaining Buddhahood) have come to be used in Buddhism. Similar conceptions in Daoism, such as "deep contemplation," correspond to these terms.

15.3 (Chapter 52)

There was a beginning of the universe,
  Which may be called the mother of the universe.[1]
He who has found the mother
  Thereby understands her sons;[2]
  He who has understood the sons
  And still keeps to the mother
  Will be free from danger throughout his life.
Block up the holes;[3]
  Shut up the doors;[4]
  And till the end of life there will be no toil.
Open the holes;
  Meddle with affairs;
  And till the end of life there will be no salvation.
Seeing what is small is called enlightenment.
Keeping to weakness is called strength.
Use the light.[5]
Revert to enlightenment.

And thereby avoid danger to one's life—
This is called practicing the eternal.[6]

Annotations:

[1] Both "the beginning" and "the mother" refer to the *Dao* as an initiator and productive agency of all things.

[2] "The sons" here means all things produced by "the mother" (the *Dao*).

[3] "The holes" represent the mouth, ears, eyes and nostrils which function as channels for perceiving and conveying knowledge or information.

[4] "The doors" is here used metaphorically for the means for communicating and absorbing knowledge or information.

[5] "The light" stands for the pure experience encountered in the higher stages of *qigong* practice. When one reaches this state through deep contemplation, one may see a light sparkling in front of one's eyes, which is symbolic of the attainment of true enlightenment.

[6] "The eternal" here stands for the constant *Dao*.

Commentary:

This chapter deals, according to Prof. Ren Jiyu, "with the foundation of all beings—the Mother, viz. the *Dao*." Lao Zi points out that no one will encounter danger if he or she follows the principle of the *Dao*. The principle teaches avoiding the search for knowledge and keeping the eyes closed and the ears blocked. It recommends not being occupied with any enterprise and maintaining a weak position. Lao Zi believes retreat to be a means of self-defence, and holds that one can avoid disaster by observing the minute (he calls this "sagaciousness") and remaining soft and weak (he calls this "powerfulness"). (see *A Taoist Classic: The Book of Lao Zi*, p. 72)

Prof. Chen Guying proclaims that the key idea of this chapter lies in Lao Zi's advising people to explore the *Dao* as the origin of all things by penetrating their appearances. This is additionally mirrored in his encouraging people to pursue and perceive the inward instead of the outward, so as to eradicate desire and enterprise, and meanwhile to foster inner enlightenment and true wisdom. Only by means of this light of wisdom, according to Lao Zi, may one get close to the attainment of the *Dao* and preserve the whole of the real self.

Here it is worth clarifying that Lao Zi looks down upon knowledge but lauds wisdom characterized by simplicity and purity of mind. Thus he believes that it is wise not to have any knowledge or any desire for knowledge since this is detrimental and destructive in view of self-preservation. As regards the approach to wisdom proposed by Lao Zi, it seems to be somewhat mysterious and incomprehensible when judged from a normally logical and epistemological perspective. Yet, if one has basically experienced what Chinese *qigong* is all about, as a way of spiritual meditation and mental cultivation, one may well understand the approach proposed by Lao Zi. This corresponds with the content of the previously-discussed chapter. The principal objective of practicing *qigong* is to reduce all one's desires for external things in a materialistic sense and ambitions for personal achievement in a social sense. In short, *qigong* is aimed at helping one return to the mental state of simplicity, having-no-knowledge and pure-mindedness. Such being the case, you become what you are by achieving your real self. Consequently, you hanker after nothing and accordingly remain undisturbed by nothing. Thus you are always free from cares and worries, anxieties and frustrations, etc. Then you do not see the point of taking any risk or adventure. If you manage to get into this frame of mind, how could it be possible that there would be any danger or harm threatening you?

15.4 (Chapter 56)

He who knows does not speak,
He who speaks does not know.[1]
He blocks the vent,
Closes the door,
Blunts the sharpness,
Unties the tangles,
Softens the glare,
And mixes with the dust.[2]
This is called Profound Identification.[3]

Therefore people cannot get intimate with him,
  Nor can they estrange themselves from him.
People cannot benefit him,
  Nor can they harm him.
People cannot ennoble him,
  Nor can they debase him.[4]
For this reason he is esteemed by all-under-the-sky.

Annotations:

[1] These two lines indicate that he who really knows and attains the *Dao* hardly talks about it, whereas he who claims to know and displays his knowledge of the *Dao* is actually ignorant of what it is. Some Chinese Lao Zi scholars tend to interpret the lines as follows: "The wise are not talkative and eloquent; the talkative and eloquent are not wise."

[2] We must read between the lines here to uncover this statement's metaphorical implications. "He blocks the vent," for instance, suggests that one stay away from the knowledge of the world because it will plunge one into the mire of cares and worries; he "closes the door" suggests that one shut the door of desires because it is the fountain head of miseries and sufferings; he "blunts the sharpness" suggests that one conceal or hide one's aggressiveness even though one is competent and talented; he "unties the tangles" suggests that one manage to free oneself from social entanglements and disturbances; he "softens the glare" suggests that one be modest by covering up one's brightness; and finally, he "mixes with the dust" suggests that one mingle with the profane world or society.

[3] By the concept Profound Identification (*xuan tong*) is meant the sphere of realizing the *Dao*. It is equivalent in meaning to such terms as "embracing the One" (*bao yi*) and "attainment of the One" (*de yi*) used by Lao Zi elsewhere.

[4] These lines are meant to illustrate the general traits related to the sphere of Profound Identification with the *Dao*.

Commentary:

Like Chapter 52 discussed earlier, this chapter exposes Lao

Zi's condemnation of pretentious knowledge and preference for genuine wisdom derived from the *Dao*. His advocacy of Profound Identification with the *Dao* can be seen as the highest form of life, and the essential quality of his ideal personality, who is expected to be broad-minded and selfless enough to treat impartially all things in the world.

The advice to "block the vent, close the door, blunt the sharpness, untie the tangles, soften the glare and mix with the dust" serves as a workable strategy for self-defence and self-preservation, in chaotic times in particular. This in effect corresponds to the Chinese saying, "Hide one's capacities and bide one's time" (*tao guang yang hui*). However, if one stays passive all the time, so that one misses one's time when it comes, the whole strategy will turn out to be in vain. Hence it would be better to develop a dialectical approach to Lao Zi's advice.

15.5 (Chapter 71)

It is best to know that you don't know.[1]
It is an aberration to pretend to know when you don't know.
The sage is free from this aberration
  Because he recognizes it as such.[2]
He can be free from this aberration
  Only when he recognizes it as such.

Annotations:

[1] There are generally two major interpretations of the original expression *zhi bu zhi*. One is given above; the other is "It is best for one not to claim oneself to know even when one really knows."

[2] The pronoun "it" here stands for "pretending to know when you don't know."

Commentary:

This chapter chiefly reveals Lao Zi's recommendation of self-knowledge as a fundamental part of true wisdom. It is fairly common around us that some people pretend to know when they don't really know, and some others tend to scratch the surface and thus get some form of superficial knowledge. Yet, they make a big display of their "half knowledge and half understanding" (*yi zhi ban jie*). In striking contrast, the sage or the wise man in the pure sense of these terms maintain a sincere and faithful attitude toward truth and wisdom. They do not rush to make any assertion, but first investigate matters inside out and grasp their respective essences.

With regard to Lao Zi's stress on the self-consciousness of the "aberration" concerned, it inevitably reminds us of Confucius' remark on real knowledge, that is, "When you know a thing, say that you know it; when you don't know a thing, say that you don't know it. That is knowledge" (*The Analects of Confucius*, II:17). And elsewhere he exclaims, "Do I have knowledge? Yes. That is, I know that I don't know (many things)." Socrates once made a similar statement, "I know that I myself don't know." And he also says, "I am a bit more intelligent than others simply because I know that I am ignorant. But others don't know that they are ignorant." It is fascinating to find that these three thinkers in ancient times happened to share more or less the same view of true knowledge or wisdom. We may presume to conclude that if truth is naked, he who genuinely pursues truth ought to be naked as well in respect of his attitude. That is to say, he must develop a sincere and honest attitude by ridding himself of all fallacies and follies, pretensions and guises. Otherwise, the more he strives for truth, the further will he deviate from it. This principle is figuratively described by the old Chinese saying, 'Trying to go south by driving the chariot north" (i.e. Acting in a way that defeats the purpose).

16 On Fortune and Misfortune

Good fortune or happiness is what all people hanker after. At the same time, misfortune or misery is what people try to avoid. However, they go hand in hand as though in a kind of twinship. Being two opposites in unity, they are mutually interdependent and transformational. This emerges in Lao Zi's dialectical thinking as expressed in Chapter 58 (DDJ).

16.1 (Chapter 58)

When the government is generous and non-discriminatory,
  The people will remain honest and sincere;[1]
When the government is severe and discriminatory,
  The people will become crafty and cunning.[2]
Misfortune is that beside which fortune lies;
  Fortune is that beneath which misfortune lurks.[3]
Who knows what may be their ultimate cause?
There is no fixed and normal frame of reference.
The normal can suddenly turn into the abnormal,
  The good can suddenly turn into the evil.[4]
The people have been deluded for a long time.

Therefore, the sage is as pointed as a square, but never stays stiff;
He is as sharp as a knife, but never cuts anybody;
He is frank and straightforward, but never aggressive;
He is bright and shining, but never dazzling.[5]

Annotations:

[1] The Chinese expression *men men* is here rendered as "being generous and non-discriminatory." It carries a similar meaning in Chapter 20 where Lao Zi claims that he "alone intends to make no distinctions" (*wo du men men*). This state of "making no distinctions" is meant to describe either a generously non-discriminatory way of governmental administration or a simple mode of social conduct.

[2] If the government is incessantly severe and discriminatory, the people have no alternative but be crafty and cunning in their own self-defence.

[3] These two lines are also translated as follows: "O Misery! Happiness lies by its side; O Happiness! Misery lurks beneath it" (He Guanghu and Gao Shining) and "Disaster is that on which good fortune depends; good fortune is that in which disaster is concealed" (Robert G. Henricks).

[4] "The normal" (*zheng*) means the normal force while "the abnormal" (*qi*), the abnormal or extraordinary force; "the good"

(*shan*) means the good or fortunate thing, while "the evil" (*yao*) the bad or unfortunate thing. They are mutually reproductive as though they are moving in an endless circle. The idea is also discussed in military terms by Sun Zi in his book *The Art of War* (Chapter V, Use of Energy).

[5] Presented here are the basic virtues and qualities of the Daoist sage, who is, according to Lao Zi, able to free himself from all troubles.

Commentary:

As has been detected in Lao Zi's dialectical viewpoint as an essential component of his political philosophy, the more severe political control is, the more resistance there is from the people; and the more generous governmental administration is, the less resistance there is from the people. As a matter of fact, evidence is easily available from the history of mankind to prove that whenever and wherever a government strives to set up more rules and regulations to control and punish people, the people will in turn seek all possible means to shake them off and escape from the imposed penalties. The situation is somewhat like Wang Bi's conclusion: "The more sophisticated and elaborate the system of control is, the more adaptable and changeable will the wiles of the people become; the harder the attack or punishment is, the quicker will the people flee" (see Beijing Daxue Zhexuexi. *Zhong Guo Zhe Xue Shi*. Vol. 1, p. 253). That is why Lao Zi advises governments to be generous and non-discriminating (i.e. by taking no arbitrary actions) instead of being severe and discriminating (i.e. by taking arbitrary actions) in order to make the people become plain and simple. This is a case in which Lao Zi applies his philosophy of take-no-action into the political field. This expresses in effect Lao Zi's recommendation that governments should not keep disturbing the people, but instead should make it possible for them to enjoy a peaceful and tranquil life. The expectation itself naturally developed from his social ideal of bringing order to the chaotic society of his time.

The dialectical thinking of Lao Zi is further reflected in his exposition of the interactions or interrelations between fortune and misfortune, normal and abnormal, good and evil. The notion that "Misfortune is that beside which fortune lies; fortune is that beneath which misfortune lurks" is reminiscent of a parable in *The Book of Huainan Zi* which may be fully cited here: There lived an old man near China's northern borders, whose horse by chance wandered into the territory of the northern tribes. All his neighbors commiserated with him over the loss. "Perhaps this will turn out to be a blessing," said the old man. After a few months, the horse came back accompanied by another fine horse from the north. Seeing this, all his neighbors congratulated him. "Perhaps this will turn out to be a cause of misfortune," said the old man. He prospered and had many fine horses. One day his son, who was fond of riding, fell from a horse and broke his leg. All the neighbors came to commiserate with the family. "Perhaps this will turn out to be a blessing," said the old man. One year later, the northern tribes mounted an invasion of the border regions. All able-bodied young men were enlisted to fight against the invaders except for the old man's son, because he was a cripple, and so the old man and his son survived the consequent slaughter. (see Ren Jian Xun, in *The Book of Huainan Zi*). The lesson of this is that an apparent blessing is often misfortune in disguise, and vice versa. Lao Zi holds this viewpoint since he believes that the normal can change into the abnormal and vice versa, and the good can become the evil and vice versa. They are as two opposites in a perpetual circle. Then, what should be done in such a situation? Lao Zi suggests that one should not fix one's eyes on the appearances of things, or even on their positive aspects; one should see through the surface of things and keep alert against their potentially negative aspects. In addition, one should not go too far, but instead should manage to stop at the right place in everything, in order to keep things from reversing to their opposites. Finally, Lao Zi assumes that man has no control over the transformation of opposites unless he succeeds in achieving the *Dao*, by the virtue of which opposites are reduced to their original state of non-discrimination.

The dialectical ideas in Lao Zi's philosophy are, according to Prof. Fung Yu-lan, the reflection of the public thought resulting from the drastic reforms that took place during both the Spring and Autumn Period and the Warring States Period in Chinese history. Lao Zi's contribution to philosophy was to discover that everything has two opposite sides. When these two sides (e.g. fortune and misfortune, normal and abnormal, good and evil, etc.) develop to a certain point they are transformed into one another, corresponding to the old saying that "things are sure to return to their opposites when they go to extremes" (*wu ji bi fan*). However, his dialectic still features some grave drawbacks as follows: First of all, Lao Zi realizes the fact that all opposites are mutually interdependent and transformational. This is factually the aspect of "unity" in view of the law of opposites in unity. And yet, he fails to see the dynamic aspect of the struggle between each pair of opposites. In addition, while Lao Zi acknowledges that everything in the universe is on the move and changing, he supposes that the movement and changes go around in a perpetual circle instead of in a process of linear development and progression. Secondly, with regard to movement and tranquility as two important categories in Chinese philosophy, Lao Zi assumes that tranquility or stillness is more essential and decisive than movement or motion as is implied in his statement, "Though all things flourish with a myriad of variations, each one eventually returns to its root. This return to the root is called tranquility" (DDJ, Ch. 16). The "root" here means the *Dao* as the origin of all things. His preference for tranquility is compatible with his philosophy of keeping to the tranquil as a whole (also see DDJ, Chs. 26 and 60). Thirdly, opposites can only be transformed into one another under certain conditions. Otherwise, they will remain what they are. This is the same with fortune and misfortune, since their mutual transformation requires relevant conditions such as subjective initiative or efforts. Nevertheless, Lao Zi absolutizes the transformation by advocating a kind of passive wait-for-one's-turn attitude, as if initiative or subjective endeavor is dispensable and unnecessary. This seems to be wishful thinking, because mutual transformation of that kind can never occur automatically. Hence it is concluded that Lao Zi's dialectics is incomplete, simplistic and somewhat naive (see Fung Yu-lan. *Zhong Guo Zhe*

Xue Shi Xin Bian, Vol. II, pp. 39-42).

17 On Life and Death

The conceptions of life and death are crucially important to all human beings. Almost all philosophers, East or West, were and are preoccupied one way or another with various and respective perspectives on life and death. Lao Zi, as the founder of Daoism, asserts that both life and death are as natural as anything else in the world. Zhuang Zi, who inherits this attitude, thinks that they are neither to be welcomed nor rejected. Therefore, these two thinkers advise people to view life and death as nothing but natural phenomena to the extent that the former is not to be overvalued and the latter not to be feared. The best way to preserve life is, according to Lao Zi, to live out one's natural term free from cares and worries. This could be possible only when one sees through the value of life and the nature of death. Let us look at Chapter 50 (DDJ) and some relevant ideas of Zhuang Zi.

17.1 (Chapter 50)

Man comes alive into the world
  And goes dead into the earth.[1]
Three out of ten will live longer.[2]
Three out of ten will live shorter.
And three out of ten will strive for long life
  But meet premature death.
And for what reason?
It is because of excessive preservation of life.[3]
Only those who don't value their lives are wiser
  Than those who overvalue their lives.[4]

I have heard that those who are good at preserving life
  Will not meet rhinoceroses or tigers when traveling the byways,
  And will not be wounded or killed when fighting battles.[5]
The rhinoceroses cannot butt their horns against them.
The tigers cannot fasten their claws upon them.

And weapons cannot thrust their blades into them.
And for what reason?
Because they are out of the range of death.[6]

Annotations:

[1] Life and death are considered to be natural phenomena in the perspective of Daoist naturalism. This notion of life and death is further discussed and developed in *The Book of Zhuang Zi*.

[2] The original expression *shi you san* is somewhat ambiguous. Han Fei Zi assumes that it refers to the four limbs and the nine cavities—the latter being the ears, eyes, nose (which has two holes, like the ears and eyes), mouth, tongue and throat (or heart). Wang Bi interprets it as "three out of ten." Yang Xingshun reckons that life followed by death in a cycle is one of the natural laws radiating from the *Dao*. Thus, he translates *shi you san* as "a third" (of all the people in human society). Like many other Lao Zi scholars, Chen Guying keeps to Wang Bi's interpretation and thinks that the remaining one out of ten are those who "are good at preserving life." So, the total of all human beings consists of those (three out of ten) who will live longer, those (three out of ten) who will live shorter, those (three out of ten) who will strive for long life but meet premature death and those (one out of ten) who are good at preserving life. I accept Chen's interpretation in this context.

[3] The "excessive preservation of life" is against the natural law of the *Dao*. It indicates here the lavish and luxurious way of life that was only accessible to the rich and powerful of Lao Zi's time, who were obsessed with material enjoyments.

[4] Here Lao Zi criticizes those who overvalue their lives, for their efforts to preserve their lives in a excessive and unnatural fashion will surely lead to premature death.

[5] Rhinoceroses, tigers and battles are here symbolic of the dangers and violence that threaten and extinguish life.

[6] "They are out of the range of death" because they are adept at preserving life by going beyond life-consciousness; in other words they are enlightened by the *Dao* to the extent that they look upon life and death as natural phenomena and follow the way of spontaneity.

Commentary:

This chapter expounds Lao Zi's attitude toward life and death, which he regards as natural phenomena from his Daoist perspective. The implicit criticism of the rich and powerful, who were obsessed with material enjoyments, reflects Lao Zi's indignation of the social reality of his time. The "excessive preservation of life" that is liable to result in premature death comes about through exposure to the destructive effects of the "five colors" that cause blindness, the "five tones" that cause deafness, the "five flavors" that cause the loss of taste, and "racing and hunting" that cause madness (see Part III, 10.1). Observant and critical as he was, Lao Zi could do nothing to change or improve the situation. He therefore stuck to his philosophy of plainness and simplicity by advising people in general to learn how to preserve life according to the principle of the *Dao*. Under such circumstances, a practical approach lies in belittling the value of life or clinging less tightly to life-consciousness, since only by so doing can one be "out of the range of death" in Lao Zi's words.

In Zhuang Zi's philosophy there is frequent explication of the naturalness of both life and death. Once he even goes so far as to proclaim that life is an excrescence, a tumor, and death is taken as the bursting of the tumor. Zhuang Zi also contends that all living beings in the world evolve from *qi*, as the vital force. Thus one comes to be alive when this vital force gathers together, and dies when this vital force disperses. He then describes the stages of existence: A man toils throughout his life; he lives an easy life when old and retired; and he finally enjoys rest after death. Describing life and death in such a circle, Zhuang Zi tells people not to welcome life when it comes along, and not to resist death when it too comes along. Zhuang Zi, in fact, is said to have beaten a drum and sung on the occasion of the natural death of his beloved wife.

According to Daoist thought, one can achieve freedom in the pure sense of the word only when he sees through the essence of death as a natural phenomenon or an inevitable end. This argument is of course open to criticism and counter-argument as well. The argument is also somewhat shrouded in obscurity and paradox. Thus it could be viewed as something pessimistically negative. That is to say, one could be crushed by such a dark and tragic sense of death, and might thereby reduce oneself to a passive being due to the consciousness of the inevitability of death. In other words, one would set no aims but muddle through life simply because death is like a sword hanging over one, ready to fall at any minute. In short, one may have no drive to take any action but wait for the coming of death. Such being the case, whether to be or not to be is no longer a question, simply because this kind of life is not distinct from death. This easily reminds us of the Chinese saying, "The suffering of misery is no worse than the death of the heart (i.e. loss of hope)."

On the other hand, this view of death can also result in a positive attitude to life itself. Since one is highly aware of the inevitability of death, one may first of all attach a meaning or a purpose to life as a passage from birth to death. Thus one may make the most of one's life because every minute is precious. One knows well that time is on the wing and can never repeat itself once it passes by. (We therefore have an old saying that "He who has high aspirations tends to sigh that the day is rather short.") Hence, one grasps every second and works extremely hard. Consequently one contributes and constructs more in one's lifetime, expecting such achievements to extend the significance of one's existence into human society and history.

Secondly, a person who accepts death as a natural phenomenon just as life is will be able to make light of whatever hardships, difficulties, miseries, sufferings and other negative experiences he encounters. In Nietzsche's phrase, he will be able to "laugh at all tragedies."

Thirdly, a person who accepts death as normal may devote himself or sacrifice his life for a cause as a revolutionary, religious martyr, etc. He may choose to die a hero's death for his ideals. Confucianism recommends that a gentleman should give up his body for the sake of humanity. This spirit of devotion obviously demands a positive sense of death, and this is in fact regarded as a way of becoming immortal.

In conclusion, when we argue that one can become free in the real sense of the word by identifying the nature of death we are encouraged to face death without fear. Thus we have no reason to be either panicked or enslaved by death to the degree that we have to crawl under its imagined claws. We should accordingly be masters of our own fate and of death as well. In this case we can afford to improve the quality of our lives in all possible aspects.

18 On the Merits of Contentment

A saying widespread among the Chinese people goes: "He who is contented (with what he has) is always merry and happy." This notion is in fact derived from Lao Zi's view on the causes of social problems in his own day. His recommendation of contentment, or self-contentment, if properly interpreted and received, still has a certain instructive import in modern times, when society is just as obsessed with material desires as in Lao Zi's time. The focus of the discussion falls on chapters 44 and 46 (DDJ).

18.1 (Chapter 44)

Which is more dear, fame or life?
Which is more valuable, life or wealth?
Which is more detrimental, gain or loss? [1]
Thus an excessive love of fame
  Is bound to cause an extravagant expense.[2]
A rich hoard of wealth
  Is bound to suffer a heavy loss.[3]
Therefore he who is contented will encounter no disgrace.
He who knows when and where to stop will meet no danger.
And in this way he can endure longer.

Annotations:

[1] "Gain" means the gain of fame and wealth, whereas "loss" means the loss of life or the body.

[2] It would be "an extravagant expense" or waste of energy, vital force and real self.

[3] It would be "a heavy loss" of what has been gained in case

of disaster, robbery, theft and even life itself.

Commentary:

It is easily detectable that Lao Zi advises people to value and treasure life instead of fame and wealth. He sees the latter as causes of danger in one sense, and in another sense as something that can be gained but never maintained, for they are "external things" and not beneficial to life at all. In human society as a whole, what the common folks desire and pursue are chiefly fame and wealth. They may go so far as to be enslaved by "the reins of fame and the shackles of wealth" as metaphorically depicted in Chinese.

As a result, Lao Zi recommends the merit of being contented with what one has. By virtue of self-contentment one can be free from disgrace and danger, and endure longer. This idea seems to be an extension of that "he who is contended is rich," as Lao Zi states in Chapter 33 (see Part III, 15.1).

As regards his preference for life, Lao Zi does not necessarily expect any excessive preservation of it. He rounds out the value of life in contrast with fame and wealth, that he rejects external things. The implied message in this context turns out to be a warning to the greed-ridden rich and fame-thirsty people. In respect of the emphasis on self-contentment, Lao Zi preaches the notion that the more easily one is contented with what one has, the closer will he get to the principle of the *Dao*. It can be perceived that one is most apt to live a more tranquil and peaceful life embellished with rich spiritual nourishment if one is contented with whatever material possessions one has. Nevertheless, a static or distorted interpretation of the concept of self-contentedness would be rather misleading for it may seduce one into justifying his passivity, laziness and even parasitism.

18.2 (Chapter 46)

When the world has the *Dao*,[1]
  Warhorses are used in farming.[2]
When the world lacks the *Dao*,
  Even mares in foal have to serve in battle.[3]
There is no guilt greater than lavish desires.

There is no calamity greater than discontentment.
There is no defect greater than covetousness.
Therefore, he who is contented with knowing contentment
Is always contented indeed.

Annotations:

[1] The *Dao* is employed here to suggest political stability and social order.

[2] That "warhorses are used in farming" implies peace and a pastoral life.

[3] That "even mares in foal have to serve in battle" indicates the harsh conditions during wartime, when the peasants were deprived of all their horses. The sentence is a free translation of the original one, which is literally "war horses thrive in the suburbs."

Commentary:

All wars and social conflicts are, in Lao Zi's mind, unexceptionally ascribed to lavish desires, discontentment, greed or ambition. Lao Zi is known to oppose war, hence he repeatedly advocates the importance of acting upon the principle of the *Dao* and meanwhile protests against any resorting to force at the expense of political stability and social order.

His sharp criticism of discontentment underlines the necessity and significance of contentment, in striking contrast. From an epistemological perspective, the statement "he who is contented with knowing contentment is always contented" can be understood as a high dimension in Lao Zi's doctrine of self-contentment. It seems to be an initial contentment when one is contended with what he has. Then it seems to be a sublimated contentment when one is contented with knowing contentment. It is through the former that the latter is possible as a consequence of a higher sphere of personal cultivation.

19 On the Possibilities of Achievement

Lao Zi is often misunderstood as an advocator of "doing nothing" or "non-action," through which one is expected to abstain from society or reject any social role. The fact of the matter is that Lao Zi keeps advising people to take no (arbitrary) action, follow the *Dao* of spontaneity, and act for others but not compete with them. A close reading of chapters 63 and 64 (DDJ) will help one grasp Lao Zi's notion of so-called "doing nothing" (*wu wei*) at all.

19.1 (Chapter 63)

Consider take-no-action as a code of conduct.
Consider make-no-trouble as a way of deed.
Consider have-no-flavor as a method of taste.[1]

It is a rule in the world that
The most difficult things begin with the easy ones,
And the largest things arise from the minute ones.[2]
Hence, tackle the difficult while it is still easy;
Achieve the large while it is still minute.[3]
For this reason, the sage never strives for the great,
And thereby he can accomplish it.[4]

He who makes promises too readily will surely lack credibility.
He who takes things too easily will surely encounter difficulties.
Therefore, even the sage regards things as difficult,
And he is free from difficulties as a result.[5]

Annotations:

[1] These are in fact three general principles or criteria of human conduct in accordance with the characteristics of the *Dao* in Lao Zi's formulation. "Consider having-no-flavor as a method of taste" seems to reflect the idea presented in Chapter 35 that "The *Dao*, if spoken out, is insipid and tasteless" (*Dao zhi chu kou, dan hu qi wu wei*).

[2] These lines intend to expose and reinforce the notion that the great develops from the small and the many from the few —encapsulating Lao Zi's sharp observation of the inner development of things in general and their dynamic transformation in

particular.

[3] These lines represent one of Lao Zi's dialectical views which appears to be fairly identical with the concept of "quantitative change toward qualitative change."

[4] This suggests the process of great achievement accomplished by the Daoist sage or the man who is in harmony with the *Dao*. During this process, he remains modest and prudent instead of being ambitious and arrogant; he starts with the small and easy things, and then, bit by bit and step by step, accumulates more and more, and advances further and further.

[5] This is obviously an encouragement to foster a consistently prudent and cautious attitude when coping with matters. Otherwise, one is likely to fail on the threshold of success merely due to carelessness or cocksureness.

Commentary:

The main theme of this chapter is strategies of dealing with difficult matters on the one hand, and the possibilities of making achievements on the other. The former requires constant prudence and care, apart from an all-round view of things. That is to say, one must see things from both the difficult and easy aspects. Then, one should commence with the easy, at the same time as being conscious of taking even the easy as the difficult. Making great achievements involves a dialectical insight into the process of the inherent progression from the small to the great. Hence, one must remain modest and persevering, and adopt a step-by-step or bit-by-bit policy. One should begin with the small, which then rolls and gathers matter like a snowball pushed forward with continuous efforts.

19.2 (Chapter 64)

What is stable is easy to hold.
What is not yet manifest is easy to handle.
What is brittle is easy to disintegrate.
What is minute is easy to eliminate.
Deal with matters before they occur.
Put them in order before disorder arises.
A tree as huge as one's embrace grows from a tiny shoot.[1]

A tower of nine stories rises from a heap of earth.[2]
A journey of a thousand *li* starts from the first step. [3]
People often fail when they are on the point of success
In their conduct of affairs.
If they remain still as careful at the end as at the beginning,
They will never suffer failures.

Annotations:

[1] This simile is used to suggest the hugeness of a tree. The actual size may go beyond the circumference of a man's embrace.

[2] The number of stories is rather symbolic in this context. In Chinese culture the number nine (*jiu*) usually symbolizes "the ultimate height" or "many."

[3] The Chinese expression "a thousand *li*" (*qian li*) is arithmetically equivalent to "five hundred kilometers" in concrete measurement. However, it is employed in this context to indicate a very long distance in an allegorical sense.

Commentary:

This chapter attempts to illustrate through specific examples the interrelationship or interaction between the big and the small, the high and the low, and the long and the short. It also advises people to cultivate a spirit of both persistency and patience in pursuit of their targets. In addition, it encourages people to become more prudent and cautious when they are approaching the end of any task. Otherwise they are most likely to ruin the whole business when they are right on the threshold of success.

Experience teaches that identifying the cause of a potential catastrophe enables measures to be taken to prevent it. That is why we have such sayings springing from the collective wisdom as follows: "Prevention is better than cure," "take an umbrella with you when there is a sign of rain," etc.

It is equally important to take into account the potential changes and developments of things encountered. According to Lao Zi, the great develops from the small, the high from the low, and the long from the short. During this process of change and development, one must take relevant and precautionary steps so as to bring things under control. That is to say, it is highly advisable to tackle a problem "in the cradle" so to speak, otherwise it will grow to an unmanageable size and eventually turn into its opposite. A dam of a thousand "*li*" (a Chinese measurement of length equivalent to half a km that is metaphorically used to mean a great dam in length and size) long, for instance, may be destroyed as a result of an ant boring a hole in it. Likewise, a building of 10,000 feet high may be destroyed by a single spark. These two parabolic cases are popular among the Chinese people and often cited to justify the above-mentioned argument. Accordingly, he who is regarded as wise is a man observant enough to pinpoint the problem at the very beginning, and then is ready to cope with it at the earliest possible moment.

In view of Lao Zi's warning that "People often fail when they are about to succeed in their conduct of affairs," we may arrive at the conclusion that whatever one tries to do, one will be rebuffed in the end if one lacks prudence and perseverance. It is noticeable in everyday life that most people tend to be overpleased with preliminary success or self-contented with minor gains at the first stages of their endeavors. Thus they overlook the hard reality that "He who laughs last laughs best." Others (especially opponents or enemies) are eager to take advantage of such carelessness to the extent of setting a trap by dangling bait first, and then knocking the victim down with a club when he takes it (see Part III, 20.4).

20 On the Art of Leadership

Lao Zi's political philosophy is amply reflected in his discussion of the art of leadership. Generally speaking, it features "take-no-action," "non-competition," "retreat for the sake of advance," and "keeping to tenderness as a strategy." Driven or stimulated by their experiences and practical demands, many readers of the *Dao De Jing* project their own ideas or read modern themes into the book. That is why it is continually read and reread and new discoveries are constantly surfacing. Scrutiny of the following 11 chapters (DDJ) will illustrate this.

20.1 (Chapter 3)

Try not to exalt the worthy,[1]
So that the people shall not compete.[2]
Try not to value rare treasures,
So that the people shall not steal.
Try not to display the desirable,
So that the people's hearts shall not be disturbed.
Therefore the sage governs the people by
Purifying their minds,[3]
Filling their bellies,[4]
Weakening their ambitions,[5]
And strengthening their bones.[6]
He always keeps them innocent of knowledge and desires,[7]
And makes the crafty afraid to run risks.
He conducts affairs on the principle of take-no-action,
And everything will surely fall into order.

Annotations:

[1] By "the worthy" (*xian ren* or *xian shi*) is meant the kind of people who claim to be learned, talented and capable of helping the ruler conduct state affairs. At that time there were many scholars traveling from one state to another in search of a so-called wise ruler to employ them. They tended to indulge in grandiloquent discourses and make extravagant promises about helping the ruler concerned to expand his territory, wealth and power. A few of them actually did render useful services, but most turned out to be puffed-up frauds. This led to widespread competition for favors from the rulers of the various states.

[2] According to Heshang Gong, *bu zheng* (not compete) indicates that the people are freed from any desire or intention to contest and struggle against each other for social achievement and reputation. They thus grow inclined to return to the Nature of which they partake.

[3] The advice *xu qi xin* (purify their minds) suggests keeping their minds vacuous and free from all greedy ideas or competitive intentions. According to Chan Wing-tsit, the Chinese term *xu* literally means "empty," which implies here absolute peace and

purity of mind, and freedom from worry and selfish desires (see Chan Wing-tsit. *A Source Book in Chinese Philosophy*, p. 141).

[4] The proposal *shi qi fu* (fill their bellies) literally denotes the satisfaction of people's basic needs, such as their physical needs for food and drink. The implied message is related to the possibility of easy contentment with what one has in contrast to insatiable greed stimulated by external things (i.e. wealth and fame). This expression should be read with particular reference to Lao Zi's saying, "The sage therefore cares for the belly instead of the eyes" in Chapter 12 (see Part III, 10.1). Historically speaking, however, deeply rooted in Chinese thinking is the notion that "people give the food supply priority," and this has had a chronic influence on governmental policies from ancient times until today. One of its negative aspects can be seen in the typical Chinese over-emphasis on food or eating in daily life and at festivals as well. The Chinese people tend to consider a festival a special occasion for a big feast. Although the modern trend is to frown on the traditional extravagance displayed at feasts, such celebrations can be regarded as a distinct cultural phenomenon with its own special features, such as the rich variety of cuisine and the enjoyment of a harmonious ambiance.

[5] The idea *ruo qi zhi* (weaken their ambitions) is meant as a strategy to reduce people's desire or impulse for competition: The petty man (*xiao ren*) gets up early in the morning to pursue profit, and the superior man (*jun zi*) does the same in order to promote his reputation and standing. They act so simply because they are motivated only by their ambitions. It is clear that this kind of obsession, at the very least, heats up the competition in society and bring about disorder on the one hand, and on the other, it results in the loss of one's real self owing to the fact that one constantly falls a victim to alienation and enslavement by either one's ambitions or external things. In addition, it stirs up the tendency of people to play tricks upon each other.

[6] The idea *qiang qi gu* (strengthen their bones) literally means to make people healthy and strong. It might also imply making them satisfied and contented by doing so.

[7] The phrase *wu zhi wu yu* (innocent of knowledge and

desires) may well be comprehended as being without knowledge of how to resort to crafty ideas in order to gain the upper hand, and as being without desire to compete or struggle for more gains.

Commentary:

This chapter has long been interpreted as a strategy of leadership. It advises the ruling class not to elevate the worthy, not to value rare treasures and not to display or show off the desirable, so that the human competitive instinct may be diminished. This is precisely because competition among people tends to stir up social confusion and chaos.

On the other hand, it advises the ruler to learn government from the sage. That is to empty the people's minds by purifying them of all desires for either reputation or social rank. Meanwhile, it calls for the fulfillment of the people's basic needs, for example, their need for daily provisions and necessities. According to an ancient Chinese scholar, the ruler is likened to a boat and the people to water. The boat can sail smoothly when the water is calm, whereas it can be turned over when the water swirls in anger. This analogy illustrates vividly the interaction between the ruling class and the ordinary people. It thus attempts to warn the ruling class that they can not afford to ignore their subjects in general, and their fundamental needs in particular. Otherwise, the tables will be bound to turn in their disfavor. Such being the case, we can better understand the following remarkable statement by Mao Zedong: "The masses are ready to hanker after social reform and to stir up political revolution when they are poverty-stricken." This implies that as human beings all work and struggle to survive, they may have no other choice but to rise in revolt if their subsistence is threatened. This does not necessarily mean that all humans are the same, for it is granted that some people live for ideals rather than for making their ends meet or filling their bellies.

"He conducts affairs on the principle of take-no-action." This is a notion running throughout Lao Zi's ideology. It calls up a ruler to do things or conduct state affairs in the most natural way possible, without being arbitrary and high-handed in ruling his subjects.

It must be pointed out that the notion of being "without knowledge" is conceived by some Lao Zi scholars as something to do with making people ignorant and stupid. It actually means reducing people's motives to play tricks or engage in craftiness in the competition involved in human activities. Correspondingly, the expression "without desires" is employed to mean that instinctive desire is to be conserved, while greedy or social desire for material possessions is to be eschewed since it is a crucial cause of all the problems arising in human society.

The expression *shang xian* (exalt or elevate the worthy) seems to me not simply to be a strategy utilized by a ruler to attract the worthy, but also a way of attaining a good name for himself. Throughout the course of Chinese history, there are many examples of emperors who made good use of men who were qualified or worthy in terms of social accomplishments, although others who were promoted to high positions were mere frauds.

The development of material civilization is prone to foster and reinforce people's desires for possessions. A close observation of modern advertising bears this out. It thus reduces people to the plight of being passive consumers or slaves of commodities. A considerable proportion of human anxiety, frustration and depression, which together comprise psycho-cultural problems, can be perceived as a consequence of the commercial display of desirable things. If by any chance all the mass media ceased to display such things, I assume that tension, either in a social or psychological sense, may well be relaxed to a great extent. If we approach Lao Zi's thought from this perspective in relation to the present human condition, we are most likely to rediscover new and rich implications in his canons. This explains why his book, short as it is—only 5,000 words or so—can be read and re-read, continually revealing fresh messages and enlightenment.

20.2 (Chapter 26)

The heavy is the root of the light.[1]
The tranquil is the lord of the hasty.[2]
Therefore the sage travels all day

Without leaving behind his baggage cart.[3]
Although he enjoys a magnificent and comfortable life,
He remains at leisure and without self-indulgence in it.
How is it that a king with ten thousand chariots
Governs his kingdom so lightly and hastily?[4]
Lightness is sure to lose the root.[5]
Hastiness is sure to lose the lord.[6]

Annotations:

[1] Being an English rendering of *zhong wei qing gen*, the word "heavy" (*zhong*) is metaphorically used to suggest a sophisticated way of managing things that features steadiness, firmness, stability and reliability. The word "light" (*qing*), on the other hand, means the opposite. The former is essentially decisive in comparison with the latter such that it is likened to be "the root" (*gen*).

[2] This is a somewhat literal translation of *jing wei zao jun*. The notion "tranquil" (*jing*) is repeated here to reflect Lao Zi's positive affirmation of tranquility as an extension of and a strategy against "take-(arbitrary)-action." Lao Zi stresses that by staying tranquil and observant one is bound to overcome arbitrary or blind action. In comparison, the idea of "hasty" (*zao*) is seen to be characteristically negative, since it is, in Lao Zi's mind, a display of "take-(arbitrary)-action." The term "lord" (*jun*) means in this context the mastery, control or command of the relevant matter.

[3] In ancient times a traveller took along his food and other necessities in a baggage cart. If he happened to leave it behind, he would be in serious trouble.

[4] "A king with ten thousand chariots" in antiquity was the ruler of a large state.

[5] "The root" here refers to the steady and reliable policy, as explained in [1]. Gao Heng, a leading Lao Zi scholar, takes this line as "Lightness is sure to lose ministers" (*qing ze shi chen*). He interprets it to mean the ruler will, if he governs his kingdom lightly, surely lose the loyalty of his ministers, who may then plot to overthrow him.

[6] "The lord" refers here to the tranquil strategy as has been

discussed in [2]. Gao Heng takes this last line as "Hastiness is sure to lose the people" (*zao ze shi min*). That is to say, the ruler will, if he conducts state affairs hastily, certainly bring about social disorder, and thus lose the support and respect of the people, who may in turn rebel against his rule.

Commentary:

This chapter presents four approaches to government —heavy, tranquil, light and hasty. The contradictions between them are ostensible. With the former favored and the latter rejected, Lao Zi persistently advises the ruler to adopt his political philosophy of "take-no-(arbitrary)-action," which he thinks is the general principle of competent and sound government.

In reality the ruler functions as the hub of a state or governmental machine. Hence what he does will naturally affect the entire operation of that machine. If he governs his kingdom lightly and hastily, in Lao Zi's terms, the ruler will plunge not only himself but also the whole country into trouble or chaos. It is for this reason that he is recommended to be prudent and play safe in respect of his political policy and governmental administration.

20.3 (Chapter 36)

In order to contract it,
It is necessary to expand it first.
In order to weaken it,
It is necessary to strengthen it first.
In order to destroy it,
It is necessary to promote it first.
In order to grasp it,
It is necessary to offer it first.
This is called subtle light.[1]

The soft and the tender overcome the hard and the strong.[2]
(Just as) fish should not be taken away from deep water,
The sharp weapons of the state should not be displayed to the people.[3]

Annotations:

[1] The original expression *wei ming* is literally rendered as "subtle light," which figuratively means "profound and predictive insight into what is going to take place the other way round." It is conceptually illustrated and justified by the subsequent line: "The soft and the tender overcome the hard and the strong." Some Lao Zi scholars assume that *wei ming* indicates a natural law of change appearing shrouded in obscurity but remaining manifest in reality.

[2] This is one of the most important notions put forth by Lao Zi. It is elaborated earlier. (See Part III, 11).

[3] "Sharp weapons of the state" is the literal translation of *guo zhi li qi*. Being ambiguous, this expression is reckoned to suggest metaphorically "the political power of the state," "the system of punishments and rewards," or "the strategies of both governmental and military administration."

Commentary:

Lao Zi consistently holds on to his observation that everything has two sides which seem to be in a state of continuous opposition and mutual transformation. That is to say, when one of the two sides develops to its extreme or acme, it will inevitably be transformed into its opposite. This dialectical thought is reflected in his description in this chapter of the interrelations and interactions between contraction and expansion, weakening and strengthening, and destruction and promotion, as well as grasping and giving. His analysis of the development of these matters and phenomena naturally leads to his generalization that "Reversion is the movement of the *Dao*" presented in Chapter 40.

A flower, for example, will naturally wither or close up (contraction) when it is in full bloom (expansion). Thus the latter can be viewed as a sign of the former state. Conversely, an inchworm draws itself together when it wants to stretch out. Dragons and snakes hibernate in order to preserve their lives and activities. It is therefore concluded that "contraction and expansion act upon each other, and hereby arises that which furthers" (see *Yi Jing Xi Ci* [*The Great Treatise on The Book of Changes*]).

As regards this dialectical thought of Lao Zi, Shi Deqing made an interesting and illustrative comment. He said, "What Lao Zi argues in this context concerns the natural development of things that is beyond human perception in general. All things in the world are sure to reverse themselves when they reach their extremes. The sun will, for instance, start to descend and set in the west when it is overhead shining to its fullest; the moon will begin to wane as soon as it is completely full. So natural is the movement of things. Expansion is therefore a sign of the imminence of contraction; the strong is therefore the sprouting of the weak; the flourishing is therefore a harbinger of the declining; the given is therefore a symptom of the taken. Both natural phenomena and human affairs develop and change in such a natural and inevitable way. Ordinary people who encounter these things are unable to predict or recognize what is behind them. It is for this reason that the *Dao* is called the "subtle light" (see Shi Deqing, *Lao Zi Dao De Jing Jie*).

It is noteworthy that these lines are often misconceived and misinterpreted as conspiratorial tactics applied to power-games. And accordingly, Lao Zi himself is often labeled a political conspirator. This is understandable to the extent that each reader of the *Dao De Jing* is liable to form his or her own image of Lao Zi by reading personal or modern ideas and feelings into his book. It is no wonder that there are, as the saying goes, as many types of Hamlet as there are audiences. The same is also true of Lao Zi. We tend to maintain that Lao Zi describes the interactions between all those categories simply in order to justify his conception of the inexorable transformation between opposites. According to Gao Heng, Lao Zi is here talking about the *Dao* of Heaven or the natural law. Hence it is groundless to accuse him of being a conspirator. (see Gao Heng. *Lao Zi Zheng Gu*, p. 81.) As can be noticed throughout the *Dao De Jing*, Lao Zi often exposes his theses first, and then leaves off by warning the ruling class of what they should not do. This chapter is no exception. That "the sharp weapons of the state should not be displayed to the people" is advice to the rulers not to apply severe laws, orders and regulations when controlling, punishing or threatening the people. This may bring about more trouble than benefit because when driven into a corner the people will rise in revolt against "the sharp weapons of the state" and the ruling class which wields them. These "weapons" are in fact symbolic of the strong, who can not last long since they are, in Lao Zi's terms, the companions of death.

20.4 (Chapter 59)

To rule people and to serve Heaven
Nothing is better than the principle of frugality.[1]
Only by frugality can one get ready early.[2]
To get ready early means to accumulate *De* continuously.
With the continuous accumulation of *De*,
One can overcome every difficulty.
If one can overcome every difficulty,
He will then acquire immeasurable capacity.
With immeasurable capacity,
He can achieve the *Dao* to govern the country.[3]
He who has the *Dao* of the country can maintain sovereignty.
This is called the way in which the roots are planted deep
And the stalks are made firm;
Longevity is achieved and sovereignty is made everlasting.

Annotations:

[1] The expression "to serve Heaven" means to preserve one's energy and life for the sake of one's natural term of existence. "The principle of frugality" implies the principle of cherishing and treasuring the vital energy, contextually referring to "the way in which the roots are planted deep and the stalks are made firm, longevity is achieved and sovereignty is made everlasting."

[2] The implications of this line could be that only by frugality can one become ready in time to act upon the *Dao* or return to the *Dao*.

[3] *You guo zhi mu* literally means to "have the mother of the country." The word "mother" suggests protection and preservation as important functions of the *Dao*.

Commentary:

Lao Zi recommends in this chapter "the principle of frugality" in a spiritual rather than material sense. He warns the ruling class not to display "the sharp weapons of the state" frequently or use them indiscreetly, otherwise disorder and revolt may result. Meanwhile he advises people not to do what should not be done; instead they should preserve their energy and nourish their spirit by reducing acquisitive desires and arbitrary actions. As a strategy, frugality is conducive to longevity and the maintenance of sovereignty.

20.5 (Chapter 60)

Governing a large country is like cooking a small fish.[1]
If the *Dao* is applied to the world,
Ghosts will lose their supernatural influence.[2]
It is not that they will actually lose it,
But that their influence will no longer be able to harm men.
It is not that their influence will no longer be able to harm men,
But that the sage also will not harm men.
Since these two do not harm men, and vice versa,[3]
They all enjoy peaceful co-existence.[4]

Annotations:

[1] *Zhi da guo, re peng xiao xian* (Governing a large country is like cooking a small fish) has become a well-known aphorism in political science. It is often taken as a strategy for conducting state affairs, widely noted for its long, historical and even international influence. US President Ronald Reagan, for instance, once cited it in one of his public speeches. The implicit warning is that, just as a small fish can be ruined if it is turned over too often while being cooked, so too can disorder be brought about in a state if the people are disturbed by too many orders and decrees. Such being the case, a ruler should become highly conscious that the mystique of, or the key to, good and stable government lies in the *Dao* of cherishing tranquility and taking no (arbitrary) action, for the sake of the public interest.

[2] This line is also rendered as "The spirits will lose their spiritual power" and "Applying the *Dao* to the kingdom can render ghosts harmless." This suggests that the *Dao* is more determinative and powerful than anything else, including the deities or other supernatural beings.

[3] The expression *fu liang bu xiang shang* (which is rendered here as "Since these two do not harm men, and vice versa") is ambiguous. Some Lao Zi scholars (e.g. Chan Wing-tsit and Ai Qi) suppose that it means the non-harmful interrelationship between the divine beings and the sage. Others (e.g. Gu Di, Chen Guying and Sha Shaohai) maintain that it means that neither ghosts nor the sage will harm people, and vice versa. I personally prefer the second interpretation.

[4] The subject "they" here stands for supernatural beings, the sage and the people involved. According to Han Fei Zi, the original expression *de jiao gui yan* means that *De*, as virtue or power, will grow completely intermingled with all beings and be given back to the people. That is to say, the world will achieve peace and the people live in harmony so long as disturbances are avoided.

Commentary:

The art of government as recommended by Lao Zi is factually an extension of his philosophy of taking no (arbitrary) action and following the way of spontaneity. Lao Zi offers advice of this kind not simply as a strategy for the benefit of the ruling class, but also due to his concern about the harsh conditions the ordinary people had to endure at that time.

As can be discerned in this chapter, Lao Zi demonstrates his atheist stance in respect of the imagined preternaturalness of ghosts and deities. This argument can be supported in a twofold way. Firstly, these supernatural beings would no longer function if the *Dao* were applied to governing the world. This obviously implies that the *Dao* is more decisive than beings in whatever form (i.e. divine, supernatural, sagely or human). Secondly, the practitioner of the *Dao* is certainly a human being who has achieved the *Dao*. Hence, it can be safely said that a human being of this type can maintain his own dignity in the face of supernatural beings. The implications of this have a great historical significance. Therefore, there is scarcely any surprise in Xun Zi's remark that "Man is bound to conquer Heaven."

It can be also observed by reading between the lines that Lao Zi intends to tell the reader in a roundabout way that disasters or scourges are caused by men themselves, and not other beings. If men act upon the *Dao* as Lao Zi advises, they will remain free from any danger or harm which is supposed to be emanated from without—from ghosts, for example. This naturally reminds us of Lao Zi's persistent opposition to acquisitive desires and competitive drives on the part of human beings.

20.6 (Chapter 61)

Governing a large country is like lying in a lower place.
This country may be likened to rivers and streams
Flowing into the sea.
It lies lower such that all in the world runs to it.
It is the converging point of all in the world.[1]
It is the female of the world
That always overcomes the male via tranquility,[2]
And with tranquility she lies lower.[3]
Hence a big state can rally small states around it
If it lowers itself to them.[4]
Small states can win trust from a big state
If they lower themselves to it.[5]
Thus a big state can rally small states by lowering itself.
Small states can win trust from a big state by lowering themselves.
What a big state wants is to unite and lead small states.
What small states want is to be rallied and protected by the big state.
When both sides get what they respectively want,
The big state should learn to keep itself lower.

Annotations:

[1] The first four lines of this text have been revised as a result of the philological studies of such scholars as Gao Heng and Gu

Di. They are transposed into this chapter in accordance with the contextual analysis of Gu Di.

[2] The interaction between the female and the male reflects Lao Zi's conviction that the *Yin* (or the tender and weak) will overcome the *Yang* (or the hard and strong). This notion is already articulated in Part III, 11.

[3] The female power is regarded by Lao Zi as derived from humility and tranquility.

[4] Lao Zi advises the large country to remain modest and friendly toward the small states.

[5] The small states are also advised to be modest and friendly toward the large country because of the demands of their bilateral relationships.

Commentary:

Lao Zi expounds in this chapter on his political philosophy, i.e., how to develop and maintain good relationships between large and small states. His notion of being friendly and modest by "lying in a lower place" is highly advisable to large and powerful countries even today. Only by doing so can they win the trust of small states and contribute to global stability and peace. The current policy of peaceful co-existence can be seen as an extension of Lao Zi's doctrine.

Lao Zi's political recommendations are based on the historical situation of his time, when China was composed of a group of states of varying sizes, and no longer a unified country. There were constant clashes between the states, among which the larger and stronger tended to bully the smaller and weaker. The unity of China then was gradually achieved through wars annexation. Lao Zi himself was preoccupied with the attainment and maintenance of peace, but persistently opposed brutal warfare, which only resulted in the suffering of the common people. That is why he advises states, whether large or small, to remain friendly and modest to each other for the sake of mutual understanding, trust and acceptability. It must be borne in mind that the large and powerful countries are assumed by Lao Zi to play the major role in this realm in general.

20.7 (Chapter 66)

The great rivers and seas can be the kings of the mountain streams
Because they skillfully stay below them.[1]
That is why they can be their kings.
Therefore, in order to be above the people,
The sage must place himself below them in his words.
In order to be ahead of the people,
He must place himself behind them in his person.[2]
In this way, the sage is above the people,
But they do not feel his weight.
He is ahead of the people,
But they do not feel his hindrance.[3]
Therefore the whole world delights in praising him
And never gets tired of him.
Simply because he does not compete with others,
Nobody under Heaven can compete with him.

Annotations:

[1] This implies metaphorically wise rulers or leaders in general who are able to win over the hearts of the people by being modest.

[2] A sage of this kind can be a qualified leader simply because he remains cautious with his words and modest with his deeds.

[3] The sage neither harms nor threatens anybody. Thus he is accepted and supported by the people, who do not feel any burden or pressure from above.

Commentary:

In this chapter Lao Zi expresses his leadership tactics that feature non-competition and modesty. He advises the ruling class to stay "below" and "behind" instead of "above" and "ahead" of the ruled so as to win them over, just like the great rivers and seas into which all mountain streams run. This is the way the powerful or the authorities avoid disturbing or putting too much pressure on the populace. Otherwise the people's lives will become rather negative and miserable.

Lao Zi lauds the image of the sage ruler, who is held up as a model simply because he is not at all arrogant or self-important in his treatment of people; he does things without competing for fame or personal gain, and he leads the people without threatening them by showing off his power. If he is by any chance so self-centered that he always thinks of his own benefits first and pushes himself ahead of others, he is liable to be detested, and even overthrown by his subordinates or subjects, or both.

20.8 (Chapter 72)

When people do not fear the power of the ruler,
Something terribly dreadful will take place.[1]
Do not force the people out of their dwellings.[2]
Do not exploit the people to the point that they cannot live.[3]
They will not detest and overthrow the regime
Only when they are not excessively oppressed.

Annotations:

[1] By "something terribly dreadful" is meant social disorder, uprisings, turmoil, etc., which usually result from the abuse of power or harsh political dictatorship.

[2] Excessive disturbances are the last straw for the long-suffering people, who then rise in revolt.

[3] When people cannot make a living any more, they have no choice but to turn to other (violent and risky) means for survival even if it means putting their lives on the line. That is the time that "something terribly dreadful" will take place.

Commentary:

In the case of governing a country, Lao Zi strongly opposes all high-handed policies. Thus he warns the ruling class not to push the people to extremes. Otherwise, they will be driven to rebel in desperation.

History provides a wealth of examples showing that the abuse of power or despotism in any conceivable form will eventually lead to self-defeat or self-destruction. The relationship between the government and the people is allegorically identical to the interaction between a boat and the water. The water below not only sustains the boat as it flows on its surface, it can also capsize it if the waves are stirred up.

20.9 (Chapter 73)

He who is brave in daring will be killed.[1]
He who is brave in not daring will survive.[2]
Of these two kinds of bravery,
One is advantageous, while the other is harmful.
Heaven detests what it detests.
Who knows its cause?
The *Dao* of Heaven does not compete, and yet it is good at winning.[3]
It does not speak, and yet it is good at responding.
It is not called, and yet it comes along on its own.
It is frankly at ease, and yet it plans well.
The net of Heaven is large and vast,[4]
It lets nothing escape, despite its wide meshes.

Annotations:

[1] The meaning of this sentence can be completed by expanding it to "He who is brave in daring to be hard and stiff will perish," which is an extension of the idea that "The hard and stiff are the companions of death."

[2] The idea embedded in this line can be completed by expanding it to "He who is brave in not daring to be hard and stiff but in being tender and weak will survive." This obviously includes the notion that "The tender and weak are the companions of life."

[3] "The *Dao* of Heaven" here refers to the natural law that is usually characterized by helping things develop without competition, and with diminishing the excessive so as to supplement the deficient.

[4] "The net of Heaven" is used as a metaphor to signify the all-embracing coverage or realm of Nature.

Commentary:

"This chapter lays forth," according to Ren Jiyu, "Lao Zi's attitude toward life and the idea of predestination. In Lao Zi's opinion, all things are disposed of by Nature. Man has to put himself at the disposal of nature, striving for nothing, doing nothing, saying nothing, which is all to the good, whereas action brings unfavorable consequences" (see *The Book of Lao Zi*, p. 94).

It is fairly apparent that Lao Zi seems to stress only the functions of the natural law while neglecting the initiative of man. It is on this point that his argument turns out to be somewhat lop-sided. However, we assume that Lao Zi attempts to distinguish between two kinds of bravery from his naturalistic perspective on the one hand, and on the other, from his affirmative stance toward the tender and weak and his negative one toward the hard and stiff. He believes that the *Dao* of Heaven or the natural law as such remains tender, weak and noncompetitive, but at the same time it is beneficial and not harmful to anything. Therefore it is highly appreciated and recommended, as contrasted with the *Dao* of man, which features how to compete against and outshine others by means of power or strength. By his advocacy of the *Dao* of Heaven Lao Zi expects people in general to modify their conduct according to the noncompetitive principle of the *Dao*, and the ruler in particular to improve his leadership based on the model of the *Dao* of Heaven. In other words, Lao Zi advises the ruler to follow the *Dao* of spontaneity or naturalness by taking no arbitrary or competitive action. Thus the ruler can successfully follow the road of the *Dao* of Heaven as described in the following: It "does not compete, and yet it is good at winning. It does not speak, and yet it is good at responding. It is not called and yet it comes along on its own. It is frankly at ease and yet it plans well." This way would manifest Lao Zi's political philosophy known as "governing the country without taking action (*wu wei er zhi*)."

20.10 (Chapter 74)

If the people are not afraid of death,
  What is the point of trying to frighten them with death?
In order to make people always afraid of death,
  We can catch and kill the trouble-makers.
Then, who will dare to make trouble?

There is always a master in charge of executions.[1]
To carry out executions in place of the master
Is like hewing wood in place of a skilled carpenter.[2]
Of those who hew wood in place of the carpenter,
Very few escape cutting their own hands.[3]

Annotations:

[1] "The master in charge of executions" means the professional executioner or headsman in the past. Some scholars (e.g. Zhang Mosheng and Cheng Guying) reckon that "a master" here stands for the *Dao* of Heaven, which determines the natural death of all things.

[2] This implies that the ruler or leader should leave actual punishments to "the master in charge" to carry out. Instead, he should strive to construct a self-image of kindness, charity and benevolence.

[3] This is apparently a warning of the destructive consequences of presuming to take over another's job.

Commentary:

This chapter expresses a very crucial aspect of Lao Zi's political philosophy. "If people are not afraid of death, what is the point of trying to frighten them with death?' is really a challenging question. In most times of chaos or social disorder, the ruler who tries to stabilize the situation tends to resort to punishments. He therefore catches and kills the "trouble-makers" or leading rebels in order to frighten other would-be rebels. This corresponds to the old Chinese adage about "killing the chicken to scare the monkeys." But if the people are not afraid of death, punishment cannot be a deterrent.

Seeing the limited function of execution as a widely applied instrument of social and political control, Lao Zi warns the ruling class not to go too far. The implied message of the last five lines in this chapter seems to be that those who carry out such a severe punishment as execution to an excessive degree will only injure themselves in the end. Hence leadership in general should be cautious enough not to drive the people into a corner by waving the club. Otherwise the latter are apt to rise in rebellion and overthrow their masters.

20.11 (Chapter 75)[1]

The people suffer from famine
  Because the ruler levies too much tax-grain.[2]
Thus they suffer from famine.
The people are difficult to rule
  Because the ruler too often takes action.[3]
Thus they are difficult to rule.
The people take life lightly
  Because the ruler longs for life so avidly.[4]
Thus they take life lightly.

Annotations:

[1] In most of the versions of the *Dao De Jing*, this chapter has one more line, which reads "Only those who don't value their lives are wiser than those who overvalue their lives." This has been inserted in Chapter 50 (DDJ), for it fits the context there, according to the textual and philological studies made by Gu Di (see Gu Di and Zhou Ying. *Lao Zi Tong*, p. 398 and also see Part III, 17 of the present book).

[2] This indicates the problems of heavy taxation and the avariciousness of the ruling class.

[3] Acting too often on the part of the rulers causes unwarrantable disturbance. The people adapt to such meddling by, for instance, evading taxes.

[4] This line contains a critique of the ruling class, who tend to overvalue life and live in a lavish way at the expense of the common people.

Commentary:

This chapter exposes the interactions between the rulers and the ruled. The latter suffer a lot simply because the former have too much enjoyment. Thus there arise conflicts between the two parties. And accordingly the social order will be at stake. It is due to this potential crisis that Lao Zi advises the ruling class to be on guard against "blood-sucking." They should learn not to abandon themselves to luxury and prolonging their lives. Rather, they ought to care whether the people they rule are contented or so miserable that they "take life lightly." By "taking life lightly" is meant that the people are driven by desperation to revolt.

21 On Warfare

The *Dao De Jing* is taken by some people (e.g. Mao Zedong) to be a book filled with military thoughts and strategies, in spite of the fact that Lao Zi himself generally maintains a negative attitude to warfare. In the military arena, Lao Zi proposes a defensive policy that is firmly based on his notion of retreat as advance. Developed from this defensive policy are such military strategies and tactics as "wait at one's ease for an exhausted enemy," "defend in order to attack," and "retreat in order to advance," which are all intended to "gain mastery or win victory by striking only after the enemy has struck." In addition, Lao Zi's exposure of the interactions between the "normal way" (*zheng*) and the "unusual or extraordinary way" (*qi*) contains a rich dialectical message and character. Chapters 57, 68 and 69 (DDJ) also touch upon this theme.

21.1 (Chapter 57)

A state should be governed in a normal way.[1]
An army should be operated in an unusual way.[2]
The world should be administered by doing nothing.
How do I know that it should be so?
Through the following:
The more prohibitive enactments there are in the world,
  The poorer the people will become;[3]
The more sharp weapons men have,[4]
  The more troubled the state will be;
The more crafts and techniques men possess,
  The more vicious things will appear;[5]
The more laws and orders are made prominent,
  The more robbers and thieves will spring up. [6]
Therefore the sage says:
"I take no action and the people of themselves become

transformed.[7]

I love tranquility and the people of themselves become righteous.

I disturb nobody and the people of themselves become prosperous.

I have no desires and the people of themselves become simple."[8]

Annotations:

[1] By "normal way" (*zheng*) is meant the *Dao* of tranquility and freedom from desires.

[2] By "unusual way" is meant the whole gamut of secret, tricky and unexpected strategies and tactics.

[3] This is because the people are too often disturbed by demands upon them.

[4] By "sharp weapons" is referred to severe laws, regulations and official orders. If the government of a country depends on all these things to carry out its administration, it will possibly plunge the country into trouble (i.e. rebellions, uprisings, social disorder, etc.).

[5] People would be influenced to the degree that they may lose the virtue of simplicity and cheat each other for gain.

[6] There often arises a situation as follows: Some of the powerful and greedy people will take advantage of their positions for gain when swept away by desires; some of the powerless and the poor people will take risk of theft or robbery when they want more. In order to prevent these mischievous doings some more laws are introduced and exercised in many possible ways. Nevertheless, the laws are made to break simply because some people tend to voilate them in pursuit of their own interest and profit. In the eyes of Lao Zi, so to speak, nothing can stop the self-seeking people when they rush into their purposes.

[7] By "transformed" is meant that people would follow the example of the sage and conscientiously transform themselves into the good via self-cultivation.

[8] By "become simple" is meant that people will reduce their desires and thus embrace simplicity.

Commentary:

In this chapter Lao Zi proposes three major strategies for three different tasks. The first is the "normal way" (*zheng*), employed to govern a state; the second is the "unusual way" (*qi*), applied to operate an army; and the third is the principle of "take-no-action" (*wu shi*), to administer the world. The first and the third seem to somewhat overlap. They are both intended to stabilize the society and the world. Yet, the second strategy is abnormal in itself, for it is set out in striking contrast to other doctrines of simplicity, non-competition, retreat, and take-no-action, etc., which in effect comprise the main content of Lao Zi's philosophical system.

"All warfare is," as Sun Zi says when talking about strategic assessments in his *The Art of War* (*Sun Zi Bing Fa*), "based on deception. Therefore, when able to attack, we must pretend to be unable; when employing our forces, we must seem inactive; when we are near, we must make the enemy believe we are far away; when far away, we must make him believe we are near. Offer a bait to allure the enemy, when he covets small advantages; strike the enemy when he is in disorder.... Launch attack where the enemy is unprepared; take action when it is unexpected. These are the keys to victory for a strategist." These strategies and tactics chime in with Lao Zi's argument that "an army should be operated in an unusual or extraordinary way" (*yi qi yong bing*).

Being a pair of opposite and yet complementary categories, *zheng* and *qi* (that are rendered here as "normal way" and "unusual way") were not only used by Lao Zi himself, but by other ancient thinkers, including Sun Zi. In *The Art of War*, the latter arrives at the conclusion that "it is due to the operation of the *qi* and *zheng* (the extraordinary and the normal tactics) that the whole army can sustain the enemy's all-out attack without suffering defeat." "Generally, in battle," continues Sun Zi, "use the normal force (*zheng*) to engage and use the extraordinary (*qi*) to win. Now, to a commander adept at the use of extraordinary force (*qi*), his resources are as infinite as Heaven and earth, as inexhaustible as the flow of the running rivers.... In battle, there are not more than two kinds of postures—the operation of the extraordinary way (*qi*) and that of the normal way (*zheng*), but their combinations give rise to an endless line of maneuvers. For these two ways (or forces) are mutually reproductive. With a circular motion, they never come to an end. Who can exhaust the possibilities of their combinations?" (see Sun Zi. *The Art of War*, Ch. V.) The use of the combinations and interactions between the extraordinary way and the normal way has been ever since accepted as a law of warfare and put into practice from time to time oblivious to the modernization of weapons of all conceivable kinds.

21.2 (Chapter 68)

In the past—
An adept commander did not display his martial prowess.[1]
An adept warrior did not become angry.[2]
An adept conqueror did not tussle with his enemy.[3]
An adept manager of men placed himself below them.[4]
This is called the virtue of non-competition.
This is called the use of others' force.
This is called the supreme principle of matching Heaven.[5]

Annotations:

[1] This idea corresponds to Lao Zi's negative attitude toward warfare, for he holds that "Weapons are nothing but instruments of evil; they are used only when there is no other choice." (Ch. 31, DDJ)

[2] An adept warrior would remain so cool and calm that he would be able to fight in battle by taking the most advantageous position. If a warrior happened to be swept away by his anger or passion, he would surely lose his temper and reason together. Such being the case he would get into trouble when engaged in a battle.

[3] This means that the conqueror would manage to win by way of strategies and tactics instead of face-to-face conflicts and clashes.

[4] This shows the function of modesty in leadership.

[5] This refers to the highest strategy that is in accord with the *Dao* of Heaven, characterized by naturalness or spontaneity.

Commentary:

Even in his consideration of military strategies and tactics as presented in this chapter, Lao Zi still holds on to his notion that the tender and soft are bound to overcome the hard and strong. It is noteworthy that the characters of the adept commander, warrior and conqueror, and the use of others' forces all contain rich dialectical messages related to the art of war. As Sun Zi points out in his remarks on attack by stratagem: "To subdue the enemy without fighting is the supreme excellence. Thus, the best policy in war is to attack the enemy's strategy. The second-best way is to disrupt his alliances through diplomatic means. The next-best method is to attack the enemy in the field. The worst policy is to attack walled cities, since this is the last resort when there is no other alternative.... Therefore, the adept commander subdues the enemy without confrontation. He captures the enemy's cities without assaulting them and overthrows the enemy's rule without protracted operations.... However, an adept warrior wins victories without showing his brilliant military prowess...." (see Sun Zi. *The Art of War*, Chs. III and IV). If we make a close comparison between these ideas about warfare, we find them strategically identical in a broad sense. It is no wonder that some readers, such as Mao Zedong, take the *Dao De Jing* as a book on warfare.

21.3 (Chapter 69)

In the past, a military strategist said:
"I dare not take the offensive, but I take the defensive.[1]
I dare not advance an inch, but I retreat a foot." [2]
This means (to make the invading force):
Advancing onward without battle formation,
  Raising his arm without morale enhancement,
  Holding his weapons without normal function,
  And tackling the enemy without meeting him.[3]
There is no greater disaster than underestimating the enemy.
Such underestimation is tantamount to self-abandonment.
Therefore, when two well-matched armies clash in battle,
  It is the side which retreats first that will win.[4]

Annotations:

[1] This implies a passive stance toward warfare because warmongers will come to no good end in Lao Zi's opinion. However, this passive stance can change into such military strategies as "Wait at one's ease for an exhausted enemy" (*yi yi dai lao*) and "Defend in order to attack" (*yi shou wei gong*).

[2] This shows a concrete application of the principle of retreat to warfare. It could turn into such military strategies as "Retreat in order to advance" (*yi tui wei jin*) or "Make concessions in order to gain advantages" (*xian shi hou de*).

[3] These are the consequences that come from the policy of retreat. Whenever confronted in a battle, the invading force tends to be full of strength, and its morale is high at the very beginning so that it seems to be irresistible. Yet, these advantageous elements will gradually fade away if they fail to be put into action as a result of the enemy's avoidance of battle.

[4] This is a rendering of *gu kang bing xiang ruo, ze rang zhe sheng yi*, revised according to Gu Di's version (see Gu Di and Zhou Ying. *Lao Zi Tong*, p. 579-580). Found in many other versions of the *Dao De Jing* is the sentence *gu kang bing xiang ruo, ai zhe sheng yi*, which is usually translated as "Therefore, the side in grief conquers in case of a balance of forces between the two sides." By "the side which retreats" is meant *rang zhe* and by "the side in grief" is meant *ai zhe*. The former can be justified as a military strategy termed "Gain mastery by striking only after the enemy has struck" (*hou fa zhi ren*), corresponding well to the above-mentioned strategy: "Retreat in order to advance" (*yi tui wei jin*). As for the latter, it is often interpreted as a tactic to show kindness, sympathy and affection so as to soften the fighting spirit of the enemy. Such an interpretation seems to be rather far-fetched in the case of warfare. However, it must be pointed out that Lao Zi seems to absolutizes the potential force of "the side which retreats." It is well known that a military victory or conquest depends on a variety of factors and conditions, and not just on a single policy—of retreat or whatever. Hence, the absolutization of retreat as a strategy ends up playing down its dialectical content.

Commentary:

This chapter continues to expound upon the laws and rules of warfare. Under the circumstances of warfare, Lao Zi proposes a number of policies which can be developed and summarized into three major military strategies as follows: (1) Wait at one's ease for the exhausted enemy; (2) defend in order to attack; and (3) retreat in order to advance. All these three strategies are intended to "gain mastery by striking only after the enemy has struck."

It is worthy reading this chapter with particular reference to Sun Zi's analyses of manoeuvering (*jun zheng pian*) and the nine varieties of ground (*jiu di pian*) covered in *The Art of War*. The two relevant passages are cited in full here:

"A whole army may be robbed of its spirit, and its commander deprived of his presence of mind. Now, at the beginning of a campaign, the spirit of soldiers is keen; after a certain period of time, it declines; and in the later stage, it may dwindle to nought. An adept commander, therefore, avoids the enemy when his spirit is keen, and attacks him when it is lost. This is the art of attaching importance to moods. In good order, he awaits a disorderly enemy; in serenity, a clamorous one. This is the art of retaining self-possession. Close to the field of battle, he awaits an enemy coming from afar; at rest, he awaits an exhausted enemy; with well-fed troops, he awaits hungry ones. This is the art of husbanding one's strength. He refrains from intercepting an enemy whose banners are in perfect order, and desists from attacking an enemy whose formations are in impressive array. This is the art of assessing circumstances." (see Sun Zi. *The Art of War*, p. 49.)

"In ancient times, an adept commander knew how to make it impossible for the enemy to unite his van and his rear, for his large and small divisions to cooperate, for his officers and men to support each other, and for the higher and lower levels of the enemy to establish contact with each other. When the enemy's forces were dispersed, the adept commander managed to prevent them from assembling; even when assembled, he managed to throw them into disorder. In this case, the commander led his army to move forward when it was advantageous to do so, and he halted his men when it was disadvantageous to move forward" (see Sun Zi. *The Art of War*, p. 79).

22 On Peace

Lao Zi values peace and stability more than anything else in the social domain. This is reflected in his staunch anti-war attitude. Thus he regards weapons as instruments of evil that may be used only when there is no other alternative. He emphasizes that the use of military force is dangerous, for "as soon as great wars are over, years of famine are sure to afflict the land." Accordingly he denounces all excessive military operations and discourages any delight in military victory. In addition, he even goes so far as to advise the winning side to cherish humanism by mourning the multitudes killed in the fighting. Lao Zi's argument on pre-war and post-war peace is presented in chapters 30 and 31 (DDJ).

22.1 (Chapter 30)

He who assists the ruler with the *Dao*
Never seeks to dominate the world with military force.[1]
The use of force is intrinsically dangerous:[2]
Wherever armies are stationed,
Briers and thorns grow wild.[3]
As soon as great wars are over,
Years of famine are sure to afflict the land.[4]
Therefore an adept commander (of a defensive force) will
Stop when he has achieved his aim.[5]
He does not use force to dominate the world.
He achieves his aim but does not become arrogant.
He achieves his aim but does not boast about it.
He achieves his aim only because he has no other choice.
This is called achieving the aim without using force to dominate.[6]
The strong and powerful rob and harm the old and weak.[7]
This is called contrary to the *Dao*.
Whatever is contrary to the *Dao* will soon perish.

Annotations:

[1] Lao Zi's concerns are made perfectly clear at the start of this chapter. He obviously recommends the *Dao* as a principle of government while condemning war as a cause of disaster.

[2] The English rendering is based on Gu Di's annotation, according to which the original expression *hao huan* (meaning "soon incur requital") would have been pronounced *hao xuan* (very dangerous) in the northern dialect of ancient China.

[3] and [4] These lines describe the disastrous and destructive consequences of the use of military force and the occurrence of warfare.

[5] This line implies Lao Zi's negation of any excessive employment of military action.

[6] The winning side in a war is advised not to take the advantage of its victory, for instance, by transforming the occupied land into its colony and enslaving the local people.

[7] This translation is based on the revision by Gao Heng (see *Lao Zi Zheng Gu*, pp. 71-72.) and Gu Di (see *Lao Zi Tong*, pp. 544-547). Most the Lao Zi scholars interpret the expression *wu zhuang ze lao* as "Things must grow old after reaching their prime." This interpretation seems to fit Lao Zi's doctrine that "Reversion is the movement of the *Dao*." Nevertheless, it fails to fit logically into the context in which we read, "This is called contrary to the *Dao*." Having seen the paradox here, Gao Heng and Gu Di read *ze* as *zei* which means "rob and harm."

Commentary:

Nothing has been more catastrophic than war in the course of human history. War destroys peace, order and stability on the one hand, and can cause famine, devastation and myriads of other miseries on the other. In short, war takes an enormous toll of mankind.

From his own observation and experience of the continual chaos and wars that marked the Spring and Autumn Period, Lao Zi came to know that the rivalry among the feudal lords striving for ever-more power and territory through the use of military force led to the disasters of war. However, he could do nothing to stop it, apart from warning people of the dangerous and disastrous aspects of war. Meanwhile, he denounces any excessive military operations by advising the winning side not to go too far (e.g. by colonizing the defeated state and enslaving its people) in their triumph. Otherwise they will betray the *Dao* and, as a consequence, soon perish.

22.2 (Chapter 31)

Weapons are nothing but instruments of evil.[1]
They are used only when there is no other choice.
Therefore, he who wins a battle is not praiseworthy.[2]
If he thinks himself praiseworthy,
He delights in the victory.
He who delights in the victory,
Delights in the slaughter of men.[3]
He who delights in the slaughter of men
Will not succeed under Heaven. [4]
For the multitude killed in the war
Let us mourn them with sorrow and grief.[5]
For the victory won by force,
Let us observe the occasion with funeral ceremonies.

Annotations:

[1] Weapons as "instruments of evil" are so dangerous and detestable that they should be carefully stored instead of being recklessly used. Otherwise they will bring great disasters and sufferings.

[2] This implies Lao Zi's negative attitude toward war and victors in general.

[3] and [4] These lines express Lao Zi's strong condemnation of and warning to those who delight in winning victory through, as he puts it, "the slaughter of men."

[5] Lao Zi proposes his idea of humanism even in his view of warfare.

Commentary:

This chapter continues with the discussion of the same theme expounded in the previous one. The denunciation of war and the condemnation of delight in slaughter turn into an appeal for peace in his chaotic and war-torn age. The urging of the winning side or the occupying force not to do further harm to the country and people involved is still of great relevance and significance nowadays. It has been historically proved that it is immensely difficult for the winning side or the occupying force, no matter how powerful it may be, to conquer another nation, even though the latter may be relatively small and weak. Incidentally, Lao Zi's proposal that the multitude killed in the war should be properly mourned springs from his humanistic ideal. It is coincidentally compatible with the relevant laws and rules of international warfare formulated in modern times.

23 On Returning to Antiquity

Lao Zi assumes that primeval society was characterized by peace, harmony and stability because the ancients acted inaccordance with the *Dao* and embraced simplicity and integrity. Appalled at the social problems and chaotic political situation of his own time, Lao Zi hankers for the "good old days" of antiquity, where, he implies, solutions to contemporary problems can be found. The relevant chapters are 17, 18, 19 and 65 (DDJ).

23.1 (Chapter 17)

The best kind of rulers are those whose existence
Is merely known by the people below them.[1]
The next-best are those who are loved and praised.
The next-best are those who are feared.
The next-best are those who are despised.
If trust in others is not sufficient,
It will be unrequitted.[2]
(The best rulers) are cautious, [3]
And seldom issue orders.
When tasks are accomplished and affairs completed,
The common people will say,
"We simply follow the way of spontaneity."[4]

Annotations:

[1] This is a rendering of *tai shang, xia zhi you zhi*. Found in other versions of the *Dao De Jing* is the sentence *tai shang, bu zhi you zhi*, which is sometimes translated as "In the best times people did not know of the existence of the rulers" or "The best kind of rulers are those whose existence is not known to the people." I think the word should be *xia* (the people below or the subordinates) instead of *bu* (not), according to the Mawangdui versions of *The Book of Lao Zi* and those annotated by Heshang Gong, Wang Bi and many other subsequent Lao Zi scholars including the contemporary Gu Di (see Gu Di and Zhou Ying. *Lao Zi Tong*, pp. 296-298).

[2] This means that if a ruler does not have enough trust or faith in the people, he will not be able to get enough trust from them in return. It also implies that if the ruler fails to honor his words or promises, the people can not trust him any more.

[3] In some versions of the *Dao De Jing* (e.g. the Mawangdui, Heshang Gong's, Fu Yi's, and so on), the word *you*, meaning "cautious, prudent or hesitant," is kept. Some other versions (e.g. Wang Bi's) they use another *you*, meaning "idle, at ease or free." I think the first *you* fits the context better.

[4] The original sentence *bai xing jie wei wo zi ran* is also rendered as "All the common people will say 'We are in ourselves.'" The implied message refers to the highest stage of government under which the people do things naturally or act upon the *Dao* of spontaneity or naturalness and thus remain undisturbed by official orders or pressures.

Commentary:

Lao Zi expresses in this chapter his political ideal, which is considered as being drawn and developed from his bitter experience of the harsh reality of his time. On the basis of his concept of the *Dao* of take-no-action (*wu wei*) as the supreme principle for government, he distinguishes between four types of rulers. He definitely recommends "the best kind of rulers" as contrasted to the other three kinds merely because the former conduct state affairs according to the principle of take-no-action or the *Dao* of spontaneity.

Throughout the *Dao De Jing*, Lao Zi time and again denounces the power-oriented and despotic type of leadership or government, for it will disturb, control and alienate the people by confusing their minds and spoiling their simplicity. He thus values social stability and order, which he thinks can be possible only when the rulers remain honest and trustworthy, use government as a instrument to serve the people and never use their power to force their will on their subjects. Therefore, Lao Zi deliberately refers back to the "good old days" of antiquity as a standard to measure the functions of government of his time. Meanwhile, he strongly objects to rulers who manipulate the people by resorting to all kinds of orders, which are useless in Lao Zi's opinion. Nevertheless, the political ideal that Lao Zi advocates has obvious Utopian features.

23.2 (Chapter 18)

When the great *Dao* is rejected,
  The doctrines of Ren and Yi will arise.[1]
When knowledge and craftiness appear,[2]
  Great hypocrisy will also emerge.
When the six family relations are not in harmony,[3]
  Filial piety and parental affection will be advocated.[4]
When a country falls into chaos,
  Loyal ministers will be praised.

Annotations:

[1] The Chinese concept of *ren* can be rendered as "humanity," "benevolence," "kindness," etc., and *yi* as "righteousness," "uprightness," etc. In most cases, "humanity and righteousness" together are used to express the concept of *ren yi*.

[2] In the Chinese language, the expression *zhi hui* usually means "knowledge and wisdom." However, here it is rendered as "knowledge and craftiness" in terms of the context. Actually this rendering is in accord with Lao Zi's negative stance toward "knowledge and craftiness" in general.

[3] "The six family relations" is an English rendering of the Chinese term *liu qin*, which has different interpretations. Accord-

ing to an early interpretation, it includes the father, mother, elder brother(s), younger brother(s), wife and children in a family. Nowadays people tend to accept that it refers to the father, son(s), elder brother(s), younger brother(s), husband and wife in a family. Here it means the relationships among them in a broad sense.

[4] "Filial piety" (*xiao*) is a kind of virtue exercised by the younger generations and directed toward the elders like parents, grandparents, etc. In contrast, "parental affection" (*ci*) is a kind of virtue is rendered by older generations toward the younger ones such as children, grandchildren, etc. A traditional Chinese family usually has several generations living together. Conventionally it would be a matter of pride when a family is composed of five generations under one roof.

Commentary:

Throughout the *Dao De Jing* it can seen that Lao Zi recommends "the great *Dao*" as the one and only solution to all the social problems of his time. Yet, reality goes against his will and develops along its own course. For instance, "humanity and righteousness" (*ren yi*) as social values are advocated instead of the *Dao* as a remedy for the disorders of the age.

With regard to the harsh condition of his time despite the influence of "humanity and righteousness" and other so-called value systems, Lao Zi deals a sharp attack at them all. His critique is conducted in a roundabout way, coinciding with his notion that "positive words seem to be negative" (*zheng yan ruo fan*). "In the eyes of Lao Zi," as Prof. Ren Jiyu puts it, "humanity and righteousness (*ren yi*), knowledge and craftiness (*zhi hui*), filial piety and parental affection (*xiao ci*) and loyal ministers (*zhong chen*) are all abnormal symptoms of an unhealthy society. So-called moral codes are never properly lived up to in a rational society. This reveals Lao Zi's dialectical thought about the relations and interactions between the great *Dao*, humanity, righteousness, knowledge, craftiness, hypocrisy, family relations in dispute, filial piety, parental affection, political disorder and loyal ministers. Historically and realistically speaking, it is fairly true that there must be something out of order whenever those values or morals are in urgent need. They are somewhat like medicine; valuable and desirable as it might be, people take it only when they fall ill. Such being the case, the demand for such a "good" thing merely indicates the existence of a bad situation.

It is worth noticing that "the great *Dao*" seems to Lao Zi to stand for what is perfect, encompassing perfect humanity and righteousness, and all other perfect values. If the *Dao* of this type is easily available and practiced in a society, there will be simply no need to propagate humanity and righteousness, etc., because people are all living in the harmonious and peaceful atmosphere of the *Dao*.

It must be pointed out that humanity and righteousness (*ren yi*) is typical of Confucianist terminology. That is why some Lao Zi scholars both in China and overseas opine that Lao Zi as a thinker appeared after Confucius. They reach such a judgment mainly by means of the Hegelian Triad—thesis, antithesis and synthesis. That is to say, they hold that "humanity and righteousness" is the thesis, and the critique of this then serves as the antithesis. So logically speaking, Confucius precedes Lao Zi. Yet, I think that this is a hasty conclusion, for it features a "leap in dark." Whenever we approach the history of Chinese thought we ought to keep in mind that Confucius is a latinized name for Kong Fu Zi, a honorific title for Kong Zi (a literal translation of which could be Master Kong); likewise, Confucianism is a latinized form of term for *Ru Jia* or *Ru Jia Xue Pai* (school of *Ru* thought). It is widely acknowledged that it was Confucius who developed the thoughts and doctrines of *Ru Jia* and made it into a system. But this does not necessarily mean that it was Confucius who originated all the ideas of *Ru Jia*. In fact, *Ru Jia* as a school of thought existed before Confucius himself, and so did some of the doctrines or theses comprising the Confucianist system, which include "humanity and righteousness" for example. Confucius claimed that he was a "transmitter" rather than an originator. This corresponds to historical fact. Nowadays modern studies of Confucianism in China have a general tendency to make a distinction between primitive Confucianism (*Yuanshi Ru Jia*),

Confucianism (*Ru Jia*), Neo-Confucianism (*Xin Ru Jia or Song-Ming Li Xue*), and Modern Confucianism (*Xiandai Ru Xue*). We mention all this to justify the conclusion that Lao Zi preceded Confucius, and not the other way round.

23.3 (Chapter 19)

Only when sageness is eliminated and craftiness discarded,
Will people benefit a hundredfold.[1]
Only when humanity is eradicated and righteousness abandoned,
Will people return to filial piety and parental affection.[2]
Only when skill is thrown away and profit ignored,
Will there be no more robbers or thieves.[3]
Yet, these three are inadequate as a doctrine.[4]
We therefore urge the following:
Manifest plainness and embrace simplicity;
Reduce selfishness and have few desires;
And get rid of learning and have no worries.[5]

Annotations:

[1] Lao Zi uses the word "sageness" (*sheng*) in a negative sense here, referring to the way in which one thinks oneself clever in making suggestions or offering solutions to social problems, etc. Similarly, he uses the word "craftiness" (*zhi*) to indicate one of the negative consequences of learning or knowledge as has been discussed above (see Part III, 15, and Part IV, 28.6). The whole statement implies the necessity and merit of returning to simplicity, as Wang Anshi interprets this.

[2] Both "humanity" (*ren*) and "righteousness" (*yi*) had been advocated as possible solutions to social problems ever since the time of King Wen of Zhou, whom Confucius respected as one of the sage rulers. However, Lao Zi excludes them from his perspective of the *Dao* as the final solution in one sense, and from his observation of the worsening reality of his time in another sense.

[3] Lao Zi maintains that "skill" (*qiao*) and "profit" (*li*) work together to stimulate people's acquisitive desires on the one hand, and tempt people to take the risk of robbing and stealing the "profit" by means of the "skill."

[4] By "these three" is meant the three pairs of categories: "sageness and craftiness," "humanity and righteousness" and "skill and profit." Lao Zi regards them as superficial excrescences of civilization advocated at a time when the principle of the *Dao* had been rejected (see Part III, 23.2).

[5] By "learning" (*xue*) is meant the learning of humanity, righteousness, sageness, craftiness, skill, etc.

Commentary:

As noted in the foregoing chapter (Ch. 18, DDJ), a diagnosis of the problematic and somewhat moribund society in Lao Zi's time is critically made by Lao Zi, who concludes that all the problems arise fundamentally from the rejection of the "great *Dao*." He then continues in this chapter (Ch. 19, DDJ) to describe more specifically the pros and cons of such social phenomena as sageness, craftiness, humanity, righteousness, skill and profit. His negation of them is ostensibly reflected in his arguments and set out in striking contrast with his three proposals as follows: "Manifest plainness and embrace simplicity. Reduce selfishness and have few desires. Get rid of learning and have no worries." It is noticeable that these three proposed solutions to the social problems are profferred in opposition to what Lao Zi terms "these three," pointing to the three pairs of categories listed above (see [4]). In the final analysis, Lao Zi's proposals are all intended to make it possible for the mind's return to simplicity as the original human nature or the highest stage of self-cultivation, and for the return to antiquity as an idealized social living environment.

Incidentally, we must keep in mind the fact that Lao Zi denies and condemns "sageness and craftiness" because they produce self-importance and misused intelligence which tend to endanger human relations, "humanity and righteousness" because they produce vanity, pretentiousness and hypocrisy, which tend to disguise base intentions, and "skill and profit" in view of prevailing trickiness and overflowing desires, which tend to stir up more troubles.

23.4 (Chapter 65)

In ancient times he who practiced the *Dao* well

Did not use it to enlighten the people.[1]
Instead he used it to make them simple.[2]
Now the people are difficult to govern
Because they have too much craftiness.[3]
Thus, governing a country by craftiness is a disaster for it.[4]
And not governing it by craftiness is a blessing for it.[5]
He who knows these two also knows the principle.[6]
It is called profound *De* to always know the principle.
Profound *De* is deep and far-reaching;
It returns to the origin with all things,[7]
And then leads to the great naturalness.[8]

Annotations:

[1] By "to enlighten the people" is meant to expose the people to crafts and skills which are assumed by Lao Zi to soil human simplicity.

[2] This is a contextual rendering of *jian yi yu zhi*. The Chinese word *yu* literally means "make one foolish." It is simply due to its literal meaning that the idea as presented in this text has been misunderstood by many readers throughout history, and thus Lao Zi himself is often labeled an advocate of obscurantism. According to Wang Bi and Heshang Gong, the word *yu* is employed here to suggest having simplicity, genuineness and naturalness—instead of knowledge, craftiness and trickiness. As observed in Chapter 20 (DDJ), Lao Zi describes his mentality and compares it to the simplicity and innocence of a new-born baby. In the same text (DDJ, Ch. 20) is the self-confession that Lao Zi seems to make as follows: "My mind is that of a stupid man" (*wo yu ren zhi xin ye*). The mind of a stupid or foolish man represents that of simplicity and genuineness, which Lao Zi thought was embraced by people in antiquity.

[3] By "too much craftiness" is implied too much trickiness and acquisitiveness.

[4] This is because it goes against the governing principle of simplicity in Lao Zi's view.

[5] This is because it accords with the governing principle of simplicity.

[6] By "the principle" is meant the governing principle of simplicity, which Lao Zi thought would lead to peace and harmony, as it had, in his view, in primeval society.

[7] By "the origin" is meant the *Dao* characterized by simplicity and genuineness.

[8] The expression *da shun* is rendered here as "the great naturalness." It is also interpreted as "the great harmony" or "the greatest conformity." I think it is another term for the *Dao*, in which all things originate, or the state of the *Dao*, in which all things are harmoniously reunified.

Commentary:

It is difficult to rule those who have too many desires, and equally difficult to rule those who have too much craftiness. It is Lao Zi's conviction that people become so mainly because they are under the negative influence of the ruling class. Hence Lao Zi believes that the leaders should first of all set themselves up as a good model of simplicity and genuineness in their styles of both governing and living. Then it will be possible for the people to become simple and genuine, or, in short, easy to rule. Subsequently, human relations can be improved, and social stability correspondingly maintained.

As a matter of fact, Lao Zi was born in a chaotic age which featured political conflicts and military clashes between a number of states. Moreover, in fighting and power games within the courts of the states were an ever-present complication in the process of government. The result was an eager pursuit of stratagems, tricks and conspiracies. Under such circumstances, Lao Zi found the chief cause of confusion and disorder lay in nothing but craftiness, trickiness, competitiveness and hypocrisy. He therefore called on people, as Chen Guying says, to get rid of all forms of struggle and dispute related to possessive values, and advised them to return to the mentality of genuineness and simplicity, which he held to be the key to the solutions to all the crises of his time. In order to hammer this point home to the reader, his remarks are noticeably sharp and cynical (see Chen Guying. *Lao Zi Zhu Yi Ji Ping Jie*, p. 315).

As regards the tactics for government recommended by Lao Zi, they tend to be understood as a kind of obscurantism. They are thus approached and appreciated (by the rulers of almost all the dynasties in China) with a particular reference to the similar arguments presented in Chapter 3 (DDJ), as follows: "Therefore the sage governs the people by purifying their minds, filling their bellies, weakening their ambitions, and strengthening their bones" (see Part III, 20.1).

24 On the Ideal Society

Throughout his book, Lao Zi proposes the principle of the Dao, advocates simplicity of mind, appreciates the environment of tranquility, denounces the catastrophe of war and admires antiquity. All these elements naturally lead to his conception of the ideal society, featureing "a small state with few people." It is ostensibly out of the range of feasibility or possibility. It is therefore taken as a spiritual refuge for those who tend to frown upon over-civilization and shun the problematic world.

24.1 (Chapter 80)

Let there be a small state with few people.[1]
It has various kinds of instruments,
  But let none of them be used.
Let the people not risk their lives, and not migrate far away.[2]
Although they have boats and carriages,
  Let there be no occasion to ride in them.[3]
Although they have armor and weapons,
  Let there be no occasion to display them.[4]
Let the people return to knotting cords and using them.[5]
Let them relish their food,
  Beautify their clothing,
  Feel comfortable in their homes
  And delight in their customs.[6]
Although the neighboring states are within sight of one another,

And the crowing of cocks and the barking of dogs
On both sides can be heard,
Their peoples may die of old age without even meeting each other.[7]

Annotations:

[1] "A small state with few people" is Lao Zi's social ideal, as contrasted with the striving to build up large countries with big populations which was prevalent in his day.

[2] This suggests that the people there are life-conscious, peace-loving and home-oriented, due to the favorable environment they live in.

[3] The people there prefer the simple way of life.

[4] The people there are free from warfare and other forms of violent conflicts.

[5] This implies returning to the ways of antiquity or simplicity.

[6] The people there seem to be contented with what they have, so that they live happy lives.

[7] By "meeting each other" is meant clashing with or fighting against one another.

Commentary:

Exemplified in this chapter is Lao Zi's ideal society that features "a small state with few people." As has been observed, the small state as such is basically structured on the model of a community in antiquity, and the people living there are characteristically simple, honest and peace-loving in general. They remain contented with what they have, and thereby live enjoyable lives. There are no disputes or conflicts among the neighboring states because they all take care of their own affairs without bothering each other. This social ideal was later on extended by Tao Yuanming, an influential poet (c. 372 or 376-427), into a Chinese Utopia known as Peach Blossom Village (*Tao Hua Yuan*), which is in fact the title of an essay by him.

It is noticeable that Lao Zi's ideal society is a natural outcome of his admiration for antiquity, his advocacy of simplicity, his appreciation of tranquility, his anti-war attitude, his pursuit of stability, and, above all, his principle of the *Dao*. It goes without saying that Lao Zi fictionizes and idealizes such a society, which is in sharp contrast to the harsh and chaotic reality of his time. He lauds such an ideal society while implicitly criticizing the traits of acquisitiveness, vanity and competitiveness found in human nature. Obviously his ideal society is far beyond attainment. It thus serves as a spiritual refuge for those who are disgusted with the over-civilized world.

It is generally acknowledged that Lao Zi calls for a return to the primitive community, as exemplified in his idealized society. However, it is a kind of return at a higher level with regard to the following characteristics: First of all, Lao Zi's idealized society is similar to the primitive community in the aspects of equality, co-production, shared consumption, non-possessiveness and non-control. Yet, the former is different from the latter to the extent that it is governed by "taking no action" and following the way of naturalness. As a result, people there do not need to run the risk of leaving home in order to make a living elsewhere. Secondly, in the idealized society of Lao Zi there are various kinds of instruments—boats, carriages, armor, weapons, etc. —which were scarcely available to the primitive community. Nevertheless, they are hardly used because there is no occasion for using them. This indicates that the members of this ideal society stick to simplicity in their activities, and there are no clashes or warfare between the various communities. Thirdly, primitive society featured low productivity and low living standards, such that there was scarcely any access to the pleasures of life. However, the society idealized by Lao Zi is characterized by a considerable quality of life. For it makes it possible for people to "relish their food, beautify their clothing, feel comfortable in their homes and delight in their customs." Finally, the proposed solution to "let the people return to knotting cords and using them" should not be simplistically conceived of as an idea to restore the outdated and retreat to the past. More exactly, it is an attempt to use the innocence and simplicity of antiquity to supersede the craftiness, trickery and hypocrisy of the people of Lao Zi's time. In short, the ideal society is characterized by equality, self-sufficiency, security, simplicity, peaceful coexistence, tranquility, harmony, and an idyllic life above all—all the things which have been dreamed of or cherished in either the human imagination or wishful thinking.

Part IV The Daoist Path to Personal Cultivation

Daoism as a philosophy is often reckoned to be the wellspring of the psychology of the Chinese people in general. This is due to the fact that Daoism is largely directed toward personal cultivation from within, which is then chiefly oriented to the attainment of *Dao-De* as the highest sphere of human life. Lao Zi proclaims that "The *Dao* begets all beings and *De* fosters them.... Therefore all beings venerate the *Dao* and honor *De*." When cultivated and exercised in the person, family, community, country and the world at large, both the *Dao* and *De* will become genuine, overflowing, everlasting, powerful and universal. Thereby the entire world will stay in peace and order, and mankind will enjoy harmonious relations.

To be discussed in this section is the process of realizing *Dao-De* as outlined in the book of Lao Zi. The process consists of, first, a relevant attitude toward *Dao-De* and subsequently the related experience, praxis and achievement of *Dao-De* via a number of approaches presented.

25 The Attitude to *Dao-De*

There are generally three different kinds of attitudes toward *Dao-De* categorized by Lao Zi. The first is positive and held by the highest type of *shi*; the second is doubtful and held by the average type of *shi*; and the last is negative and held by the lowest type of *shi*. Personal cultivation in Daoism depends, first and foremost, on an appropriate attitude to *Dao-De*. Close reading of chapters 41 and 70 (DDJ) may give one some basic ideas about this.

25.1 (Chapter 41)

When the highest type of *shi* hear of the *Dao*,
  They diligently practice it.[1]
When the average type of *shi* hear of the *Dao*,
  They half-believe it.
When the lowest type of *shi* hear of the *Dao*,
  They laugh heartily at it.
If they did not laugh at it,
  It would not be the *Dao*.

Therefore there is the established saying:
  The *Dao* that is bright seems to be dark;
  The *Dao* that advances seems to retreat;
  The *Dao* that is level seems to be uneven.
Thus the great *De* appears empty like a valley;[2]
  The far-reaching *De* appears insufficient;[3]
  The vigorous *De* appears inert;[4]
  The simplistic *De* appears clumsy;[5]
  The whitest appears soiled;[6]
  The greatest square has no corners;[7]
  The greatest vessel is unfinished;[8]
  The greatest music sounds faint;[9]
  The greatest form has no shape;[10]
  The *Dao* is hidden and nameless.
Yet it is the *Dao* that initiates all things
  And brings them to completion.

Annotations:

[1] The Chinese term *shi* means a man of learning. It refers here to a special social class in the pre-Qin period (before 221 B.C.). It finds no English equivalent. "Literati" as a collective term partly conveys its connotation. Here it has been transliterated rather than translated.

[2] Being empty like a valley, the great *De* can eternally have more space to fill, and accordingly be enriched.

[3] The far-reaching *De* is not concretely visible, so that people think it is insufficient.

[4] Since the vigorous *De* does not demonstrate its strength or power, it looks as if it is inert or slack.

[5] The simplistic *De* is so plain, innocent and unsophisticated that it looks as slow, naive and foolish.

[6] "The whitest" means the purest *De* in this context. Being so pure, it has no intention of displaying itself. Hence it looks like something that concealing disgrace or humility.

[7] The greatest square knows no boundaries or edges, so that it seems to have no corners at all.

[8] The line *da qi mian cheng* is modified according to one of the two Mawangdui versions of the *Dao De Jing*, for it fits better in the context. The greatest vessel as an instrument would be too large to have any fixed form or function. It is thus beyond human capacity to either use it or complete it. In most of the popular versions of the *Dao De Jing*, the line reads: *Da qi wan cheng* and it is thus translated as "The greatest vessel is always completed last."

[9] The greatest music is in fact the most fascinating and beautiful music that only exists in one's imagination. In practice what is composed can not fully express what is imagined; and what is performed can hardly be any better than what is composed. This is merely because the original beauty and charm get more or less lost during the transition from creative imagination to instrumental performance. For this reason, Tao Yuanming preferred to play the Chinese lute without cords. Coincidentally, Join Keats remarks in one of his poems titled "Ode on a Grecian Urn" as follows:

"Heard melodies are sweet,
But those unheard are sweeter;
Therefore, ye soft pipes, play on;
Not to the sensual ear, but more endear'd,
Pipe to the spirit ditties of no tone..."

[10] As the form is too great to be seen as a whole, it looks as if it is shapeless.

Commentary:

Lao Zi classifies *shi* as a social stratum into three broad types: the highest, the average and the lowest. Their respective attitudes toward *Dao-De* reflect three general attitudes. It is obvious that

Lao Zi holds a positive and commendable view of the first of the three attitudes to *Dao-De*. In order to clear away the doubts and ignorance the average *shi* and the lowest *shi* have as regards the *Dao*, Lao Zi cites some old sayings (that could be created by himself) to testify to the authentic and extraordinary functions of *Dao-De*. As can be observed nowadays in this world where materialism and nihilism are so prevalent and rampant, plenty of people are inclined to sneer or mock at the *Dao* of human conduct characterized by such *De* as simplicity, honesty, morality, selflessness, etc. Many people seem to get lost or be on the wrong track in respect of their value systems. With regard to this, the implied message in this chapter is noticeably of considerable relevance and significance since it encourages the development of the highest type of *shi* with an affirmative attitude to *Dao-De*.

25.2 (Chapter 70)

All the world says that my *Dao* is great,
　But it does not resemble anything concrete.
Just because it is great,
　It does not resemble anything concrete.
It would have been small for long if it did.[1]

My words are very easy to understand and practice.
But no one in the world can understand and practice them.
My words have their own source,[2]
　My deeds have their own master.[3]

It is merely because people do not know this
　That they fail to understand me.
Those who can understand me are very few,
　And those who can follow me are hard to meet.
Therefore the sage wears coarse garb,
　But conceals a precious jade in his bosom.[4]

Annotations:

[1] The first stanza has been transposed from Chapter 67 of other versions of the *Dao De Jing*, for it fits better in this context (see Gu Di and Zhou Ying. *Lao Zi Tong*, pp. 615-619). The *Dao*,

is in Lao Zi's mind, great and exists in everything and everywhere. However, it does not look like anything specific and concrete. Otherwise, it would not be what it is.

[2] The Chinese word *zong* literally means "ancestor." It is translated here as "source," suggesting the root (*Dao*) of Lao Zi's words.

[3] The Chinese word *jun* literally means "ruler" or "emperor." It is translated as "master" here so as to indicate the criterion or measurement (*Dao*) of Lao Zi's deeds.

[4] This metaphor is rich in meaning. It implies first of all the personality of the sage that features plainness and simplicity, without any intention to show himself off. Secondly, the "coarse garb" signifies the outside appearance which serves to cover up the "precious jade." The "jade" stands for the *Dao* and *De* as well.

Commentary:

In this chapter Lao Zi seems to be somewhat anguished because his ideas are not appreciated and his deeds not followed by the majority. Lao Zi ascribes this frustrating situation to human ignorance of the *Dao* and its manifestations. However, the reluctance to act upon his words and deeds lies, in my opinion, in the tendency of many people to become blinded with acquisitiveness and pleasure-snobbery. As a result they fix their eyes either on the dazzling appearances or the practical dimensions of things only, and naturally neglect the spiritual aspect, as exemplified by the inner and virtuous self.

Generally speaking, personal cultivation in Daoism depends on the willingness to modify one's behavior and purify one's mind on the model recommended by the Daoist sage. This requires a sincere consideration of the words and deeds of the sage. Naturally the most important thing is to foster and establish a positive attitude toward *Dao-De* just like that held by the highest type of *shi* discussed above.

26 The Experience of *Dao-De*

As a result of adopting a positive attitude to *Dao-De*, one would undergo a highly enlightened experience and change of mentality which is uniquely distinct from and well transcends any practical or empirical types. This kind of experience and mentality feature above all simplicity, tranquility, genuineness, modesty, adaptability, open-mindedness, persistency, etc., which in turn represent the fundamental aspects of the ideal personality Lao Zi advocates. A scrutiny of chapters 15 and 20 (DDJ) will offer some insights into this subject.

26.1 (Chapter 15)

He who was adept at practicing the *Dao* in antiquity
Was subtly profound and penetrating, too deep to be understood.[1]
As he was beyond people's cognitive capacity,
I can only describe him arbitrarily:
He was cautious, as if walking across a frozen river in winter;
He was vigilant, as if being threatened by an attack on all sides;
He was solemn and reserved, like a visiting guest;
He was supple and pliant, like ice about to melt;[2]
He was broad, like the boundless sea;
He was vigorous, like the untiring blowing wind;
He was genuine and plain, like the uncarved block;[3]
He was open and expansive, like a great valley;[4]
He was merged and indifferent, like muddy water.[5]
Who could make the muddy gradually clear via tranquility?
Who could make the still gradually come to life via activity?[6]
(It was nobody else but him.)
He who maintains the *Dao* does not want to be overflowing.[7]
It is just because he does not want to be overflowing
That he can be renewed when worn out.[8]

Annotations:

[1] In Wang Bi's version of Lao Zi's book, *shi* is used instead of *Dao*. It is here revised according to the Mawangdui copies of

the *Dao De Jing*.

[2] This denotes flexibility and adaptability on the part of the person who was good at following the *Dao* in ancient times.

[3] This suggests the personality that features simplicity.

[4] This means the open-mindedness which renders possible the immense capacity to receive and accommodate other things.

[5] This implies that he looks naive and clumsy, but has inward wisdom. It can be read with a particular reference to another line, "...the sage wears coarse garb, but conceals a precious jade in his bosom." (see Part IV, 25.2)

[6] Many Lao Zi scholars tend to annotate these two lines from their respective perspectives and experiences. Take Wang Bi and Heshang Gong, for example. The former views them as explaining natural phenomena which demonstrate the working of the *Dao* of spontaneity or naturalness, whereas the latter assumes that they reflect the human state and process of becoming in both a mental and physical sense. As a result, modern Lao Zi scholars also supply different annotations. With regard to the Chinese term *zhuo*, Wu Chen, Chen Guying et al. hold that it implies a state of stirring or turbulence; Sha Shaohai and others reckon that it indicates a chaotically turbid and rigid environment in a social or psychical dimension. Chan Wing-tsit (Chen Rongjie) and Ren Jiyu maintain that it refers to "muddy water." That is why we encounter such English renderings as follows: "Which of you can assume such murkiness, to become in the end still and clear? Which of you can make yourself inert, to become in the end full of life and stir?" (Arthur Waley) "Who can make the muddy water clear? As it quietens down it will become clear. Who can make stillness last? It will gradually lose its peace as change arises." (Ren Jiyu) "Who can make muddy water gradually clear through tranquility? Who can make the still gradually come to life through activity?" (Chen Wing-tsit) I personally agree with Chen and Ren, as I think Lao Zi uses the word *zhuo* as a metaphor which corresponds to the characteristics of Lao Zi's empirical observation and intuitive thinking as a whole. Comparatively speaking, Chen's version is more concise and poetic, and accordingly closer to Lao Zi's style. Here I have

changed "muddy water" into "the muddy" owing to my conviction that it is more suggestive in the physical, social, mental and moral senses, in addition to going parallel to "the still" as a collective noun employed in the following line.

[7] It indicates that he entertains no inkling of self-complacency and arrogance with regard to what he does according to the *Dao*.

[8] This means that he is always on the move in continuous pursuit of the *Dao* and *De*.

Commentary:

This chapter presents Lao Zi's description of the experience of the men in ancient times who supposedly followed the *Dao*. The *Dao* is too subtle and profound to be understood by the ordinary man. Accordingly, he who is good at practicing the *Dao* is also "subtly profound and penetrating, too deep to be understood" by the common people.

As far-fetched a depiction as it is in Lao Zi's terms, the experience of a highly enlightened type is a process of encountering and handling a variety of conditions. This process is in effect a process of personal cultivation, featuring such manners and frames of mind as cautiousness, vigilance, solemnity, adaptability, plainness, simplicity, genuineness, broad-mindedness, receptivity, tranquility, persistency, vitality, untiringness, boundlessness, modesty, and so on. These are actually the essential dimensions of an ideal personality in Lao Zi's view. Comparatively speaking, these two rhetorical questions ("Who can make the muddy gradually clear via tranquility? Who can make the still gradually come to life via activity?") contain a very crucial and instructive message. They at least expose the difficulty related to the experience and practice of *Dao-De* during the process of which tranquility and patience are highly demanded but hard to be maintained and exercised with persistency and continuity. "The muddy" has rich connotations. On one level it means "muddy water," but metaphorically it signifies a muddy mind, turbid situation, chaotic order, confused environment, decadent morality, etc. All this is the opposite of "the clear" as its antithetical counterpart. Likewise, "the still" is regarded as denoting "the dead," "the static," "the inert," "the inactive," etc. All this is antithetical to the qualities of "the alive" or "the dynamic." As regards these two pairs of opposite categories—the muddy and the clear, the still and the alive—a vehicle of transformation is highly desirable. The vehicle itself seems to be made up of such essential but contradictory elements as "tranquility" and "activity," as recommended by Lao Zi.

As has often been observed in practice and experience, it is through concentration and tranquility that one is able to get out of the mire of muddiness and confusion on the one hand, and eventually become clear-minded and remain at ease on the other. This is often true of the natural process during which muddy water becomes clear through tranquility or freedom from disturbance. Whenever one calms down and keeps oneself in a state of tranquility, one's rationality, judgment, feeling, etc., all work clearly, rationally and pleasantly. However, in terms of psychology and development, the involvement in tranquility and peace for too long a time can turn into a state of stillness, during which one may grow slack, inert or indolent. At this stage activity is required as a stimulus. When activated and motivated, one becomes renewed, energetic and creative again. This can be seen as an exposition of the reason why stillness (static state) taken to its extreme degree will turn into activity (dynamic state) and vice versa in the existence of all beings. The dialectical form of their transformation is actually extended from the general principle that "Reversion is the movement of the *Dao*" (DDJ, Ch. 40).

It is said that the philosopher Martin Heidegger (1889-1976) was deeply impressed by the two lines quoted above (*Shu neng zhuo yi jing zhi xu qing? Shu neng an yi dong zhi xu sheng?*). He had them written on a wall scroll and hung it in his study for contemplation. We guess that the German philosopher may have had a profound reason to do so, because he himself was at the time preoccupied with seeking the possibillity of "clarity."

26.2 (Chapter 20)

How much difference is there between ready approval

And outright denunciation?
How much difference is there between good and evil?
What people fear cannot but be feared.[1]
The multitude are merry, as if feasting on a day of sacrifice,
Or as if ascending a tower to enjoy the scenery in springtime.[2]
I alone remain tranquil and reluctant to distinguish.[3]
I feel broad and far-reaching, as if at a loss;
I am indifferent and without concern,
Like an infant that cannot smile;
I am wearied indeed, as if I have no home to return to.[4]
The multitude are so brilliant and self-exhibiting,
I alone seem to be lost in darkness and ignorance.[5]
The multitude are so observant and discriminating,
I alone intend to make no distinctions.[6]
The multitude possess more than enough,
I alone seem to lack everything.[7]
The multitude have their reasons for taking action,
I alone seem to be clumsy and incapable of nothing.[8]
The multitude like to be endorsed and supported,
I alone value the realization and attainment of the *Dao*.[9]

Annotations:

[1] This line implies that one should be prudent enough not to rouse people's fears. One thus becomes accustomed to social conformity or following the majority.

[2] By "merry" is meant pleasure-seeking and indulgence in earthly delights. The whole statement represents a crucial aspect of Lao Zi's view of human mentality in general.

[3] This line can be expressed more simply by saying, "He who has attained and is adept at practicing the *Dao* remains tranquil and free from seeking pleasure, and meanwhile reluctant to distinguish between so-called approval and denunciation, good and evil, for there is not much difference between them."

[4] In these lines Lao Zi describes the mentality of the Daoist sage, characterized by innocence and simplicity of mind.

[5] This sets out the difference between the multitude and the

Daoist sage.

[6] "Discriminating" means a kind of rigidly severe and demanding attitude toward people and things.

[7] The word "everything" is employed in a material and instrumental sense. In Lao Zi's mind the Daoist sage is by no means possessive; he seems to have nothing except the *Dao*.

[8] This means that the Daoist sage tends to appear clumsy and conceal his wisdom. It is an extension of the idea that "the sage wears coarse garb but conceals a precious jade in his bosom."

[9] This explains the key reason why the Daoist sage is distinct from the multitude. His ultimate objective in life lies in the pursuit and acquisition of the *Dao*.

Commentary:

This chapter represents Lao Zi's attitude to society and life in general. He thinks it rather relative and tentative with regard to the judgment of such values as nobility and humility, good and evil, beautiful and ugly, etc. Therefore, he remains indifferent and reluctant to distinguish between the so-called distinctions which are casually made by the multitude.

It is noticeable that Lao Zi could not, as Ren Jiyu remarks, display much tolerance for the society of his time. He looked on the multitude as being mean, vulgar and shameless.... In the last sentence he shows that the difference between this "I" and others is that the former has achieved the *Dao*. It can well be added that Lao Zi found the dedication by a person to a pleasure-seeking kind of life, which is a symptom of materialism or over-civilization. He exposes his way of life in order to encourage the multitude to devote themselves to spiritual nourishment instead of material possessions or physical enjoyment. He was thus different from others due to the fact that he was persistent in his pursuit of the *Dao* as his ultimate goal in life.

27 The Praxis of *Dao-De*

The praxis of the *Dao* and *De* involves relevant strategies articulated in the following chapter. The benefits of acting upon the *Dao* as the supreme principle and nourishing *De* as the highest virtue are extensive and boundless according to Lao Zi; better still, they are accessible and available to all beings alike under Heaven. Let us focus on chapters 7, 23 and 27, with reference to chapters 35, 52 and 54 (DDJ).

27.1 (Chapter 7)

Heaven is eternal and Earth everlasting.
They can be so just because they do not exist for themselves.[1]
And for this reason they can long endure.
Therefore the sage places himself in the background,
But finds himself in the foreground.[2]
He puts himself away without self-consideration,
And yet he always remains well-preserved.[3]
It is because he has no personal interests
That his personal interests are fulfilled.[4]

Annotations:

[1] This suggests the selflessness of Heaven and Earth that are taken by Lao Zi as a frame of reference for man in pursuit of the *Dao*.

[2] This shows how modesty works as a kind of virtue and strategy for self-development. As has been proved in practice, he who remains modest is most liable to be well accepted and respected by others. It is for this reason that the old Chinese saying "Modesty receives benefit whereas conceit brings harm" is widely appreciated and recommended.

[3] This means that he who thinks of others before himself is most apt to be loved and taken good care of.

[4] This represents the advantage of selflessness, which corresponds to the notion that the sage "takes no action and yet nothing is left undone."

Commentary:

Some readers of Lao Zi assume that this chapter reveals a crafty and diplomatic egoism. In other words, Lao Zi is thought to advocate taking no action for oneself simply because that is easiest way to gain profit, or attaining selfish ends through selflessness. On the other hand, some other readers of Lao Zi maintain that this chapter exemplifies a kind of objective law, as does Chapter 36 (DDJ). Hence they argue that it is only natural for the Daoist sage to "find himself in the foreground," "remain well-preserved" and have his personal interests come to fruition simply because of his modesty and selflessness. As a matter of fact, Lao Zi's description of Heaven and Earth in view of their alleged selflessness is allegorically directed toward the personality of the Daoist sage. It is largely due to his virtuous modesty and selflessness that the sage can be a beloved ruler and long endure. In reality, however, many rulers fail to restrain their selfish desires owing to external temptations and easy access to treasured objects or rare things. Bit by bit they get deeply involved in corruption and other forms of social ills. When they go too far in order to satisfy their greed at the expense of the interests of the majority, they are likely to be either overthrown or punished in the end. That is why Lao Zi advises people to follow the example of the sage by means of a genuine practice of the *Dao* and *De*, both in word and deed.

27.2 (Chapter 23)

A whirlwind does not last a whole morning;
A rainstorm does not last a whole day.[1]
What causes them to be so?
It is Heaven and Earth.
If Heaven and Earth cannot make them last long,
  How much less can man?
Therefore, he who seeks the *Dao* is identified with the *Dao*.[2]
He who seeks *De* is identified with *De*.
He who seeks Heaven is identified with Heaven.[3]
He who is identified with the *Dao*—
  The *Dao* is also happy to have him.
He who is identified with *De*—
  De is also happy to have him.
He who is identified with Heaven—
  Heaven is also happy to have him.

Annotations:

[1] By "whirlwind" is metaphorically meant the strict and severe laws and regulations enforced by despots, and by "rainstorm" is meant heavy taxation and forced labor decreed by harsh rulers.

[2] This indicates that he who pursues the *Dao* is identified with it by putting it into practice. As has often been noticed in the history of Chinese thought, the identification of words with deeds is always stressed and recommended as an essential part of personal cultivation. The same is also true of identification with *De* as the manifestation of the *Dao*.

[3] This idea is one of the important sources from which the doctrine of Heaven-and-man oneness (*tian ren he yi*—"the oneness between Nature and man") is derived and developed. It is noteworthy that in many popular versions of the *Dao De Jing* this line reads "He who seeks the loss (of the *Dao*) is identified with loss (*yu shi zhe, tong yu shi*)." It is here revised according to the recent philological studies made by Gu Di, who asserts that the Chinese word *shi* (loss) is a scribal error for *tian* (Heaven), since the two characters are almost similar in appearance, the former hardly fits the context here. Then, this line should be translated, "He who seeks Heaven is identified with Heaven" (*yu tian zhe, tong yu tian*). Accordingly, the last sentence of this chapter is similarly revised by replacing the word *shi* (loss) with *tian* (Heaven). It therefore runs like this: "He who is identified with Heaven—Heaven is also happy to have him (*tong yu tian zhe, tian yi le de zhi*)" (see GU Di. *Lao Zi Tong*, pp. 88-92).

Commentary:

This chapter explains the way to master the *Dao,*—by faithful practice and bilateral identification. In plain language, if one pursues the *Dao* with faith, he will attain it and identify himself with it by applying it to his actions. The concept of the oneness between man and the *Dao*, man and *De* as well as man and Heaven (i.e. Nature) is a thread that runs throughout the historical development of Chinese thought in general, and underlies the spirit of Chinese philosophy in particular.

It is of great significance that Lao Zi criticizes, albeit in a roundabout way, the severe laws, strict regulations, heavy taxation and forced labor that afflict the people in a country under despotic rule, for they often do more harm than good. Moreover, their very harshness ensures that such measures are short-lived. As has been noted, it is from his philosophy of keeping to tranquility and governing by non-action that Lao Zi offers his implied criticism, intending to warn the ruling class not to take any arbitrary or drastic actions in view of governmental administration. Otherwise, they are doomed to failure.

27.3 (Chapter 27)[1]

He who is adept at travelling leaves no track or trace behind.[2]
He who is adept at speaking makes no blemishes or flaws.[3]
He who is adept at counting uses no tallies or counters.[4]
He who is adept at shutting the door needs no bolts,
And yet it cannot be opened when shut.[5]
He who is adept at binding things needs no strings,
And yet they cannot be untied when bound.[6]

Annotations:

[1] The second part of this text, from "Therefore the sage is always good at saving men" to "Such is called the significant subtlety of the *Dao*," has been moved to Chapter 62 as a result of contextual analysis and philological studies made by Gu Di. (see Gu Di and Zhou Ying. *Lao Zi Tong*, pp. 499-502)

[2] This allegory suggests that he who has attained the *Dao* is good at doing things by taking no (arbitrary) action.

[3] This implies that he who has mastered the *Dao* is good at teaching without using (fine-sounding) words.

[4], [5] and [6] These are all allegorical descriptions offered to justify the merits of practicing the *Dao*.

Commentary:

This chapter exemplifies the advantage and validity of practicing the *Dao* and *De*. It seems to Lao Zi that all human affairs could be well done as naturally as possible provided one follows and acts upon the supreme principle of the *Dao*. The depiction of being adept at traveling and speaking is in fact an extended notion of Lao Zi's thesis as regards "taking no (arbitrary) action" and "teaching without using (fine-sounding) words."

It is worth pointing out that the advantages of practicing the *Dao* and *De* are reflected and stated here and there throughout the *Dao De Jing*. A wise ruler, for instance, will have all the people under Heaven come to him if he holds fast to the Great Image, which is another name for the *Dao* (see Part I, 2.2). The people in general will be free from danger throughout their lives if they have found and still keep to the *Dao* as the mother of the universe (see Part III, 10.2). Talking about *De*, it will become pure and genuine when cultivated and exercised in the person, full and overflowing when cultivated and exercised in the family, constant and everlasting when cultivated and exercised in the community, powerful and abundant when cultivated and exercised in the country, and universal when cultivated and exercised in the world (see Part II, 7.1).

28 The Attainment of *Dao-De*

It is notable that Lao Zi talks about the *Dao* from various perspectives throughout his book. Relatively speaking, one of the most important objectives lies in how to pursue *Dao* as the highest sphere or realm of the human spirit. As a matter of fact, the pursuit of the *Dao* is implied in certain hidden proposals as suggested in his discussion of the *Dao* and its characteristics. It is worth mentioning that the pursuit of the *Dao* reflects the Daoist ideal of human life. In order to illustrate Lao Zi's concept of attaining the *Dao*, we presume to break down his proposed approach to *Dao-De* into six dimensional components as follows:

(1) self-purification and deep contemplation;
(2) plainness and simplicity;
(3) vacuity and tranquility;
(4) tenderness and non-competition;
(5) have-less-selfishness and have-few-desires;

(6) naturalness and take-no-action.

The focus of the discussion can be found in chapters 10, 13, 16, 22, 28 and 49 (DDJ).

(1) Self-Purification and Deep Contemplation (Chapter 10)

This subtitle is a modified version of Lao Zi's notion (i.e. *di chu xuan jian*) initially presented in Chapter 10 (DDJ). One may as well go on to read chapters 47 and 52 (DDJ) so as to achieve a better understanding of how to purify one's mind and contemplate things in a similar form of insightful meditation or observation. The approach as such is, needless to say, oriented toward the mastery of *Dao* and the nourishment of *De*.

Can you keep the spirit and embrace the One[1]
Without departing from them?
Can you concentrate your vital force and achieve tenderness
Like an infant without any desires?[2]
Can you purify your mind and contemplate in depth
Without any flecks?[3]
Can you love the people and govern the state
Without taking action?[4]
Can you play the role of the feminine
In the opening and closing of the gates of Heaven?[5]
Can you understand all and penetrate all
Without using your reasoning powers?

Annotations:

[1] "The One" is also mentioned in other chapters (e.g. chs. 22 and 39, DDJ) as another name for the *Dao*. Yet, it is employed here to mean the inseparable unity of the spirit and the body. This kind of unity is only possible when a person is identified with the *Dao*.

[2] The expression "vital force" is an English rendering of the Chinese term *qi*, which is seen as the vital force or life energy. Ancient Chinese philosophers and doctors believed that life appears when this vital force gathers, whereas death comes along when it disperses. This notion has had such a historical impact that many Chinese people are still convinced that diseases result from a blocked or problematic flow of this vital force (*qi*) in the

meridians or the channels and collaterals (*jing luo*) of the human body. "Tenderness" is the companion of life, and "innocence" the trait of the Daoist sage in Lao Zi's view.

[3] By "purify your mind" (*di chu*) is meant cleaning and ridding your mind of all pre-existing selfish ideas and personal considerations. By "contemplate in depth" (*xuan jian*) is meant insightful observation (*dong guan*). It is also translated as "deep contemplation" or "mystical insight."

[4] This is an expression of the idea of "governing by taking no (arbitrary) action." This line is revised according to Chen Guying's version (see Chen Guying. *Lao Zi Zhu Yi Ji Ping Jie*, p. 98). However, in many other versions of Lao Zi's book, this sentence reads "Can you love the people and govern the state without personal knowledge?" (*ai min zhi guo, neng wu zhi hu?*), instead of "Can you love the people and govern the state without taking action?" (*ai min zhi guo, neng wu wei hu?*) I think the latter expression fits the context better, and Lao Zi's system as a whole.

[5] I adopt Gao Heng's explanation that "the gates of Heaven" refers to the inborn sense organs (see Gao Heng. *Lao Zi Zheng Gu*, p. 25). By "the role of the feminine" is meant tranquility. Thus, the entire sentence may imply a tranquil approach to observing all things in the world via the sense organs. This approach is commonly known as "tranquil observation" (*jing guan*). There is a popular saying that "the essence of the myriad things is naturally obtained through tranquil observation."

Commentary:

This chapter centers upon the approach to personal cultivation in the direction of attaining the *Dao* as the highest form of life. The unity of the spirit and the body embodies the identification of man with the *Dao*. The realization of this unity will naturally lead to the harmony or harmonious development of one's body (i.e. physical and emotional life) and spirit (spiritual and rational life). To concentrate one's vital force (*qi*) and obtain infant-like tenderness will inevitably lead to a peaceful and calm state of mind (*xin ping qi he*) as a healthy psychical environment, which is in fact the companion of life and ensures freedom from worries and cares. Self-purification and deep contemplation serve to help one get rid of all selfish desires and considerations in one sense, and in another sense help one achieve deep and profound insights into all things. In short, these two strategies for personal cultivation will surely result in great wisdom and even the mastery of the *Dao*. Mastery of the *Dao* in a social sense produces the Daoist sage, who can "love the people and govern the state without taking action."

It is interesting to imagine that it might be possible, by means of self-purification and deep contemplation, to know the "all-under-the-sky" and see the *Dao* of Heaven without going out of the door or looking through the window (see Part III, 15.2). In order to achieve this, Lao Zi advises people to "block the vent and close the door." (see Part III, 15.3)

(2) Plainness and Simplicity (Chapter 28)

This subtitle stresses the perception of plainness and the embracing of simplicity (*jian su bao pu*). It is taken directly from Chapter 19 of the *Dao De Jing* (see Part III, 23.3) and is proposed by Lao Zi himself as an approach to the attainment of the *Dao*. As a matter of fact, simplicity is another name for the *Dao*, which features naturalness, innocence and purity. It seems minute, simple and clumsy, yet, it can be so powerful that nothing under Heaven can subdue it. Therefore, if the rulers were able to maintain it, all the people would submit to them spontaneously (see Part I, 4.2). Now let us see what Lao Zi says about this in Chapter 28 (DDJ):

> He who knows the masculine and keeps to the feminine
> Will become the ravine of the world.[1]
> Being the ravine of the world,
> He will never depart from constant *De*,
> But return to the state of infancy.[2]
> He who knows glory but keeps to disgrace
> Will become the valley of the world.[3]
> Being the valley of the world,
> He will be proficient in constant *De*
> And return to the state of simplicity.[4]

He who knows the white but keeps to the black
Will become the principle of the world.[5]
Being the principle of the world,
He will possess constant *De*
And return to the state of ultimate infinity.[6]
(When the simplicity is broken up,
It is turned into vessels.
By using these vessels,
The sage becomes the head of officials.
Hence a perfect government is not carved out of artificiality.)[7]

Annotations:

[1] "The masculine" represents the hard and strong (*Yang*) whilst "the feminine" refers to the soft and weak (*Yin*). "The ravine of the world" is symbolic of modesty and the potential source of power or strength.

[2] "Constant *De*" implies accordance with the *Dao*. "The state of infancy" suggests innocence, plainness and simplicity.

[3] "The valley of the world" is symbolic of the humility of lying in a lower place and the capacity for accommodating all things under Heaven.

[4] "The state of simplicity" is the English rendering of *pu*, which virtually means a block of uncarved wood. This image is repeatedly employed by Lao Zi to mean the original state of complete simplicity that is equal to the *Dao*.

[5] "The white" denotes something bright, clear and outstanding, whereas "the black" denotes something dark, obscure and non-showy. This seems to mean that the sage in harmony with the *Dao* tends to disregard or ignore public fame and reputation by staying in the background.

[6] "The state of ultimate infinity" is the English interpretation of *wu ji*, which I think is another term for the *Dao* as the original and infinite source of all things.

[7] This part in parentheses is assumed by some Lao Zi scholars (e.g. see Gu Di and Zhou Ying. *Lao Zi Tong*, pp. 175-177) to be a comment made by an ancient reader of the *Dao De Jing*. "The

vessels" that come into being when the simplicity is broken up are said to stand for all things or the institutional components of a government. The sage ruler then has no other alternative but to utilize them for governance and leadership. Nevertheless, a perfect government can never be established by means of artificiality, or "take-action" in Lao Zi's terminology. It would only be possible to exist, according to Lao Zi, in the original state of complete simplicity (the *Dao*) alone.

Commentary:

In this chapter Lao Zi resorts to a number of symbols to exemplify the plain and simplistic aspects of the *Dao*. "The masculine" symbolizes the hard, strong, active, aggressive and dynamic, while "the feminine" symbolizes the tender, weak, passive, regressive, static, etc. In short, these two terms are respectively equivalent in symbolism to a pair of Chinese philosophical categories known as *Yang* and *Yin*. Lao Zi is apt to recommend his notion of the feminine for its reserved character and its potential power. This is compatible with his idea that "Weakness is the function of the *Dao*," and similarly with his conviction that "The tender and weak conquer the hard and strong."

Both "ravine" and "valley" serve as symbols of modesty and emptiness with the capability to accommodate all things. At the same time they tend to suggest that they are by no means competitive or exhibitionist. They are ready to absorb, and not repel, whatever comes to them.

"The state of infancy" indicates innocence and purity of mind and spirit. "The state of simplicity" implies perfect and natural simplicity, like a block of uncarved wood. In a mental state of simplicity, one is usually immune from any acquisitive desires or competitive instincts. In other words, he may enjoy peace and harmony with his surroundings. The last line of this chapter advises the ruler or government to put into practice the ideal of simplicity as the highest principle. Only by so acting will he be able to hold on to the *Dao* with integrity.

It is noticeable that Lao Zi uses the word "return" (*fu gui*) from time to time. Where the Daoist sage is expected to return to is a hierarchy of three interrelated spheres of mentality depicted as "the state of infancy" (plainness and innocence), "the state of the uncarved block" (purity and simplicity) and "the state of ultimate infinity" (the original *Dao*). The last sphere is the highest of all, because he who returns to that state of ultimate infinity is identified, or becomes one with the *Dao*. To attain this objective there must be a medium that is thought to lie in the persistent and deliberate decreasing of desires and selfishness. Chapters 19 and 32 (DDJ) cast a particular light on Lao Zi's advocacy of plainness and simplicity.

(3) Vacuity and Tranquility (Chapter 16)

Vacuity and tranquility are recommended by Lao Zi as two major principles for self-cultivation on the one hand, and for the attainment of the *Dao* and the nourishment of *De* on the other. The application of these two principles is expected to purify the mind of all conventional prejudices and egoistic desires. At the same time, one can free oneself from all self-indulgence and external disturbances as well as material temptations. By so doing one is able to return to the root as the state of tranquility, to the destiny as the originally good nature, and to the eternal as the everlasting and supreme principle of the *Dao*. As a consequence, he will be one, or identified with the *Dao*, *De* and Heaven; that is, he will then achieve the highest form of life in a spiritual sense. Let us examine Lao Zi's argument presented in Chapter 16 (DDJ).

> Try the utmost to get the heart into complete vacuity.[1]
> Be sure to keep the mind in steadfast tranquility.[2]
> All things are growing and developing
>   And I see thereby their cycles.[3]
> Though all things flourish with a myriad of variations,
>   Each one eventually returns to its root.[4]
> This returning to its root is called tranquility;
> This tranquility is called returning to its destiny;[5]
> Returning to its destiny is called the eternal.[6]
> To know the eternal is called enlightenment and wisdom.

Not to know the eternal is to take blind action,
Thus resulting in disaster.
He who knows the eternal can embrace all.[7]
He who embraces all can be impartial.
He who is impartial can be all-encompassing.
He who is all-encompassing can be at one with Heaven.[8]
He who is at one with Heaven can be at one with the *Dao*.
He who is at one with the *Dao* can be everlasting
And free from danger throughout his life.

Annotations:

[1] By "complete vacuity" is meant the inner world characterized by wisdom and emptiness (like a valley that is open and broad, capable of accommodating the myriad things).

[2] By "steadfast tranquility" is implied a frame of mind that features great quietude, calmness and clearness, free from disturbance from external things (e.g. fame, wealth, etc.).

[3] This suggests that everything is on the move, with reference to the interaction and replacement between, for instance, the static and the dynamic, the hard and the tender, the strong and the weak, the still and the active, etc.

[4] By "the root" is meant the origin or the original state, known as tranquility.

[5] By "the destiny" is meant the original essence from which the renewal of vitality arises.

[6] By "the eternal" is indicated the constant and ever-lasting rule or law according to which all things move, change and develop in cycles.

[7] The ability to "embrace all" reflects the function of "complete vacuity" above-mentioned.

[8] The Chinese word "Heaven" is used here, meaning nature or the universe. Being at one with Heaven and then with the *Dao* leads naturally to the attainment of eternity and infinity. This idea is further elaborated in Chapter 23 (DDJ).

Commentary:

This chapter is mainly preoccupied with the importance of how to foster and keep vacuity and tranquility as a source of spiritual nourishment and personal cultivation. Psychologically speaking, the principle of vacuity is intended to reduce and eradicate self-indulgence and egoistic arrogance in one sense, and to develop a capacity to embrace all things in another. Likewise, the principle of tranquility is meant to help a person diminish and free himself from self-opinionatedness and prejudice, which tend to cause mental confusion and disturbances. Only by means of vacuity and tranquility can one absorb more vital energy and preserve oneself well, in addition to being able to "return to the root," "destiny" and "eternal" in Lao Zi's terminology. The notion of tranquility is repeatedly emphasized in the *Dao De Jing*. In view of its potentiality, Lao Zi maintains that "the tranquil overcomes the hasty.... By remaining quiet and tranquil, one can become the ruler of the world" (DDJ, Ch. 45, also see Part III, 14.5).

As regards returning to "the root," it means to return to the origin of all beings, which refers to the *Dao* and features vacuity and tranquility. Associated with returning to "the root" is the idea of returning to "destiny," from which the Neo-Confucianist doctrine of "returning to the original nature of man" is assumed by Chen Guying to be derived and developed. Some Neo-Confucianists in the Song Dynasty (960-1279) were convinced that the human mind or nature is originally clear, pure and transparent. It becomes perplexed, confused and soiled because it is covered with social dust, influences, bias, ambitions, acquired craftiness, etc. Thus it is through sincere reflection on the inner self and self-correction of egoistic ills that one can be able to return to one's original good nature.

Lao Zi's concept of being at one with Heaven and the *Dao* is further discussed in Chapter 23 (DDJ). We may cite it here for further consideration: "He who seeks the *Dao* is identified with the *Dao*. He who seeks *De* is identified with *De*. He who seeks Heaven is identified with Heaven. He who is identified with the *Dao*—the *Dao* is also happy to have him. He who is identified with *De*—*De* is also happy to have him. He who is identified with Heaven—Heaven is also happy to have him."

In order to understand the chapter from a wider perspective, it is worth citing full the following Ren Jiyu's comments: In this chapter Lao Zi advocates emptying the mind and maintaining an impartial attitude toward change and development. From his point of view changes are no more than cyclical movement. A change will eventually come back to its point of departure. This is called *gui-gen* (returning to the root). In the final analysis, motion is not different from changelessness, that is, tranquility. Since tranquility is the general principle governing all vicissitudes, it thus acquires its identity as the eternal. To follow the principle of tranquility, one should not take any reckless action. In applying this principle to both everyday life and political activities, he holds that nonaction will become a panacea, for it runs no risk. (see Ren Jiyu. *The Book of Lao Zi*, p. 30)

(4) Tenderness and Non-Competition (Chapter 22)

Lao Zi firmly grounds his doctrine of keeping to tenderness on his conviction that "Reversion is the movement of the *Dao*." Thus he believes that the tender, soft and weak are companions of life and able to overcome the hard, stiff and strong, described as companions of death in his terminology. Conquest of this kind is only possible in Lao Zi's opinion when the *De* of non-competition is concretely applied as a code of conduct to practice with sincerity and modesty. It requires therefore such indispensable traits as "not clinging to one's opinions," "not claiming to be always right" and "not boasting of one's prowess," which are all stressed in the following chapter (DDJ, Chapter 22).

To yield is yet to be preserved intact.[1]
To be bent is yet to become straight.[2]
To be hollow is yet to become full.[3]
To be worn out is yet to be renewed.[4]
To have little is yet to gain.[5]
To have much is yet to be perplexed.[6]
Therefore the sage holds on to the One
  And thus becomes a model for the world.[7]
He does not cling to his ideas.
Therefore he is able to see things clearly.
He does not claim to be always right.

Therefore he is able to tell right from wrong.
He does not boast of himself.
Therefore he is given credit.
He does not think himself superior.
Therefore he is qualified for leadership.
It is only because he does not compete
  That the world cannot compete with him.[8]
How could such an old saying be false
  As "To yield is yet to be preserved intact?"
Truly one will be preserved wholly without going to the contrary.
This is a constant and natural precept.[9]

Annotations:

[1] This expresses the idea of timely compromise for the sake of self-preservation and defence. Whenever there is a storm, the grass is, for instance, so soft and supple that it gives in by lying down with the wind, and thus it survives. Conversely, the huge tree is so hard and strong that it refuses to yield, and thus gets blown down or snapped. This message is fairly instructive with regard to human activities in general, provided justice is taken into account.

[2] By the expression "be bent" is meant contraction or retreat, whereas "become straight" means expansion or advance.

[3] This line is an extension of the figurative term "empty valley," which is capable of receiving and embracing things in infinite quantity.

[4] This suggests a natural law that the new replaces the old. Tree leaves undergo, for example, such a change or cycle.

[5] This implies a steady and gradual progression of achievement. The greatest thing in the world begins, according to Lao Zi, with the minute or the little, and it grows bigger bit by bit. Hence Lao Zi advises people to set out by doing the minute or small in order to achieve the great or large. Some scholars (e.g. Ren Jiyu) interpret this sentence as "To have little (knowledge) is yet to gain." I am inclined to hold that Lao Zi here talks about personal development in general from the perspective of the *Dao*.

[6] This is a parallel to the preceding line, suggesting that he who is too greedy and ambitious will live in illusion and get nowhere because what he dreams about is beyond possibility. He will be somewhat like the person who cannot stand long on tiptoe or walk long in bounds. However, Prof. Ren translates it "To have much (knowledge) is yet to be perplexed," seemingly corresponding to his interpretation of the foregoing line.

[7] This is a rendering of *sheng ren bao yi wei tian xia shi*. By "the One" is meant the *Dao* that Lao Zi advocates all along. According to Ren Jiyu, Lao Zi here means "takes the *Dao* (the One) as the instrument to observedestiny under Heaven." The word *shi* does not only mean "model." It was also an instrument used in divination from the remote past to the Han Dynasty. The diviner tried to predict good or bad fortune by twirling this instrument. In this chapter, the *shi* that is used by the sage is not a material object, but is the principle of the *Dao*. Some scholars (e.g. Ai Qi) have this sentence as *sheng ren bao yi wei tian xia mu* based on the two versions of the *Dao De Jing* unearthed in 1973 from the ancient tombs of Mawangdui. It is then explained as "Therefore the sage who embraces the One will be able to govern the world." I think there is not much difference between these seemingly different interpretations in view of their implied message.

[8] This reflects Lao Zi's idea of non-competition and its merits. It is actually an extension of his philosophy of keeping to tenderness and his principle of advance by means of retreat.

[9] "This" refers to the notion that "To yield is yet to be preserved intact."

Commentary:

The first six lines in this chapter are assumed to be old sayings which pre-date Lao Zi. They take into consideration both the positive and negative aspects of almost all things and situations. Lao Zi uses them to reveal and justify his dialectical perspective, which is in fact recommended as a general principle with regard to the observation and treatment of social matters.

In everyday life, attention is often drawn to the outside of things rather than the inside of them. Thanks to his concrete experience and sharp observation, Lao Zi tends to contemplate and penetrate with insight social life and human activities. Thus he maintains that everything has two sides, which may be termed the positive and negative aspects. Both of them should be taken into account. Opposite as they are, they are interrelated and dependent upon one another, so they should be approached in respect of their interactions. For this reason, Lao Zi points out that the action of "yielding" will lead to preservation intact; the tolerance of "being bent" will lead to the advantage of becoming straight; the state of being "hollow" will lead to the merit of becoming full; the state of being "worn out" will lead to being renewed; and the situation of having "little" will lead to more gains, greater achievements, etc. In the final analysis, the *De* of non-competition is concluded as the key to realizing all possible benefits. Being a code of conduct, the *De* of non-competition lies in the virtues of not clinging to one's ideas (*bu zi jian*), not claiming oneself to be always right (*bu zi shi*), and not boasting about oneself (*bu zi jin*). However, non-competition is obviously contrary to the competition that is all around us. The interrelations between these two distinct strategies can also be observed from a dialectical and complementary viewpoint. Some things can be, as it were, accomplished by means of non-competition, whereas other things can only be accomplished by means of competition. It all depends on the specific situation. Hence, the way in which Lao Zi overemphasizes non-competition turns out to be lop-sided or half-dialectical.

It is noteworthy that Lao Zi's advice "to yield" and "to be bent" is derived from his recommended philosophy of keeping to the tender and supple, which he regards as "companions of life." As for his notion of non-competition, it is the actual praxis of his principle of subsequent advance via initial retreat. Lao Zi discusses elsewhere the importance of tenderness or softness, for he believes that "the soft and tender are companions of life" whilst "the hard and stiff are companions of death;" and accordingly, "the tender and weak stay in the superior position" whilst "the hard and strong fall in the inferior position" (see Part III, 11.2).

Similarly, Lao Zi concludes that the tender and weak can overcome the hard and strong (see Part III, 11.3). As regards the necessity for and advantages of non-competition, Lao Zi repeats it with reference to the *Dao* of Heaven, which he thinks does not compete and yet is good at winning (DDJ, Ch. 73). Thus he encourages people to model their behavior upon the *Dao* of Heaven. Consequently, if a person does not compete with others, nobody under Heaven can compete with him (DDJ, Ch. 66). Such being the case, one should stay in an advantageous position if one is to fulfill one's wishes and hopes.

(5) Have-Less-Selfishness and Have-Few-Desires (chs. 13, 49)

Presented in Chapter 19 (DDJ) is the idea of reducing one's selfishness and having few desires in order to approach the *Dao* as the model for the world. As has been read in his book, Lao Zi respectively recommends having less selfishness by forgetting one's body and having few desires by developing a state of infancy. If one's self-cultivation reaches this stage, one is well on the path to the attainment of the *Dao* and *De* together. Let us first examine Chapter 13 (DDJ), and then Chapter 49 (DDJ).

A. (Chapter 13)

One is alarmed when in receipt of favor or disgrace.
One has great trouble because of one's body that he has.
What is meant by being alarmed by favor or disgrace?
Favor is regarded as superior, and disgrace as inferior.
One is alarmed when one receives them
  And equally alarmed when one loses them.[1]
This is what is meant by being alarmed by favor or disgrace.
What is meant by having great trouble because of the body?
The reason why I have great trouble is that I have a body.
If I had no body,
  What trouble could I have?[2]
Hence he who values the world in the same way as he values his body
  Can be entrusted with the world.[3]
He who loves the world in the same way as he loves his body
  Can be entrusted with the world.[4]

Annotations:

[1] By the pronoun "them" is meant favor and disgrace, the gain and loss of which will be most likely to startle those who try hard to win and maintain the former while avoiding and rejecting the latter.

[2] This implies that trouble comes from possession of the body, which is here symbolic of personal life, egoism and selfishness. Hence one can be free from all troubles and worries if only one can forget or reject one's body (i.e. egoism or selfishness).

[3] and [4] Judging from the context, we can conclude that Lao Zi thinks that the world can be a better place to live in if it is left to the selfless to govern. Lao Zi's idea of "valuing the body" (*gui shen*) is presented in Chapter 44, in contrast to valuing such external things as material acquisitions, pleasure-snobbery, vanity, reputation, etc. Yet, his notion of "having no body" (*wu shen*) is expressed in chapters 13 and 7 with a reference to selfishness or egoism. That is why we need to be highly conscious of the different contexts involved.

Commentary:

In this chapter Lao Zi presents his thought of "having no body" (*wu shen*), which can be viewed as identical with "having no ego or self" (*wu ji*). "The body" as such is considered the root cause of troubles and worries because it is symbolic of egoism or selfishness. As a matter of fact, it is only due to "the body" that one is apt to be alarmed when receiving or losing favor or disgrace. This mentality underlines personal vanity and preoccupation with self-interest.

Therefore, one will be able to make light of any favor or disgrace, and better still, be free from troubles or worries provided one rejects the body, or to be exact, eschews egoism. Having reached this stage of self-cultivation, one will surely, according to Lao Zi, attain the *Dao* as the supreme principle and act upon it accordingly, no matter what one is engaged in.

B. (Chapter 49)

The sage has no fixed mind of his own.[1]
He takes the mind of the people as his mind.

I treat those who are good with goodness
And I also treat those who are not good with goodness,
Then everyone will try to become good.[2]
I trust those who are trustworthy
And I also trust those who are not trustworthy,
Then everyone will try to become trustworthy.[3]
When the sage governs the world,
He seeks to put away his personal will
And to help everyone return to the sphere of simplicity.[4]
While the people all concentrate on their own eyes and ears,
He renders them back to the sphere of infancy without desires.[5]

Annotations:

[1] By "fixed mind of his own" is meant a selfish mind or persistent egoism.

[2], [3] These expressions demonstrate that the Daoist sage rejects nobody and embraces the spirit of helping all people by way of self-transformation.

[4] "The sphere of simplicity" features the attainment of *Dao*. It is the highest form of spiritual life in Lao Zi's opinion.

[5] "The sphere of infancy without desires" is a figurative illustration of "the sphere of simplicity." A genuine, innocent and pure state of soul is supposed to be the ultimate pursuit of the Daoist sage as characterized by Lao Zi.

Commentary:

This chapter reveals Lao Zi's political ideal exemplified by the lofty personality of the Daoist sage. Since he is selfless and rejects nobody, the sage is most liable to be well received and trusted by the people, thus establishing his moral influence over them.

The probability of realizing this political ideal as well as cultivating this idealized personality is, in the final analysis, determined by such crucial virtues as selflessness and broad-mindedness. They in turn make it possible for the common people to return to "the sphere of simplicity" or "the sphere of infancy without desires."

It should be stressed that the virtue of treating and trusting all people (with or without goodness) accounts for an important dimension of the sage's personality. This conduct of rejecting nobody as an idealized trait is also conclusively credited with remarkable consequences elsewhere. Take Chapter 62 (DDJ), for example. Lao Zi assumes that honored words can gain respect from others, and likewise, fine deeds can have an impact on others. "Therefore the sage is always good at saving men, and consequently nobody is rejected. He is always good at saving things, and consequently nothing is rejected. This is called the hidden light." (see Part III, 13.2)

(6) Naturalness and Take-No-Action (Chapter 48)

Lao Zi proclaims that the *Dao* follows the way of naturalness or spontaneity (chs. 25 and 22, DDJ) and features take-no-action (chs. 37, 38 and 48, DDJ). In turn, we may as well take them as an approach to achieving the *Dao*. The application of this approach can be effective only when the pursuit of the *Dao* is firmly established as the ultimate goal of life. A relevant and instructive message is contained in Chapter 48 (DDJ).

The pursuit of learning is to increase day after day.[1]
The pursuit of the *Dao* is to decrease day after day.[2]
It decreases and decreases again
  Till one gets to the point of take-no-action.
He takes no action and yet nothing is left undone.
In order to govern all under Heaven
  One should adopt the policy of doing nothing.[3]
A person who likes to do anything arbitrary,[4]
  Is not qualified to govern all under Heaven.

Annotations:

[1] Heshang Gong assumes that the content of this "learning" chiefly concerns studies of governmental administration, moral education, rites and music. By learning one's knowledge of these matters accumulates day after day. Nevertheless, this is a negative kind of knowledge tending to develop craftiness and cunning, which in turn intensify desires and wants. Consequently, there will arise competition, conspiracies and other social problems.

[2] The *Dao* features the origin of all things and "invariably takes no action." Hence, the pursuit of the *Dao* helps one reduce his desires as one gets closer to it.

[3] "Doing nothing" (*wu shi*) means not doing anything to disturb and control the people. It is derived from the supreme principle of "take-no-action."

[4] "To do anything arbitrary" (*you shi*) is the exact opposite of "doing nothing" (*wu shi*).

Commentary:

This chapter makes a distinction between the pursuit of learning and that of the *Dao*. According to Lao Zi, the former leads to a continuous increase in practical knowledge associated with ambitions and desires, whereas the latter leads to a continuous increase in spiritual nourishment and freedom from desires. He who strives for more knowledge of such external things as social crafts and values is apt to have more ambitions and desires. The consequence will be that he will become enslaved and alienated with regard to his real self or genuine nature. But he who approaches the *Dao* will be steadily freed from these matters and able to return to simplicity as a kind of spiritual destination.

Once again, Lao Zi emphasizes the importance of 'take-no-action'. He views it as a principle to be adopted by the ruler when conducting state affairs. At the same time he advises the ruler to model himself on the Daoist sage by "doing nothing" (*wu shi*) to disturb and control the people under his reign. Otherwise there will be no chance for him to become a qualified ruler and govern all under Heaven. This notion of Lao Zi in effect corresponds to his recommendation of "self-transformation" (*zi hua*) to people in general.

"To do anything arbitrary" (*you shi*) is the implication of "take-action" (*you wei*) in Lao Zi's terminology. It is considered to be negative and disadvantageous in the long run, contrasting sharply with "doing nothing" or "take-no-action." It needs to be stressed that "doing nothing" or "take-no-action" simply means doing whatever does not disturb people or go against natural law. However, he tends to absolutize the advantages of his favorite principle of "take-no-(arbitrary or blind)action." That is why it is taken more often than not as something extremely passive.

To sum up, naturalness or spontaneity is characteristic of the *Dao* of Heaven, which is assumed by Lao Zi to be the final standard or frame of reference for the *Dao* of man. The former is claimed to "reduce whatever is excessive and supplement whatever is insufficient," whilst the latter contrarily "reduces the insufficient and offers more to the excessive" (see Part I, 5.1). Yet the *Dao* of man will change into the *Dao* of the sage if it is modeled properly upon the *Dao* of Heaven. In this case it is "to benefit all things and to cause no harm"; and correspondingly, it is "to act for others but not to compete with them." (see Part I, 5.1).

With respect to "take-no-action" as an essential feature of the *Dao*, it is so capable and functionable that it can leave nothing undone, as described in chapters 37, 38, 48 and so on (DDJ). Thus it plays an indispensable role in a political or social sense, because it can help rulers to subdue all things to their sway as a result of self-transformation. The importance of "take-no-action" lies in the effect Lao Zi depicts in the following statements: "I take no action, and the people of themselves become transformed.... I disturb nobody, and the people of themselves become prosperous." (see Part III, 21.1)

Appendix 1 *The Dao De Jing of Lao Zi* (Translation)

With particular reference to the Mawangdui silk-copy versions of the *Dao De Jing* and other old versions, including those of Wang Bi and Heshang Gong, this revised edition is largely based on the recent philological studies done by such leading Lao Zi scholars as Gu Di, Zhou Ying, Chen Guying, Ren Jiyu, Gao Heng, Ma Shulun, Yan Lingfeng, Sha Shaohai and Ai Qi. It has benefited considerably from two works in Chinese, namely, *Lao Zi Tong* (Gu Di & Zhou Ying) and *Lao Zi Zhu Yi Ji Ping Jie* (Chen Guying), which are virtual encyclopedias of Lao Zi studies at the present stage. In addition, the English rendering of the book owes a great deal to the existing translations by Chan Wing-tsit, Robert G. Henricks, He Guanghu, Gao Shining, Song Lidao and Xu Junyao. I would like take this opportunity to acknowledge my gratitude to all these scholars.

Chapter 1 (see Part I, 1.1)

The *Dao* that can be told is not the constant *Dao*.
The Name that can be named is not the constant Name.
The Being-without-form is the origin of Heaven and Earth;
The Being-within-form is the mother of the myriad things.
Therefore it is always from the Being-without-form
  That the subtlety of the *Dao* can be contemplated;
Similarly it is always from the Being-within-form
  That the manifestation of the *Dao* can be perceived.
These two have the same source but different names,
  They both may be called deep and profound.
The Deepest and most profound
  Is the doorway to all subtleties.

Chapter 2 (see Part III, 12.1)

When the people of the world know the beautiful as beauty,
There arises the recognition of the ugly.
When they know the good as good,
There arises the recognition of the evil.

This is the reason why
Have-substance and have-no-substance produce each other;
Difficult and easy complete each other;
Long and short contrast with each other;
High and low are distinguished from each other;
Sound and voice harmonize with each other;
Front and back follow each other.

Thus, the sage conducts affairs through take-no-action;
He spreads his doctrines through wordless teaching;
He lets all things grow without his initiation;
He nurtures all things but takes possession of nothing;
He promotes all things but lays no claim to his ability;
He accomplishes his work but takes no credit for his contribution.
It is because he takes no credit
That his accomplishment stays with him for ever.

Chapter 3 (see Part III, 20.1)

Try not to exalt the worthy,
So that the people shall not compete.
Try not to value rare treasures,
So that the people shall not steal.
Try not to display the desirable,
So that the people's hearts shall not be disturbed.
Therefore the sage governs the people by
Purifying their minds,
Filling their bellies,
Weakening their ambitions,
And strengthening their bones.
He always keeps them innocent of knowledge and desires,

And makes the crafty afraid to run risks.
He conducts affairs on the principle of take-no-action,
And everything will surely fall into order.

Chapter 4 (see Part I, 1.2)

The *Dao* is empty (like a bowl),
Its usefulness can never be exhausted.
The *Dao* is bottomless (like a valley),
Perhaps the ancestor of all things.
Invisible or formless, it appears non-existing
But actually it exists.
I don't know whose child it is at all.
It seems to have even preceded the Lord.

Chapter 5 (see Part I, 2.4)

Heaven and Earth are not humane.
They regard all things as straw dogs.
The sage is not humane.
He regards all people as straw dogs.
The space between Heaven and Earth is like a bellows, isn't it?
While vacuous, it is never exhaustible.
When active, it turns out even more.
(To talk too much will surely lead to a quick demise.
Hence it is better to keep to tranquility.)

Chapter 6 (see Part I, 1.3)

The spirit of the valley is immortal.
It is called the subtle and profound female.
The gate of the subtle and profound female
Is the root of Heaven and Earth.
It is continuous and everlasting,
With a utility never exhausted.

Chapter 7 (see Part IV, 27.1)

Heaven is eternal and Earth everlasting.
They can be so just because they do not exist for themselves.

And for this reason they can long endure.
Therefore the sage places himself in the background,
  But finds himself in the foreground.
He puts himself away without self-consideration,
  And yet he always remains well-preserved.
It is because he has no personal interests
  That his personal interests are fulfilled.

Chapter 8 (see Part III, 14.1)

The supreme good is like water.
Water is good at benefiting all things
  And yet it does not compete with them.
It dwells in places that people detest,
  And thus it is so close to the *Dao*.

In dwelling, (the best man) loves where it is low.
In the mind, he loves what is profound.
In dealing with others, he loves sincerity.
In speaking, he loves faithfulness.
In governing, he loves order.
In handling affairs, he loves competence.
In his activities, he loves timeliness.
Since he does not compete,
  He is free from any fault.

Chapter 9 (see Part III, 14.2)

To talk too much will lead to a quick demise.
Hence, it is better to keep to tranquility.
To keep what is full from overflowing
  Is not as good as to let it be.
If a sword-edge is sharpened to its sharpest,
  It will not be able to last long.
When your rooms are filled with gold and jade,
  You will not be able to keep them safe.
If you become arrogant because of honor and wealth,
  It will bring upon you misfortune.
Retreat as soon as the work is done.

Such is the *Dao* of Heaven.

Chapter 10 (see Part IV, 28.1)

Can you keep the spirit and embrace the One
Without departing from them?
Can you concentrate your vital force and achieve tenderness
Like an infant without any desires?
Can you purify your mind and contemplate in depth
Without any flecks?
Can you love the people and govern the state
Without taking action?
Can you play the role of the feminine
In the opening and closing of the gates of Heaven?
Can you understand all and penetrate all
Without using your intelligence?

Chapter 11 (see Part III, 8.1)

Thirty spokes are united around the hub to make a wheel,
But it is on the central hole for the axle
That the utility of the chariot depends.
Clay is kneaded to mold a utensil,
But it is on the empty space inside it
That the utility of the utensil depends.
Doors and windows are cut out to form a room,
But it is on the interior vacancy
That the utility of the room depends.
Therefore, have-substance brings advantage
While have-no-substance creates utility.

Chapter 12 (see Part III, 10.1)

The five colors make one's eyes blind.
The five tones make one's ears deaf.
The five flavors dull one's palate.
Racing and hunting unhinge one's mind.
Goods that are hard to get tempt people to rob and steal.
Hence, the sage cares for the belly instead of the eyes;
And he rejects the latter but accepts the former.

Chapter 13 (see Part IV, 28.5A)

One is alarmed when in receipt of favor or disgrace.
One has great trouble because of one's body that he has.
What is meant by being alarmed by favor or disgrace?
Favor is regarded as superior, and disgrace as inferior.
One is alarmed when one receives them
  And equally alarmed when one loses them.
This is what is meant by being alarmed by favor or disgrace.
What is meant by having great trouble because of the body?
The reason why I have great trouble is that I have a body.
If I had no body,
  What trouble could I have?
Hence he who values the world in the same way as he values his body
  Can be entrusted with the world.
He who loves the world in the same way as he loves his body
  Can be entrusted with the world.

Chapter 14 (see part I, 2.1)

You look at it but can not see it;
  It is called the imageless.
You listen to it but can not hear it;
  It is called the soundless.
You touch it but can not find it;
  It is called the formless.

These three cannot be further inquired into,
  For they are the inseparable One.
The One is not bright when it is up,
  And not dark when it is down.
Infinite and indistinct, it cannot be named,
  Thus reverting to a state of non-thingness.

This is called shape without shape,
  Or image without image.
It is also called the Vague and the Elusive.
When meeting it, you cannot see its head,

When following it, you cannot see its back.
Hold on to the *Dao* of old
In order to harness present things.
From this you may know the primeval beginning.
This is called the law of the *Dao*.

Chapter 15 (see Part IV, 26.1)

He who was adept at practicing the *Dao* in antiquity
Was subtly profound and penetrating, too deep to be understood.
As he was beyond people's cognitive capacity,
I can only describe him arbitrarily:
He was cautious, as if walking across a frozen river in winter;
He was vigilant, as if being threatened by an attack on all sides;
He was solemn and reserved, like a visiting guest;
He was supple and pliant, like ice about to melt;
He was broad, like the boundless sea;
He was vigorous, like the untiring blowing wind;
He was genuine and plain, like the uncarved block;
He was open and expansive, like a great valley;
He was merged and indifferent, like muddy water.
Who could make the muddy gradually clear via tranquility?
Who could make the still gradually come to life via activity?
(It was nobody else but him.)
He who maintains the *Dao* does not want to be overflowing.
It is just because he does not want to be overflowing
That he can be renewed when worn out.

Chapter 16 (see Part IV, 28.3)

Try the utmost to get the heart into complete vacuity.
Be sure to keep the mind in steadfast tranquility.
All things are growing and developing
And I see thereby their cycles.
Though all things flourish with a myriad of variations,
Each one eventually returns to its root.
This returning to its root is called tranquility;

This tranquility is called returning to its destiny;
Returning to its destiny is called the eternal.
To know the eternal is called enlightenment and wisdom.
Not to know the eternal is to take blind action,
  Thus resulting in disaster.
He who knows the eternal can embrace all.
He who embraces all can be impartial.
He who is impartial can be all-encompassing.
He who is all-encompassing can be at one with Heaven.
He who is at one with Heaven can be at one with the *Dao*.
He who is at one with the *Dao* can be everlasting
  And free from danger throughout his life.

Chapter 17 (see Part III, 23.1)

The best kind of rulers are those whose existence
  Is merely known by the people below them.
The next-best are those who are loved and praised.
The next-best are those who are feared.
The next-best are those who are despised.
If trust in others is not sufficient,
  It will be unrequited.
(The best rulers) are cautious,
  And seldom issue orders.
When tasks are accomplished and affairs completed,
  The common people will say,
  "We simply follow the way of spontaneity."

Chapter 18 (see Part III, 23.2)

When the great *Dao* is rejected,
  The doctrines of Ren and Yi will arise.
When knowledge and craftiness appear,
  Great hypocrisy will also emerge.
When the six family relations are not in harmony,
  Filial piety and parental affection will be advocated.
When a country falls into chaos,
  Loyal ministers will be praised.

Chapter 19 (see Part II, 23.3)

Only when sageness is eliminated and craftiness discarded,
Will people benefit a hundredfold.
Only when humanity is eradicated and righteousness abandoned,
Will people return to filial piety and parental affection.
Only when skill is thrown away and profit ignored,
Will there be no more robbers or thieves.
Yet, these three are inadequate as a doctrine,
We therefore urge the following:
Manifest plainness and embrace simplicity;
Reduce selfishness and have few desires;
And get rid of learning and have no worries.

Chapter 20 (see Part IV, 26.2)

How much difference is there between ready approval·
And outright denunciation?
How much difference is there between good and evil?
What people fear cannot but be feared.
The multitude are merry, as if feasting on a day of sacrifice,
Or as if ascending a tower to enjoy the scenery in springtime.
I alone remain tranquil and reluctant to distinguish.
I feel broad and far-reaching, as if at a loss.
I am indifferent and without concern,
Like an infant that cannot smile.
I am wearied indeed, as if I have no home to return to.
The multitude are so brilliant and self-exhibiting,
I alone seem to be lost in darkness and ignorance.
The multitude are so observant and discriminating,
I alone intend to make no distinctions.
The multitude possess more than enough,
I alone seem to lack everything.
The multitude have their reason for taking action,
I alone seem to be clumsy and incapable of nothing.
The multitude like to be endorsed and supported,
I alone value the realization and attainment of the *Dao*.

Chapter 21 (see Part I, 2.3)

The character of the great *De*
 Follows from the *Dao* alone.
What is called the *Dao*
 Appears elusive and vague.
Vague and elusive as it is,
 There is the image in it.
Elusive and vague as it is,
 There is the real in it.
Profound and obscure as it is,
There is the essence in it.
The essence is very concrete
 And contains the proof inside itself.
From the present back to the past
 Its name continues to ever last,
 By which alone we may know the beginning of all things.
How do I know their beginning as such?
Only through this.

Chapter 22 (see Part IV, 28.4)

To yield is yet to be preserved intact.
To be bent is yet to become straight.
To be hollow is yet to become full.
To be worn out is yet to be renewed.
To have little is yet to gain.
To have much is yet to be perplexed.
Therefore the sage holds on to the One
 And thus becomes a model for the world.
He does not cling to his ideas.
Therefore he is able to see things clearly.
He does not claim to be always right.
Therefore he is able to tell right from wrong.
He does not boast of himself.
Therefore he is given credit.
He does not think himself superior.
Therefore he is qualified for leadership.
It is only because he does not compete

That the world cannot compete with him.
How could such an old saying be false
As "To yield is yet to be preserved intact?"
Truly one will be preserved wholly without going to the contrary.
This is a constant and natural precept.

Chapter 23 (see Part IV, 27.2)

A whirlwind does not last a whole morning;
A rainstorm does not last a whole day.
What causes them to be so?
It is Heaven and Earth.
If Heaven and Earth cannot make them last long,
How much less can man?
Therefore, he who seeks the *Dao* is identified with the *Dao*.
He who seeks *De* is identified with *De*.
He who seeks Heaven is identified with Heaven.
He who is identified with the *Dao*—
The *Dao* is also happy to have him.
He who is identified with *De*—
De is also happy to have him.
He who is identified with Heaven—
Heaven is also happy to have him.

Chapter 24 (see Part III, 14.3)

He who stands on tiptoe is not steady.
He who doubles his stride cannot go far.
He who displays himself is not wise.
He who justifies himself is not prominent.
He who boasts of himself is not given any credit.
He who feels self-important is not fit for leadership.
From the perspective of the *Dao*,
These are like remnants of food and tumors of the body,
So disgusting that the one with the *Dao* stays away from them.
Likewise the sage knows himself but does not display himself.
He loves himself but does not feel self-important.

Hence, he rejects that and accepts this.

Chapter 25 (see Part I, 1.4)

There was something undifferentiated and all-embracing,
Which existed before Heaven and Earth.
Soundless and formless, it depends on nothing external
And stays inexhaustible.
It operates with a circular motion
And remains inextinguishable.
It may be considered the mother of all things under Heaven.
I do not know its name, and hence call it the *Dao* far-fetchedly.
If forced to give it another name, I shall call it the Great.
The Great is boundless and thus functioning everywhere.
It is functioning everywhere and thus becoming far-reaching.
It is becoming far-reaching and thus returning to the original point.
Therefore the *Dao* is great.
Heaven is great.
Earth is great.
And Man is also great.
There are four great things in the universe,
And Man is one of them.

Man follows the way of Earth.
Earth follows the way of Heaven.
Heaven follows the way of the *Dao*.
And the *Dao* follows the way of spontaneity.

Chapter 26 (see Part III, 20.2)

The heavy is the root of the light.
The tranquil is the lord of the hasty.
Therefore the sage travels all day
Without leaving behind his baggage cart.
Although he enjoys a magnificent and comfortable life,
He remains at leisure and without self-indulgence in it.
How is it that a king with ten thousand chariots

Governs his kingdom so lightly and hastily?
Lightness is sure to lose the root.
Hastiness is sure to lose the lord.

Chapter 27 (See Part IV, 27.3)

He who is adept at travelling leaves no track or trace behind.
He who is adept at speaking makes no blemishes or flaws.
He who is adept at counting uses no tallies or counters.
He who is adept at shutting the door needs no bolts,
And yet it cannot be opened when shut.
He who is adept at binding things needs no strings,
And yet they cannot be untied when bound.

Chapter 28 (see Part IV, 28.2)

He who knows the masculine and keeps to the feminine
Will become the ravine of the world.
Being the ravine of the world,
He will never depart from constant *De*,
But return to the state of infancy.
He who knows glory but keeps to disgrace
Will become the valley of the world.
Being the valley of the world,
He will be proficient in constant *De*
And return to the state of simplicity.
He who knows the white but keeps to the black
Will become the principle of the world.
Being the principle of the world,
He will possess constant *De*
And return to the state of ultimate infinity.
(When simplicity is broken up,
It is turned into vessels.
By using these vessels,
The sage becomes the head of officials.
Hence a perfect government is not carved out of artificiality.)

Chapter 29 (see Part III, 9.2)

I think that one will not succeed

When he desires to govern the state and act upon it.
The state as a sacred vessel should not be acted upon,
Nor should it be held on to.
He who acts upon it will harm it.
He who holds on to it will lose it.
Thus the sage takes no action, and therefore fails in nothing;
He holds on to nothing, and therefore loses nothing.

Of all the creatures some lead and some follow;
Some breathe and some blow;
Some are strong and some are weak;
Some rise up and some fall down.
Hence the sage discards the extremes,
The extravagant and the excessive.

Meanwhile, he desires to have no desires.
He does not value rare treasures.
He learns what is unlearned.
He returns to what is missed.
Thus he helps all things in natural development,
But does not dare to take any action.

Chapter 30 (see Part III, 22.1)

He who assists the ruler with the *Dao*
Never seeks to dominate the world with military force.
The use of force is intrinsically dangerous:
Wherever armies are stationed,
Briers and thorns grow wild.
As soon as great wars are over,
Years of famine are sure to afflict the land.
Therefore an adept commander (of a defensive force) will
Stop when he has achieved his aim.
He does not use force to dominate the world.
He achieves his aim but does not become arrogant.
He achieves his aim but does not boast about it.
He achieves his aim only because he has no other choice.
This is called achieving the aim without using force to dom-

inate.
The strong and powerful rob and harm the old and weak.
This is called contrary to the *Dao*.
Whatever is contrary to the *Dao* will soon perish.

Chapter 31 (see Part III, 22.2)

Weapons are nothing but instruments of evil.
They are used only when there is no other choice.
Therefore, he who wins a battle is not praiseworthy.
If he thinks himself praiseworthy,
He delights in the victory.
He who delights in the victory,
Delights in the slaughter of men.
He who delights in the slaughter of men
Will not succeed under Heaven.
For the multitude killed in the war
Let us mourn them with sorrow and grief.
For the victory won by force,
Let us observe the occasion with funeral ceremonies.

Chapter 32 (see Part I, 4.2)

The *Dao* is eternal and has no name.
Though it is simple and seems minute,
Nothing under Heaven can subordinate it.
If kings and lords were able to maintain it,
All people would submit to them spontaneously.
Heaven and Earth unite to drip sweet dew,
Without the command of men, it drips evenly over all.
Once a system comes into being,
Names are instituted.
Once names are instituted,
One has to know where and when to stop.
It is by knowing where and when to stop
That one can be free from danger.
Everything under Heaven is embraced by the *Dao*,
Just like every river or stream running into the sea.

Chapter 33 (see Part III, 15.1)

He who knows others is knowledgeable.
He who knows himself is wise.
He who conquers others is physically strong.
He who conquers himself is mighty.
He who is contented is rich.
He who acts with persistence has will.
He who does not lose his place will endure.
He who dies but is not forgotten enjoys a long life.

Chapter 34 (see Part I, 4.3)

The great *Dao* flows everywhere.
It may go left, it may go right.
All things rely on it for existence,
  And never does it turn away from them.
When it accomplishes its work,
  It does not claim credit for itself.
It preserves and nourishes all things,
  But it does not claim to be master over them.
Thus it may be called the minute.
All things come to it as to their home,
  Yet it does not act as their master.
Hence it may be called the great.
This is always the case with the sage
  Who is able to achieve his greatness
  Just because he himself never strives to be great.

Chapter 35 (see Part I, 2.2)

If you hold fast to the great image,
  All the people under Heaven will come to you.
They will come and do no harm to each other,
  But will all enjoy comfort, peace and health.
Music and dainties can make passers-by tarry,
  While the *Dao*, if spoken out, is insipid and tasteless.
Being looked at, it is imperceptible.
Being listened to, it is inaudible.
Being utilized, it is inexhaustible.

Chapter 36 (see Part III, 20.3)

In order to contract it,
  It is necessary to expand it first.
In order to weaken it,
  It is necessary to strengthen it first.
In order to destroy it,
  It is necessary to promote it first.
In order to grasp it,
  It is necessary to offer it first.
This is called subtle light.

The soft and the tender overcome the hard and the strong.
(Just as) fish should not be taken away from deep water,
The sharp weapons of the state should not be displayed to
  the people.

Chapter 37 (see Part III, 9.1)

The *Dao* invariably takes no action,
  And yet there is nothing left undone.
If kings and lords are able to maintain it,
  All things will submit to them due to self-transformation.
If, after submission, they have resurging desires to act,
  I should subdue them by the nameless simplicity.
When they are subdued by the nameless simplicity,
  They will be free of desires.
Being free of desires, they will be tranquil,
  And the world will of itself be rectified.

Chapter 38 (see Part II, 6.2)

The man of superior *De* is not conscious of his *De*,
  And in this way he really possesses *De*.
The man of inferior *De* never loses sight of his *De*,
  And in this way he has no true *De*.
The man of superior *De* takes no action
And thus nothing will be left undone.
The man of inferior *De* takes action
  And thus something will be left undone.

The man of superior humanity takes action
And so acts without purpose.
The man of superior righteousness takes action
And so acts on purpose.
The man of superior propriety takes action,
And when people do not respond to it,
He will stretch out his arms and force them to comply.

Therefore, only when the *Dao* is lost does *De* disappear.
Only when *De* is lost does humanity appear.
Only when humanity is lost does righteousness appear.
Only when righteousness is lost does propriety appear.

Now propriety is a superficial expression of loyalty and Faithfulness, and the beginning of disorder.
The man of foreknowledge has but the flower of the *Dao*,
And this is the beginning of ignorance.
Hence the great man dwells in the thick instead of the thin.
He dwells in the fruit instead of the flower.
Therefore he rejects the latter and accepts the former.

Chapter 39 (see Part I, 4.4)

Of those in the past that obtained the One:
Heaven obtained the One and became clear;
The earth obtained the One and became tranquil;
The Gods obtained the One and became divine;
The valleys obtained the One and became full;
All things obtained the One and became alive and kept growing;
Kings and lords obtained the One and the world became peaceful.

Taking this to its logical conclusion we may say:
If Heaven had not thus become clear,
It would soon have cracked;
If the earth had not thus become tranquil,
It would soon have broken apart;

If the Gods had not thus become divine,
They would soon have perished;
If the valleys had not thus become full,
They would soon have dried up;
If all things had not thus become alive and kept growing,
They would soon have become extinct;
If kings and lords had not thus become honorable and noble,
They would soon have toppled and fallen.

It is always the case
That the noble takes the humble as its root.
And the high takes the low as its base.
Hence kings and lords call themselves
The orphaned, the solitary or the unworthy.
This is regarding the humble as the root of the noble,
Is it not?
People disdain the "orphaned," "solitary" or "unworthy."
And yet kings and lords call themselves by these terms.
Therefore the highest honor needs no flattering.
Thus with everything—
Sometimes it may increase when decreased,
And sometimes it may decrease when increased.
For this reason—
They desire not to dazzle and glitter like jade,
But to remain firm and plain like stone.

Chapter 40 (see Part I, 3.1)

Reversion is the movement of the *Dao*.
Weakness is the function of the *Dao*.
All things under Heaven come from Being-within-form.
And Being-within-form comes from Being-without-form.

Chapter 41 (see Part IV, 25.1)

When the highest type of *shi* hear of the *Dao*,
They diligently practice it.
When the average type of *shi* hear of the *Dao*,

They half-believe it.
When the lowest type of *shi* hear of the *Dao*,
They laugh heartily at it.
If they did not laugh at it, it would not be the *Dao*.

Therefore, there is the established saying:
The *Dao* that is bright seems to be dark;
The *Dao* that advances seems to retreat;
The *Dao* that is level seems to be uneven.
Thus the great *De* appears empty like a valley;
The far-reaching *De* appears insufficient;
The vigorous *De* appears inert;
The simplistic *De* appears clumsy;
The whitest appears soiled;
The greatest square has no corners;
The greatest vessel is unfinished;
The greatest music sounds faint;
The greatest form has no shape;
The *Dao* is hidden and nameless.
Yet it is the *Dao* that initiates all things
And brings them to completion.

Chapter 42 (see Part I, 4.1)

The *Dao* produces the One.
The One turns into the Two.
The Two give rise to the Three.
The Three bring forth the myriad of things.
The myriad things contain *Yin* and *Yang* as vital forces,
Which achieve harmony through their interactions.

Chapter 43 (see Part III, 11.1)

The softest thing in the world
Runs in and out of the hardest thing.
The invisible force penetrates any creviceless being.
Thereby I come to know the advantage of take-no-action.
Few in the world can realize the merits of wordless teaching
And the benefits of do-nothing.

Chapter 44 (see Part III, 18.1)

Which is more dear, fame or life?
Which is more valuable, life or wealth?
Which is more detrimental, gain or loss?
Thus an excessive love of fame
  Is bound to cause an extravagant expense.
A rich hoard of wealth
  Is bound to suffer a heavy loss.
Therefore he who is contented will encounter no disgrace.
He who knows when and where to stop will meet no danger.
And in this way he can endure longer.

Chapter 45 (see Part III, 14.5)

What is most perfect seems to be incomplete,
  But its utility cannot be impaired.
What is most full seems to be empty,
  But its utility cannot be exhausted.
The most straight seems to be crooked.
The greatest skill seems to be clumsy.
The greatest eloquence seems to stutter.
The tranquil overcomes the hasty.
The cold overcomes the hot.
By remaining quiet and tranquil,
  One can become a model for all the people.

Chapter 46 (see Part III, 18.2)

When the world has the *Dao*,
  War horses are used in farming.
When the world lacks the *Dao*,
  Even mares in foal have to serve in battle.
There is no guilt greater than lavish desires.
There is no calamity greater than discontentment.
There is no defect greater than covetousness.
Therefore, he who is contented with knowing contentment
  Is always contented indeed.

Chapter 47 (see Part III, 15.2)

Without going out of the door
  One may know the all-under-the-sky.
Without looking through the window
  One may see the *Dao* of Heaven.
The further one goes,
  The less one knows.
Therefore the sage knows without going about,
  Understands without seeing,
  And accomplishes without taking action.

Chapter 48 (see Part IV, 28.6)

The pursuit of learning is to increase day after day.
The pursuit of the *Dao* is to decrease day after day.
It decreases and decreases again
  Till one gets to the point of take-no-action.
He takes no action and yet nothing is left undone.
In order to govern all under Heaven
  One should adopt the policy of doing nothing.
A person who likes to do anything arbitrary,
  Is not qualified to govern all under Heaven.

Chapter 49 (see Part IV, 28.5B)

The sage has no fixed mind of his own.
He takes the mind of the people as his mind.
I treat those who are good with goodness
  And I also treat those who are not good with goodness,
  Then everyone will try to become good.
I trust those who are trustworthy
  And I also trust those who are not trustworthy,
  Then everyone will try to become trustworthy.
When the sage governs the world,
  He seeks to put away his personal will
  And to help everyone return to the sphere of simplicity.
While the people all concentrate on their own eyes and ears,
  He renders them back to the sphere of infancy without desires.

Chapter 50 (see Part III, 17.1)

Man comes alive into the world
  And goes dead into the earth.
Three out of ten will live longer.
Three out of ten will live shorter.
And three out of ten will strive for long life
  But meet premature death.
And for what reason?
It is because of excessive preservation of life.
Only those who don't value their lives are wiser
  Than those who overvalue their lives.

I have heard that those who are good at preserving life
  Will not meet rhinoceroses or tigers when traveling the byways,
  And will not be wounded or killed when fighting battles.
The rhinoceroses cannot butt their horns against them.
The tigers cannot fasten their claws upon them.
And weapons cannot thrust their blades into them.
And for what reason?
Because they are out of the range of death.

Chapter 51 (see Part II, 6.1)

The *Dao* begets all beings,
  And *De* fosters them.
Substance gives them physical forms,
  And environment completes them.
Therefore all beings venerate the *Dao* and honor *De*.
As for the veneration of the *Dao* and the honoring of *De*,
  It is not out of obedience to any orders;
  It comes spontaneously due to their naturalness.
Hence the *Dao* begets all beings,
  And *De* fosters them,
  Rears them and develops them,
  Matures them and makes them bear fruit,
  Protects them and helps them breed.
To produce them without taking possession of them,

To raise them without vaunting this as its own merit,
And to nourish them without controlling them,
This is called Profound *De*.

Chapter 52 (see Part III, 15.3)

There was a beginning of the universe,
Which may be called the mother of the universe.
He who has found the mother
Thereby understands her sons;
He who has understood the sons
And still keeps to the mother
Will be free from danger throughout his life.
Block up the holes;
Shut up the doors;
And till the end of life there will be no toil.
Open the holes;
Meddle with affairs;
And till the end of life there will be no salvation.
Seeing what is small is called enlightenment.
Keeping to weakness is called strength.
Use the light.
Revert to enlightenment.
And thereby avoid danger to one's life—
This is called practicing the eternal.

Chapter 53 (see Part III, 10.2)

If I have a little wisdom,
I will walk along a broad way
And fear nothing but going astray.
The broad way is very even,
But the powerful delight in by-paths.
The courts are exceedingly corrupt,
Whereas the fields are exceedingly weedy
And the granaries are exceedingly empty.
They are wearing elegant clothes,
Carrying sharp swords,
Enjoying exquisite food and drink,

And owning abundant wealth and treasures.
They can be called robber chieftains.
This is surely against the *Dao*.

Chapter 54 (see Part II, 7.1)

He who is good at building cannot be shaken.
He who is good at holding can lose nothing.
Thus his ancestral sacrifice can pass down
From generation to generation.
When cultivated and exercised in the person,
De will become pure and genuine.
When cultivated and exercised in the family,
De will become full and overflowing.
When cultivated and exercised in the community,
De will become constant and everlasting.
When cultivated and exercised nationwide,
De will become powerful and abundant.
When cultivated and exercised worldwide,
De will become universal and widespread.

Therefore, (by taking it as a standard we should)
Use this person to examine other persons,
Use this family to examine other families,
Use this community to examine other communities,
Use this country to examine other countries,
And use this world to examine other worlds.
How do I know the situation of all things under Heaven?
Precisely by the above-mentioned method.

Chapter 55 (see Part II, 7.2)

He who possesses *De* in abundance
Can be compared to a newborn infant.
Poisonous insects will not sting him.
Fierce brutes will not injure him.
Birds of prey will not attack him.
His bones are weak and his sinews tender,
But his grasp is firm.

He does not yet know about the intercourse of male and female,
But his organ is aroused,
For his physical essence is at its height.
He may cry all day without becoming hoarse,
For his innate harmony is simply perfect.
The essence and harmony as such are natural and constant.
To know this is called being wise.
The desire to multiply life's enjoyments means ill omen.
The mind to employ *qi* excessively means fatal stiffness.
Things that have grown strong commence to become old.
This is called "being contrary to the *Dao*."
Whatever is contrary to the *Dao* will soon perish.

Chapter 56 (see Part III, 15.4)

He who knows does not speak,
He who speaks does not know.
He blocks the vent,
Closes the door,
Blunts the sharpness,
Unties the tangles,
Softens the glare,
And mixes with the dust.
This is called Profound Identification.

Therefore people cannot get intimate with him,
Nor can they estrange themselves from him.
People cannot benefit him,
Nor can they harm him.
People cannot ennoble him,
Nor can they debase him.
For this reason he is esteemed by all-under-the-sky.

Chapter 57 (see Part III, 21.1)

A state should be governed in a normal way.
An army should be operated in an unusual way.
The world should be administered by doing nothing.

How do I know that it should be so?
Through the following:
The more prohibitive enactments there are in the world,
The poorer the people will become;
The more sharp weapons men have,
The more troubled the state will be;
The more crafts and techniques men possess,
The more vicious things will appear;
The more laws and orders are made prominent,
The more robbers and thieves will spring up.
Therefore the sage says:
"I take no action and the people of themselves become transformed.
I love tranquility and the people of themselves become righteous.
I disturb nobody and the people of themselves become prosperous.
I have no desires and the people of themselves become simple."

Chapter 58 (see Part III, 16.1)

When the government is generous and non-discriminatory,
The people will remain honest and sincere;
When the government is severe and discriminatory,
The people will become crafty and cunning.
Misfortune is that beside which fortune lies;
Fortune is that beneath which misfortune lurks.
Who knows what may be their ultimate cause?
There is no fixed and normal frame of reference.
The normal can suddenly turn into the abnormal,
The good can suddenly turn into the evil.
The people have been deluded for a long time.

Therefore, the sage is as pointed as a square, but never stays stiff;
He is as sharp as a knife, but never cuts anybody;
He is frank and straightforward, but never aggressive;

He is bright and shining, but never dazzling.

Chapter 59 (see Part III, 20.4)

To rule people and to serve Heaven
  Nothing is better than the principle of frugality.
Only by frugality can one get ready early.
To get ready early means to accumulate *De* continuously.
With the continuous accumulation of *De*,
  One can overcome every difficulty.
If one can overcome every difficulty,
  He will then acquire immeasurable capacity.
With immeasurable capacity,
  He can achieve the *Dao* to govern the country.
He who has the *Dao* of the country can maintain sovereignty.
This is called the way in which the roots are planted deep
  And the stalks are made firm;
  Longevity is achieved and sovereignty is made everlasting.

Chapter 60 (see Part III, 20.5)

Governing a large country is like cooking a small fish.
If the *Dao* is applied to the world,
  Ghosts will lose their supernatural influence.
It is not that they will actually lose it,
  But that their influence will no longer be able to harm men.
It is not that their influence will no longer be able to harm men,
  But that the sage also will not harm men.
Since these two do not harm men, and vice versa,
  They all enjoy peaceful co-existence.

Chapter 61 (see Part III, 20.6)

Governing a large country is like lying in a lower place.
This country in the world may be likened to rivers and streams flowing into the sea.
It lies lower such that all in the world runs to it.
It is the converging point of all in the world.
It is the female of the world.

That always overcomes the male via tranquility,
  And with tranquility she lies lower.
Hence a big state can rally small states around it
  If it lowers itself to them.
Small states can win trust from a big state
  If they lower themselves to it.
Thus a big state can rally small states by lowering itself.
Small states can win trust from a big state by lowering themselves.
What a big state wants is to unite and lead small states.
What small states want is to be rallied and protected by the big state.
When both sides get what they respectively want,
  The big state should learn to keep itself lower.

Chapter 62 (see Part III, 13.2)

The *Dao* is the storehouse of all things.
It is treasured by the good man,
  And also preserved by the bad man.

Honored words can gain respect from others.
Fine deeds can have an impact on others.
Even if a man is bad,
  Why should he be ever rejected?
Therefore, the sage is always good at saving men,
  And consequently nobody is rejected.
He is always good at saving things,
  And consequently nothing is rejected.
This is called the hidden light.
Therefore, the good man is the teacher of the bad.
And the bad is the material from which the good may learn.
He who does not value the teacher
  Or care for the material,
  Will still be greatly deluded
  Though he thinks himself clever.
Such is called the significant subtlety of the *Dao*.

Therefore, on the occasion of enthroning an emperor
Or installing the three ministers,
It is better to offer the *Dao* as a present
Though there are grand ceremonies of saluting them
With the round jadeware, followed by the four-horse chariot.
Why did the ancients value this *Dao* so much?
Did they not say, "Those who seek shall attain and
Those who sin shall be freed?"
For this reason it is valued by all under Heaven.

Chapter 63 (see Part III, 19.1)

Consider take-no-action as a code of conduct.
Consider make-no-trouble as a way of deed.
Consider have-no-flavor as a method of taste.

It is a rule in the world that
The most difficult things begin with the easy,
And the largest things arise from the minute.
Hence, tackle the difficult while it is still easy;
Achieve the large while it is still minute.
For this reason, the sage never strives for the great,
And thereby he can accomplish it.

He who makes promises too readily will surely lack credibility.
He who takes things too easily will surely encounter difficulties.
Therefore, even the sage regards things as difficult,
And he is free from difficulties as a result.

Chapter 64 (see Part III, 19.2)

What is stable is easy to hold.
What is not yet manifest is easy to handle.
What is brittle is easy to disintegrate.
What is minute is easy to eliminate.
Deal with matters before they occur.

Put them in order before disorder arises.
A tree as huge as one's embrace grows from a tiny shoot.
A tower of nine stories rises up from a heap of earth.
A journey of a thousand *li* starts from the first step.
People often fail when they are on the point of success
  In their conduct of affairs.
If they remain still as careful at the end as at the beginning,
  They will never suffer from failures.

Chapter 65 (see Part III, 23.4)

In ancient times he who practiced the *Dao* well
  Did not use it to enlighten the people.
Instead he used it to make them simple.
Now the people are difficult to govern
  Because they have too much craftiness.
Thus, governing a country by craftiness is a disaster for it.
And not governing it by craftiness is a blessing for it.
He who knows these two also knows the principle.
It is called profound *De* to always know the principle.
Profound *De* is deep and far-reaching;
It returns to the origin with all things,
  And then leads to the great naturalness.

Chapter 66 (see Part III, 20.7)

The great rivers and seas can be kings of the mountain
  streams
  Because they skillfully stay below them.
That is why they can be their kings.
Therefore, in order to be above the people,
  The sage must place himself below them in his words.
In order to be ahead of the people,
  He must place himself behind them in his person.
In this way, the sage is above the people,
  But they do not feel his weight.
He is ahead of the people,
  But they do not feel his hindrance.
Therefore the whole world delights in praising him

And never gets tired of him.
Simply because he does not compete with others,
Nobody under Heaven can compete with him.

Chapter 67 (see Part III, 10.3)

I have three treasures
Which I grasp and keep.
The first is "kindness."
The second is "frugality."
The third is "to dare not be ahead of the world."

With kindness, one can become courageous.
With frugality, one can become generous.
With not daring to be ahead of the world,
One can become the leader of the world.

Now it is a fatal mistake
To seek courage by abandoning kindness,
To seek generosity by abandoning frugality,
And to seek precedence by abandoning retreat.
With kindness, one can be victorious in the case of attack,
And remain firm in the case of defence.
Heaven will help and protect such a one through kindness.

Chapter 68 (see Part III, 21.2)

In the past—
An adept commander did not display his martial prowess.
An adept warrior did not become angry.
An adept conqueror did not tussle with his enemy.
An adept manager of men placed himself below them.
This is called the virtue of non-competition.
This is called the use of others' force.
This is called the supreme principle of matching Heaven.

Chapter 69 (see Part III, 21.3)

In the past, a military strategist said:
"I dare not take the offensive, but I take the defensive.

I dare not advance an inch, but I retreat a foot."
This means (to make the invading force):
Advancing onward without battle formation,
  Raising his arm without morale enhancement,
  Holding his weapons not at the ready,
  And tackling the foe without meeting him.
There is no greater disaster than underestimating the enemy.
Such underestimation is tantamount to self-abandonment.
Therefore, when two well-matched armies clash in battle
  It is the side which retreats first that will win.

Chapter 70 (see Part IV, 25.2)

All the world says that my *Dao* is great,
  But it does not resemble anything concrete.
Just because it is great,
  It does not resemble anything concrete.
It would have been small for long if it did.

My words are very easy to understand and practice.
But no one in the world can understand and practice them.
My words have their own source,
  My deeds have their own master.

It is merely because people do not know this
  That they fail to understand me.
Those who can understand me are very few,
  And those who can follow me are hard to meet.
Therefore the sage wears coarse garb
  But conceals a precious jade in his bosom.

Chapter 71 (see Part III, 15.5)

It is all the best to know that you don't know.
It is an aberration to pretend to know when you don't know.
The sage is free from the aberration
  Because he recognizes it as such.
He can be free from this aberration
  Only when he recognizes it as such.

Chapter 72 (see Part III, 20.8)

When people do not fear the power of the ruler,
  Something terribly dreadful will take place.
Do not force the people out of their dwellings.
Do not exploit the people to the point that they cannot live.
They will not detest and overthrow the regime
  Only when they are not excessively oppressed.

Chapter 73 (see Part III, 20.9)

He who is brave in daring will be killed.
He who is brave in not daring will survive.
Of these two kinds of bravery,
  One is advantageous, while the other is harmful.
Heaven detests what it detests.
Who knows its cause?
The *Dao* of Heaven does not compete, and yet it is good at winning.
It does not speak, and yet it is good at responding.
It is not called, and yet it comes along on its own.
It is frankly at ease and yet it plans well.
The net of Heaven is large and vast,
  It lets nothing escape, despite its wide meshes.

Chapter 74 (see Part III, 20.10)

If the people are not afraid of death,
  What is the point of trying to frighten them with death?
In order to make people always afraid of death,
  We can catch and kill the trouble-makers.
Then, who will dare to make trouble?
There is always a master in charge of executions.
To carry out executions in place of the master
  Is like hewing wood in place of a skillful carpenter.
Of those who hew wood in place of the carpenter,
  Very few escape cutting their own hands.

Chapter 75 (see Part III, 20.11)

The people suffer from famine

Because the ruler levies too much tax-grain.
Thus they suffer from famine.
The people are difficult to rule
Because the ruler too often takes action.
Thus they are difficult to rule.
The people take life lightly
Because the ruler longs for life so avidly.
Thus they take life lightly.

Chapter 76 (see Part III, 11.2)

When alive, man is soft and tender.
After death, he is hard and stiff.
All things like grass and trees are soft and tender when alive,
Whereas they become withered and dried when dead.
Therefore, the hard and stiff are companions of death
Whereas the soft and tender are companions of life.
Hence an army will be shattered when it becomes strong.
A tree will be broken when it grows huge.
The hard and strong fall in the inferior position;
The soft and tender stay in the superior position.

"The violent and strong do not die natural deaths."
I shall take this principle as the father of my teaching.

Chapter 77 (see Part I, 5.1)

Does not the *Dao* of Heaven resembles the drawing of a bow?
When the string is taut, press it down.
When it is low, raise it up.
When it is excessive, reduce it.
When it is insufficient, supplement it.
The *Dao* of Heaven reduces whatever is excessive
And supplements whatever is insufficient.
The *Dao* of man does the opposite.
It reduces the insufficient
And adds more to the excessive.
Who is able to have a surplus to offer to the world?

Only the one who has the *Dao*.
The sage does not accumulate for himself.
The more he shares with others, the more he possesses.
The more he gives to others, the richer he becomes.
The *Dao* of Heaven benefits all things and causes no harm.
The *Dao* of the sage acts for others but never competes with them.

Chapter 78 (see Part III, 11.3)

Nothing in the world is softer and weaker than water,
But no force can compare with it in attacking the hard and strong.
For this reason there is no substitute for it.
Everyone in the world knows that
The soft can overcome the hard,
And the weak can overcome the strong,
But none can put it into practice.
Therefore the sage says:
"He who shoulders the disgrace for his nation
Can be the sovereign of the country;
He who bears the misfortune of his nation
Can be the king of the world."
Positive words seem to be their opposite.

Chapter 79 (see Part I, 5.2)

To reconcile two sides in deep hatred
Is surely to leave some hatred behind.
If one returns good for evil,
How can this be taken as a proper solution?
Therefore the sage keeps the counterfoil of the tally,
Yet he does not demand repayment of the debt.
The virtuous man is as kind and generous as the tally keeper
While the non-virtuous is as harsh and calculating as a tax collector.
The *Dao* of Heaven has no preference.
It is constantly with the good man.

Chapter 80 (See Part III, 24.1)

Let there be a small state with few people.
It has various kinds of instruments,
  But let none of them be used.
Let the people not risk their lives, and not migrate far away.
Although they have boats and carriages,
  Let there be no occasion to ride in them.
Although they have armor and weapons,
  Let there be no occasion to display them.
Let the people return to knotting cords and using them.
Let them relish their food,
  Beautify their clothing,
  Feel comfortable in their homes
  And delight in their customs.
Although the neighboring states are within the sight of one another,
  And the crowing of cocks and barking of dogs
  On both sides can be heard,
  Their peoples may die of old age without ever meeting each other.

Chapter 81 (see Part III, 13.1)

True words are not beautiful;
Beautiful words are not true.
A good man is not an eloquent arguer;
An eloquent arguer is not a good man.
He who knows does not show off his extensive learning;
He who shows off his extensive learning does not know.

Appendix 2 *The Dao De Jing of Lao Zi* (Original)

老子道德经

按：自《老子道德经》传世以来，迄今历时两千余载，各式注本多达上百种。就我个人所阅版本而论，除《马王堆帛书老子甲乙本》外，要本当推河上公、王弼、傅奕、成玄英、王安石、范应元、刘师培、马叙伦、高亨、蒋锡昌、严灵峰、张松如、任继愈、陈鼓应、古棣与周英等先哲时贤所为作。

值得指出的是，陈鼓应先生的《老子注译及评介》与古棣、周英先生的《老子通》(两卷)，均属难得的善本。陈本总结先贤成果，贯通古今释义，侧重义理归纳，堪称“老子小百科”，颇具导读之功。古、周本运用书校、理校、语校、韵校、文校和字校等六种互相结合的方法反复正诂，析难排疑，内容翔实，论说通达，引述精当，更具特色。

笔者执教数载，习用中英文讲授“中国哲学与智慧”、“西方美学导论”和“跨文化学导论”等课程，所涉比较庞杂。久之，虽学养不济，然独锺旧章，意在“温故知新”与明德修身，传布华夏文化及经典要义。此番不揣浅陋，在参考上列版本基础之上，以文理通达、逻辑弗悖为原则，最终借助文本与语境分析的方法，屡经推敲，暂且修订出这一版本。英文本据此译出。诚望就正于大家。

一　章

道可道，非常道；
名可名，非常名。
无，名天地之始；
有，名万物之母。

故常无，欲以观其妙；
　常有，欲以观其皦。
此两者，同出而异名，同谓之玄。
玄之又玄，众妙之门。

二　章

天下皆知美之为美，斯恶已；
　皆知善之为善，斯不善已。
故有无相生，
　难易相成，
　长短相形，
　高下相倾，
　音声相和，
　前后相随。
是以圣人处无为之事，行不言之教；
万物作而不辞，生而不有，
为而不恃，功成而不居。
夫唯不居，是以不去。

三　章

不尚贤，使民不争；
不贵难得之货，使民不为盗；
不见可欲，使民心不乱。
是以圣人之治，
虚其心，实其腹；
弱其志，强其骨。
常使民无知无欲。

使夫知者不敢为也。
为无为,则无不治矣。

四　章

道盅,而用之或不盈。
渊兮,似万物之宗;
湛兮,似或存。
吾不知其谁之子,象帝之先。

五　章

天地不仁,以万物为刍狗;
圣人不仁,以百姓为刍狗。
天地之间,其犹橐籥乎?
虚而不屈,动而愈出。

六　章

谷神不死,是谓玄牝。
玄牝之门,是谓天地之根。
绵绵若存,用之不勤。

七　章

天长地久。
天地所以能长且久,
以其不自私,故能长久。
是以圣人后其身而身先,
外其身而身存。
以其无私,故能成其私。

八 章

上善若水。
水善利万物而不争。
处众人之所恶,故几于道矣。
居善地,心善渊,
与善人,言善信,
正善治,事善能,动善时。
夫唯不争,故无尤矣。

九 章

多言数穷,不如守冲。
持而盈之,不如其已;
揣而锐之,不可常保。
金玉满堂,莫之能守;
富贵而骄,自遗其咎。
功遂身退,天之道也。

十 章

载营魄抱一,能无离乎?
专气致柔,能如婴儿乎?
涤除玄鉴,能无疵乎?
爱民治国,能无为乎?
天门开阖,能为雌乎?
明白四达,能无知乎?

十一章

三十辐共一毂，
当其无，有车之用。
埏埴以为器，
当其无，有器之用。
凿户牖以为室，当其无，有室之用。
故有之以为利，无之以为用。

十二章

五色令人目盲；
五音令人耳聋；
五味令人口爽；
驰骋畋猎，令人心狂；
难得之货，令人行妨。
是以圣人之治也，为腹不为目。
故去彼取此。

十三章

宠辱若惊，大患有身。
何谓宠辱若惊？
宠为上，辱为下，
得之若惊，失之若惊，
是谓宠辱若惊。
何谓大患有身？
吾所以有大患者，为吾有身；
及吾无身，吾有何患？

故贵以身于天下者,则可以寄天下;
爱以身于天下者,则可以讬天下。

十四章

视之不见,名曰“夷”;
听之不闻,名曰“希”;
搏之不得,名曰“微”;
此三者不可致诘,故混而为一。
一者,其上不皦,其下不昧。
绳绳兮不可名,复归于无物。
是谓无状之状,无象之象,
是谓惚恍。

迎之不见其首,随之不见其尾。
执古之道,以御今之有;
能知古始,是谓道纪。

十五章

古之善为道者,微妙玄通,深不可测。
夫唯不可测,故强为之容:
豫兮,若冬涉川;
犹兮,若畏四邻;
俨兮,其若客;
涣兮,其若凌释;
澹兮,其若海;
飂兮,若无止;
敦兮,其若朴;

旷兮，其若谷；
混兮，其若浊。
孰能浊以静之，徐清；
孰能安以动之，徐生。
保此道者不欲盈。
夫唯不盈，故能敝而新成。

十六章

致虚极，守静笃。
万物并作，吾以观复。
夫物芸芸，各归其根。
归根曰静，静曰复命；
复命曰常，知常曰明。
不知常，妄作凶。
知常容，容乃公，
公乃全，全乃天，
天乃道，道乃久，没身不殆。

十七章

太上，下知有之；
其次，亲而誉之；
其次，畏之；
其次，侮之。
信不足焉，有不信焉。
悠兮，其贵言。
功成事遂，百姓皆谓“我自然”。

十八章

大道废,有仁义;
智慧出,有大伪;
六亲不和,有孝慈;
国家混乱,有忠臣。

十九章

绝圣弃智,民利百倍;
绝仁弃义,民复孝慈;
绝巧弃利,盗贼无有。
此三者,以为文不足。
故令有所属:
见素抱朴,
少私寡欲,
绝学无忧。

二十章

唯之与诃,相去几何?
美之与恶,相去若何?
人之所畏,不可不畏。

众人熙熙,如享太牢,如春登台。
我独泊兮,其未兆;
荒兮,其未央;
沌沌兮,如婴儿之未孩;
累累兮,若无所归。

众人昭昭,我独昏昏。
众人察察,我独闷闷。
众人皆有馀,而我独若遗;
众人皆有以,我独玩且鄙;
众人皆有异,我独贵德母。

二十一章

孔德之容,惟道是从。
道之为物,惟恍惟惚。
惚兮恍兮,其中有象;
恍兮惚兮,其中有物。
窈兮冥兮,其中有精;
其精甚真,其中有信。

自今及古,其名不去,以阅众甫。
吾何以知众甫之然哉?以此。

二十二章

曲则全,枉则直,洼则盈,
敝则新,少则得,多则惑。
是以圣人抱一为天下式。
不自见,故明;
不自是,故彰;
不自伐,故有功;
不自矜,故长。
夫唯不争,故天下莫能与之争。
古之所谓"曲则全"者,岂虚言哉!

诚全而归之,常言自然。

二十三章

飘风不终朝,骤雨不终日。
孰为此者? 天地。
天地尚不能久,而况于人乎?

故从事于道者,同于道;
于德者,同于德;
于天者,同于天。
同于道者,道亦乐得之;
同于德者,德亦乐得之;
同于天者,天亦乐得之。

二十四章

企者不立;跨者不行;
自见者不明;自是者不彰;
自伐者无功;自矜者不长。
其于道也,曰馀食赘行。
物或恶之,故有道者不处。
是以圣人自知而不自见,
自爱而不自贵,
故去彼取此。

二十五章

有物混成,先天地生。
寂兮寥兮,独立而不改,

周行而不殆，可以为天地母。
吾不知其名，故强字之曰道，
强为之名曰大。
大曰逝，逝曰远，远曰返。

故道大，天大，地大，人亦大。
域中有四大，而人居其一焉。
人法地，地法天，天法道，道法自然。

二十六章

重为轻根，静为躁君。
是以君子终日行不离辎重。
虽有荣观，燕处超然。
奈何万乘之主，而以身轻天下？
轻则失根，躁则失君。

二十七章

善行者无辙迹；
善言者无瑕谪；
善数者不用筹策；
善闭者无关楗而不可开；
善结者无绳约而不可解。

二十八章

知其雄，守其雌，为天下谿。
为天下谿，常德不离，
复归于婴儿。

知其荣，守其辱，
为天下谷。
为天下谷，常德乃足，
复归于朴。
知其白，守其黑，
为天下式。
为天下式，常德不忒，
复归于无极。

二十九章

将欲取天下，而为之者，吾见其不得已。
天下神器，不可为也，不可执也。
为者败之，执者失之。
是以圣人无为故无败，无执故无失。

夫物或行或随，或嘘或吹，
或强或羸，或载或隳。
是以圣人去甚，去奢，去泰。

是以圣人欲不欲，不贵难得之货，
学不学，复众人之所过，
以恃万物之自然，而不敢为。

三十章

以道佐人主者，不以兵强于天下。
其事好还：
师之所处，荆棘生焉；

大战过后，必有凶年。
故善者，果而已矣，勿以取强焉。
果而勿骄，果而勿矜，
果而勿伐，果而不得已，
是谓果而勿强。
物壮贼老，是谓不道，不道早已。

三十一章

夫唯兵者，不祥之器，
不得已而用之。
故胜而不美。
若美必乐之。
乐之者，是乐杀人也。
夫乐杀人者，
则不可以得志于天下矣。
杀人之众，则以悲哀泣之；
战胜者，则以丧礼处之。

三十二章

道常，无名之朴；
虽小，天下莫能臣。
候王若能守之，万物将自宾。
天地相合，以降甘露，
民莫之令而自均。
始制有名。
名亦既有，夫亦将知止，
知止可以不殆。

三十三章

知人者智，自知者明。
胜人者有力，自胜者强。
知足者富。
强行者有志。
不失其所者久。
死而不忘者寿。

三十四章

大道氾兮，其可左右。
万物恃之以生而不辞，
功成而不有。
衣被万物而不为主，
可名于小；
万物归焉而不为主，
可名为大。
是以圣人之能成大也，
以其终不为大，故能成其大。

三十五章

执大象，天下往；
往而不害，安平太。
乐与饵，过客止。
道之出口，
淡乎其无味，
视之不足见，

听之不足闻，
用之不可既。

三十六章

将欲歙之，必固张之；
将欲弱之，必固强之；
将欲废之，必固举之；
将欲取之，必固予之；
是谓微明。

柔弱胜刚强。
鱼不可以脱于渊，
国之利器不可以示人。

三十七章

道常无为而无不为。
候王若能守之，万物将自化。
化而欲作，吾将镇之以无名之朴。
镇之以无名之朴，夫将不欲。
不欲以静，天下将自正。

三十八章

上德不德，是以有德；
下德不失德，是以无德。
上德无为，而无不为，
下德为之，而有不为。
上仁为之，而无以为，

上义为之,而有以为。
上礼为之,而莫之应,
则攘臂而扔之。

故失道而失德,
失德而后仁,
失仁而后义,
失义而后礼。
夫礼者,忠信之薄,而乱之首。
前识者,道之华,而愚之始。
是以大丈夫处其厚不居其薄,
处其实而不居其华。
故去彼取此。

三十九章

昔之得一者:
天得一以清;
地得一以宁;
神得一以灵;
谷得一以盈;
万物得一以生;
候王得一以为天下正。

其致之也,谓天无以清将恐裂;
地无以宁将恐废;
神无以灵将恐歇;
谷无以盈将恐竭;

万物无以生将恐灭；
侯王无以正将恐蹶。

故贵以贱为本，高以下为基。
是以侯王自称孤、寡、不榖。
此其以贱为本也！非与？
人之所恶，唯孤、寡、不榖，
而侯王以自称，
故至誉无誉。
故物或益之而损，或损之而益。
是故不欲琭琭如玉，而珞珞如石。

四十章

反者道之动；
弱者道之用。
天下万物生于有。
有生于无。

四十一章

上士闻道，勤而行之。
中士闻道，若存若亡。
下士闻道，大笑之。
不笑不足以为道。
建言有之：
明道若昧；
进道若退；
夷道若颣。

故上德若谷;
广德若不足;
建德若偷;
质德若渝;
大白若辱;
大方若隅;
大器免成;
大音希声;
大象无形;
道隐无名。
夫唯道善始且善成。

四十二章

道生一,
一生二,
二生三,
三生万物。
万物负阴而抱阳,
冲气以为和。

四十三章

天下之至柔,驰骋于天下之至坚。
无有,入于其间。
吾是以知无为之有益也。
无言之教,无为之益,
天下希及之矣。

四十四章

名与身孰亲？
身与货孰多？
得与亡孰病？
是故甚爱必大费，多藏必厚亡。
知足不辱，知止不殆，可以长久。

四十五章

大成若缺，其用不敝；
大盈若冲，其用不穷。
大直若屈，
大巧若拙，
大辩若讷。
静胜躁，寒胜热。
清静为天下正。

四十六章

天下有道，却走马以粪。
天下无道，戎马生于郊。
罪莫大于多欲，
祸莫大于不知足，
咎莫大于欲得。
故知足之足，常足矣。

四十七章

不出户，知天下；

不窥牖，见天道。
其出弥远，其知弥少。
是以圣人不行而知，
不见而明，不为而成。

四十八章

为学日益，为道日损。
损之又损，以至于无为。
无为而无不为。
将欲取天下，常以无事。
及其有事，不足以取天下。

四十九章

圣人恒无心，以百姓之心为心。
善者，吾善之；
不善者，吾亦善之，德善矣。
信者，吾信之；
不信者，吾亦信之；德信矣。
圣人之在天下也，歙歙焉，
为天下浑其心。
百姓皆注其耳目，圣人皆孩之。

五十章

出生入死。
生之徒十有三；
死之徒十有三；
而人之生生，动之于死地，

亦十有三。
夫何故也？以其生生之厚也。
夫无以生为贵者，是贤于贵生也。

盖闻善摄生者，
陆行不遇兕虎，
入军不被甲兵；
兕无所投其角，
虎无所用其爪，
兵无所容其刃。
夫何故也？以其无死地焉。

五十一章

道生之，德畜之；
物形之，势成之。
是以万物莫不尊道而贵德。
道之尊，德之贵，
夫莫之命而常自然。
故道生之，德畜之，
长之育之，成之熟之，盖之覆之。
生而不有，为而不恃，长而不宰。
是谓玄德。

五十二章

天下有始，以为天下母。
既得其母，以知其子；
既知其子，复守其母，没身不殆。

塞其兑,闭其门,终身不勤。
开其兑,济其事,终身不救。
见小曰明,守柔曰强。
用其光,复归其明,无遗身殃。
是谓袭常。

五十三章

使我介然有知,行于大道,唯施是畏。
大道甚夷,而人好径。
朝甚除,田甚芜,仓甚虚;
服文采,带利剑,厌饮食;
资财有馀,是谓盗夸,非道也哉!

五十四章

善建者不拔,善抱者不脱,子孙以祭祀不辍。
修之于身,其德乃真;
修之于家,其德乃馀;
修之于乡,其德乃长;
修之于邦,其德乃丰;
修之于天下,其德乃溥。

故以身观身,以家观家,
以乡观乡,以邦观邦,以天下观天下。
吾何以知天下然哉?以此。

五十五章

含德之厚,比于赤子。

毒虫不螫，猛兽不据，攫鸟不搏。
骨弱筋柔而握固，
未知牝牡之合而朘作，精之至也！
终日号而不嗄，和之至也！
知和曰常，知常曰明。
益生曰祥，心使气曰强。
谓之不道，不道早亡。

五十六章

知者不言，言者不知。
塞其兑，闭其门；
挫其锐，解其纷；
和其光，同其尘，
是谓玄同。

故不可得而亲，
亦不可得而疏；
不可得而利，
亦不可得而害；
不可得而贵，
亦不可得而贱，
故为天下贵。

五十七章

以正治国，
以奇用兵，
以无事取天下。

吾何以知其然哉？以此：
天下多忌讳，而民弥贫；
民多利器，国家滋昏；
民多技巧，奇物滋起；
法令滋彰，盗贼多有。
故圣人云：
我无为而民自化；
我好静而民自正；
我无事而民自富；
我无欲而民自朴。

五十八章

其政闷闷，其民淳淳；
其政察察，其民缺缺。

祸兮，福之所倚；
福兮，祸之所伏。
孰知其极？其无正也。
正复为奇，善复为妖。
人之迷也，其日固已久矣。

是以圣人方而不割，
廉而不刿，
直而不肆，
光而不耀。

五十九章

治人事天，莫若啬。
夫唯啬，是以早服；
早服是谓重积德。
重积德，则无不克；
无不克，则莫知其极；
莫知其极，则可以有国之母；
有国之母，则可以长久。
是谓根深固柢，长生久视之道。

六十章

治大国，若烹小鲜。
以道莅天下，其鬼不神。
非其鬼不神，其神不伤人。
非其神不伤人，圣人亦不伤人。
夫两不相伤，故德交归焉。

六十一章

治大国若居下流也，譬之在天下，
犹川谷之与江海也。
大国者，天下之所流，天下之所交也。
天下之牝，牝常以静胜牡，以静为下。
故大国以下小国，则取小国；
小国以下大国，则取大国。
故或下以取，或下而取。
大国不过欲兼蓄人，

小国不过欲入事人。

夫两者各得所欲,大者宜为下。

六十二章

道者万物之奥,

善人之宝,不善人之所保。

美言可以市尊,

美行可以化人。

人之不善,何弃之有?

是以圣人常善救人,

故人无弃人;

常善救物,故物无弃物。

是谓袭明。

故善人,不善人之师;

不善人,善人之资。

不贵其师,不爱其资,虽智大迷。

是谓要妙。

故立天子,置三公,

虽有拱璧以先驷马,

不如坐进此道。

古之所以贵此道者,何也?

不曰求之以得,有罪以免邪?

故为天下贵。

六十三章

为无为。

事无事。

味无味。

天下之难事,必作于易;
天下之大事,必作于细。
图难于其易也,为大于其细也。
是以圣人终不为大,故能成其大。
夫轻诺必寡信,多易必多难。
是以圣人犹难之,故终无难矣。

六十四章

其安易持,其未兆易谋。
其脆易泮,其微易散。
为之于未有,治之于未乱。
合抱之木,生于毫末;
九层之台,起于累土;
千里之行,始于足下。
民之从事,常于几成而败之。
慎终如始,则无败事。

六十五章

古之善为道者,
非以明民,将以愚之。
民之难治,以其知之。
故以智治国,国之贼;
不以智治国,国之福。
此两者,亦稽式也。
常知稽式,是谓玄德。

玄德深矣，远矣，
与物反矣，乃至大顺。

六十六章

江海之所以能为百谷王者，
以其善下之，故能为百谷王。
是以圣人欲上民，必以言下之；
欲先民，必以身后之。
是以圣人处上而民不重，
处前而民不害，
天下乐推而不厌。
以其不争，故天下莫能与之争。

六十七章

吾有三宝，持而保之：
一曰慈，
二曰俭，
三曰不敢为天下先。
夫慈故能勇，俭故能广，
不敢为天下先，故能成器长。
今舍慈且勇，舍俭且广，舍后且先，
则必死矣！
夫慈以战则胜，以守则固。
天将以慈救之，以慈卫之。

六十八章

古之善为士者不武；

善战者不怒；
善胜敌者不与；
善用人者为之下。
是谓不争之德，
是谓用人之力，
是谓配天之极。

六十九章

古之用兵者有言曰：
“吾不敢为主，而为客；
不敢进寸，而退尺。”
是谓行无行，攘无臂，
执无兵，扔无敌。
祸莫大于轻敌，轻敌几亡吾宝。
故抗兵相若，襄者胜矣。

七十章

天下皆谓吾道大不肖。
夫唯大，故似“不肖”；
若肖，久已其细也夫。

吾言甚易知，甚易行。
天下莫能知，莫能行。
言有宗，事有君。
夫唯无知，是以不我知。
知我者希，则我者贵。
是以圣人被褐而怀玉。

七十一章

知不知，尚矣；
不知知，病矣。
圣人不病，以其病病。
夫唯病病，是以不病。

七十二章

民不畏威，则大威至。
无狎其所居，无厌其所生。
夫唯无厌，是以不厌。

七十三章

勇于敢则杀，
勇于不敢则活。
此两者，或利或害，
天之所恶，孰知其故？
天之道，
不争而善胜，
不言而善应，
不召而自来，
默然而善谋。
天网恢恢，疏而不失。

七十四章

民不畏死，奈何以死惧之？
若使民常畏死，而为奇者，

吾将得而杀之,孰敢?
常有司杀者杀。
夫代司杀者杀,
是谓代大匠斫。
夫代大匠斫者,
希有不伤其手矣。

七十五章

民之饥,
以其上食税之多,是以饥。
民之难治,
以其上之有为,是以难治。
民之轻死,
以其上求生之厚,是以轻死。

七十六章

人之生也柔弱,
其死也刚强。
草木之生也柔脆,
其死也枯槁。
故刚强者死之徒,
柔弱者生之徒。
是以兵强则灭,木强则折。
刚强处下,柔弱处上。
“强梁者不得好死”,
吾将以为教父。

七十七章

天之道,其犹张弓与?
高者抑之,下者举之;
有余者损之,不足者补之。
天之道,损有余而补不足;
人之道则不然,损不足以奉有余。
孰能有余而奉天下?
唯有道者。
是以圣人无积,
既以为人己愈有,
既以与人己愈多。
故天之道,利而不害;
圣人之道,为而不争。

七十八章

天下柔弱莫过于水,
而攻坚强者莫之能先,
以其无以易之。
柔之胜刚,弱之胜强,
天下莫能知,莫能行。
故圣人之言云:
"受国之垢,是谓社稷主;
受国不祥,是为天下王。"
正言若反。

七十九章

和大怨,必有余怨;
报怨以德,安可以为善?
是以圣人执左契,而不责于人。
有德司契,无德司彻。
天道无亲,常与善人。

八十章

小国寡民。
使有什伯之器而不用;
使民重死而不远徙。
虽有舟舆,无所乘之;
虽有甲兵,无所陈之;
使民复结绳而用之。
甘其食,
美其服,
安其居,
乐其俗。
邻国相望,鸡犬之声相闻,
民至老死,不相往来。

八十一章

信言不美,美言不信。
善者不辩,辩者不善。
知者不博,博者不知。

Appendix 3 Toward the *Dao* of Human Existence*

Lao Zi is generally acclaimed as the first Chinese thinker to coin the special concept of the *Dao*, which serves in turn as the keystone of Daoism as a philosophy.[1] As a matter of fact, he is preoccupied with the concept in his philosophy, which progresses by way of elucidating this concept. The Chinese term *Dao* literally means "way" or "road." Based on this primary meaning, it assumes a metaphorical sense and is usually identified with "the way of man," signifying human morality, code of conduct, etc. But in respect of Lao Zi's way of thought as a whole, the meaning of the *Dao* transcends the ethical and social domains. It is then found to have certain extended implications related to the origin of the universe, the root of all things, the law of natural change and social development, the principle of political and military affairs, and above all, the truth of human existence. The *Dao* can be conceived of as the constellation of Lao Zi's philosophy. The most complicated but fascinating of all its aspects is that its connotations vary with the different contexts in which it is used. This is chiefly because the *Dao De Jing* (i.e. *Tao-Te Ching*) or *The Book of Lao Zi* itself has a unique and poetic form of expression encompassing metaphors, aphorisms and apothegms. It is thereby more suggestive than articulate with regard to the ideas presented.[2] Hence, only by means of both textual scrutiny and contextual analysis can one approach the boundaries of this abstruse concept. Elsewhere I have attempted to expound on Lao Zi's doctrine of the *Dao* from eight dimensions, as follows: the *Dao* of the Universe, the *Dao* of the dialectic, the *Dao* of human

---

* A paper delivered at '97 Symposium on "Daoist Tradition and Modernity" in Bonn, Germany.

life, the *Dao* of Heaven and man, the *Dao* of personal cultivation, the *Dao* of governance, the *Dao* of warfare, and the *Dao* of peace.[3] This section will focus more on the *Dao* of human existence, with reference to other aspects of Lao Zi's philosophizing on the one had, and to the *status quo* of the human condition on the other.

I Frame of Reference: The *Dao* of Man, Heaven and the Sage

In China today, people face a paradoxical situation as a result of the country's rapid economic construction and the dilemmas this poses as regards traditional ethics and moral civilization. With the implementation of the "open-door policy," most Chinese citizens have ventured to free themselves from the spiritual yoke of chimerical ideals and to peep out of the window at the outside world. The result is that they are shocked to discover that they have been left far behind in the aspect of material civilization, and they profoundly regret that they used to live in ideological fantasies. Then, during the process of China's reform, launched in the late 1970s, economic wonders have been created and living standards obviously raised. But there arise many socio-cultural problems. As in the West, the idea of competition has been embraced as the key to getting rich, strong and prosperous. As a rule, competition does work effectively to promote economic growth, from which people benefit a great deal. Nevertheless, it is carried out to extremes in some cases and unjustly in other cases, thus turning out to be a fountain head of such problems as obnoxious competitiveness, acquisitiveness, selfishness, inequality, frustration, anxiety, etc. So, bothered by these troubles, people seem to have no sooner shaken off the spiritual yoke mentioned above than they find themselves burdened with new shackles. As we reflect on this situation, it easily reminds us of what Lao Zi thinks of as "the *Dao* of man"—characterized by competitiveness, acquisitiveness, selfishness and inequality. The *Dao* of man "reduces the insufficient and offers more to the excessive." (Ch. 77)

The *Dao* of man can be traced back to the historical background of the Spring and Autumn Period (722-481 B.C.) in ancient China. During that period conflicts and clashes were of frequent occurrence, being stirred up by acquisitive and possessive desires for more land, power and property. Lao Zi excoriates the negative aspects of the *Dao* of man as a social norm and moral code widely exercised to such a degree that it is somewhat similar to "the law of the jungle" in modern terms.

According to Lao Zi, the *Dao* of man itself is often taken for granted in human society. It will, if made the norm of conduct, excite insatiable greed or desire for more possession. This will inevitably lead to the exploitation of man by man and class discrimination, and then to interpersonal struggle, and eventually to societal disorder and suffering.... In a word, it will bring about a vicious circle in both the social and moral orders.

Because of the negative aspects of the *Dao* of man, Lao Zi recommends the "*Dao* of Heaven" as its antidote. In Chapter 77 he expounds on the *Dao* of Heaven:

> The *Dao* of Heaven resembles the drawing of a bow.
> When its string is taut, press it down.
> When it is low, raise it up.
> When it is excessive, reduce it.
> When it is insufficient, supplement it.
> The *Dao* of Heaven reduces whatever is excessive
> And supplements whatever is insufficient.
> ...
> The *Dao* of Heaven benefits all things and causes no harm.
> ....

Basically inferred from his intuitive and empirical observation of natural phenomena such as transition and change, motion and replacement, growth and decline, and the progress of time, space and all beings in the world, Lao Zi reaches the conviction that there exists the *Dao* of Heaven. The *Dao* of Heaven as the law of Nature lets everything be what it can be or become without imposing, dominating or taking any blind action. Thus it is reckoned to function as the heart of the universe and to benefit all things. It is worth mentioning in passing that the *Dao* of Heaven is also reflected in Lao Zi's statement that "Heaven and earth unite to drop sweetdew which falls evenly over all things without being forced." All this can be seen as the conceptual source of the egalitarianism or equal division of property, which is deeply rooted in the mentality of the Chinese people. Hence, when its merits are appreciated in view of its possible contribution to social stability, its demerits should not be neglected in view of its potential to block economic development.

In the *Dao De Jing*, a sharp distinction is made between the *Dao* of Heaven and the *Dao* of man. The former demonstrates itself as a symbol of naturalness, selflessness and equality in a virtuous sense, whereas the latter, as a negative product of human civilization, is the very opposite. It might be concluded from the context involved that the *Dao* of Heaven is advocated not only as a rebuff to the practitioners of the *Dao* of man, but also as an ultimate measurement or frame of reference. That is to say, the *Dao* of Heaven is idealized as a model to be imitated, followed and acted upon by man. Lao Zi advocates this as a result of his deep concern and sympathy for the people of his time, who suffered from all manner of calamities. That is why Lao Zi further emphasizes that "the *Dao* of Heaven has no preference. It is constantly with the good man."(DDJ, Ch. 79) As a consequence, there arises the *Dao* of the sage in striking contrast to the *Dao* of man. According to Lao Zi, it "acts for others but never competes with them." (DDJ, Ch. 81) I personally think that the *Dao* of the sage is the fruit on the tree rooted in the *Dao* of Heaven but planted by man, that is, the "good man" or the "virtuous man," and not the "non-virtuous man" in Lao Zi's terms. Incidentally, the sage here refers to the sage of the Daoist type. He is "the only one who has got the *Dao*" (i.e. the *Dao* of Heaven) and he possesses such virtues as universal love and generosity typical of an absolute giver. In fact, the *Dao* of the sage is the realization of the *Dao* of Heaven extended to human praxis. All men alike are encouraged not simply to admire the virtues of the Daoist sage, but to model themselves upon him via self-cultivation. Only by so doing, according to Lao Zi, can people enjoy harmonious relations and society remain at peace.

What is more, the *Dao* of the sage can be seen, if we borrow Feng Youlan's phrase, as "the highest form of achievement of which man as a man is capable." All this tends to result in and from the state of "oneness between Heaven and man." This notion itself can be also rendered as "Heaven-man oneness" or "nature-man oneness" in accordance with the word order of the Chinese expresion *tian ren he yi*. This key concept threads through the development of Chinese intellectual history. Its origin is more often than not dated back to Mencius (c. 372-289 B.C.)[4] or Dong Zhongshu (179-104 B.C.).[5] I personally think that it can be dated back to Lao Zi, or even further back to the *Yi Jing* (i.e. *I Ching* or *The Book of Changes*).[6] In the *Dao De Jing*, Lao Zi lists "four great things in the universe" including *Dao*, Heaven, Earth and Man. "Man follows the way of Earth. Earth follows the way of Heaven. Heaven follows the way of *Dao*. And *Dao* follows the way of spontaneity" (DDJ, Ch. 25), or the way of naturalness that signifies the *Dao* itself. In this context, the *Dao* or the way of naturalness, is the highest but hidden principle beyond sense perception; Heaven and earth as a whole mean nature or the universe. Man gets integrated with nature (i.e. Heaven and earth) by acting upon the *Dao*. In more straightforward language Lao Zi expounds elsewhere that "He who seeks the *Dao* is identified with the *Dao*.... He who seeks Heaven isidentified with Heaven.... He who is identified with the *Dao*—the *Dao* is also happy to have him.... He who is identified with Heaven—Heaven is also happy to have him."(DDJ, Ch. 23) [7] In this case "He who seeks..." apparently refers to man, and "Heaven" stands for nature or the universe. The identification of man with Heaven and with the *Dao* as well is surely a happy situation due to mutual receptivity.

The doctrine of Heaven-man oneness is all the more important to the Chinese people since their culture is essentially a non-religious one. Thus, their pursuit of super-moral values is mostly stimulated and guided by their pursuit of the state of Heaven-man oneness as an ideal form of spiritual life. The doctrine itself has been carried on and further developed as exemplified in Neo-Daoism, Neo-Confucianism and modern schools of thought in the course of Chinese history. As far as I understand it, the doctrine of Heaven-man or nature-man oneness can be rediscovered and more rewardingly approached nowadays from at least four dimensions: the spiritual, aesthetic, social and environmental. First of all, from the spiritual dimension, the notion of "nature-man oneness" functions as a bay where the anchor of the "lifeboat" can be dropped. In other words, it is chiefly concerned with the cultivation and sublimation of human life in an ethical sense, and with the pursuit and location of man's destination in a spiritual sense. To my mind, this idea in Daoism emphasizes self-identification with nature, unconditioned pursuit of spontaneity and absolute freedom from social ambitions. Secondly, in respect of "nature-man oneness" from an aesthetic viewpoint it primarily refers to the inspiring interaction between the limited stream of personal life and the unlimited flow of universal change, which usually takes place in one's emotional world or at the time when one contemplates external objects. Interaction of this kind can facilitate a bilateral projection, reinforcement and sublimation in a vitalistic sense. Thirdly, in a social sense, the notion of "nature-man oneness" basically means the adaptation individuals to the community as a group. It is supposed to underline the development of harmonious human relations, and meanwhile the improvement of team work in the entire society. This is actually equivalent to the realization of "unity" or "harmony" in human relations. Finally, with regard to the doctrine of "nature-man oneness" from an environmental perspective, it directs man to reconsider his place in Nature. It thereby consolidates his consciousness of environmental protection, and in turn ameliorates the quality of his life in general.[8]

In the final analysis, the *Dao* of the sage is essentially characterized by the will to eschew competition. This "virtue of non-competition" is, according to Lao Zi, equal to "the supreme principle of matching Heaven" (DDJ, Ch. 68), that is, matching the *Dao* of Heaven. Consequently, "in order to be above the people," the sage with the *Dao* "must place himself below them in his words. In order to be ahead of the people, he must place himself behind them in his person. In this way, he is above the people, but they do not feel his weight. He is ahead of the people, but they do not feel his hindrance. Therefore the whole world delights in praising him and never gets tired of him. Just because he does not compete with others, nobody under the sky can compete with him," (DDJ, Ch. 66) and moreover, "he is free from any fault." (DDJ, Ch. 8)

After all, Lao Zi's advocacy of the *Dao* of the sage is, however good-natured it may be, a kind of wishful thinking in terms of harsh reality. But this does not necessarily mean that his wish has no instructive message at all as regards the keenly competitive and frustratingly problematic society in which we live nowadays.

II Pursuit of Sageliness: Practical and Sagely Wisdom

From Lao Zi's preoccupation with the three categories of the *Dao* discussed above, it may be discerned that there arise correspondingly three forms of wisdom, namely, divine wisdom, practical wisdom and sagely wisdom. To be more specific, the *Dao* of Heaven reflects a kind of mysteriously divine wisdom, the *Dao* of man a kind of secularly practical wisdom and the *Dao* of the sage a kind of transcendentally sagely wisdom. As has been observed, the first is, as it were, an idealized frame of reference based on a personified characterization of natural phenomena and can therefore be suspended in our discussion here; rather, the second is of high frequency in social praxis and daily life against the background of human civilization; and the third serves as the highest possible goal of achievement a Daoist sage strives for.

By "practical wisdom" is generally meant the wisdom of instructive significance and instrumental usage related to human activities with obviously pragmatic purposes, say, in the aspects of self-achievement, self-development, self-interest, human relations, etc. Such wisdom can be easily identified in many of Lao Zi's sayings. In respect of self-achievement, for instance, Lao Zi says, "It is a rule in the world that the most difficult things begin with the easy, and the largest things arise from the minute. Hence tackle the difficult while it is still easy; and achieve the large while it is still minute." (DDJ, Ch. 63) In respect of self-development, Lao Zi advises metaphorically that [one should] "Deal with things before their occurrences. Put them in order before disorder arises. A tree as huge as one's embrace grows from a tiny shoot. A tower of nine-stories rises up from a heap of earth.

A journey of a thousand *li* [meaning a long distance] starts from the first step. People often fail when they are about to succeed in their conduct of affairs. If they stay as careful at the end as at the beginning, they will never suffer failure." (DDJ, Ch. 64) In respect of coping with human relations, Lao Zi warns that "He who makes promises too readily surely lacks credibility. He who takes things too easily will surely encounter difficulty." (DDJ, Ch. 63) Elsewhere he stresses that "He who knows others is knowledgeable, but he who knows himself is wise. He who conquers others is physically strong, but he who conquers himself is mighty." (DDJ, Ch. 33) In respect of self-interest, diplomatic strategies can be detected in condensed form in Chapter 36, as follows: "In order to contract it, it is necessary to expand it first. In order to weaken it, it is necessary to strengthen it first. In order to destroy it, it is necessary to promote it first. In order to grasp it, it is necessary to offer it first. This is called Subtle Light (*wei ming*)."

These lines are well-known among the Chinese people in general and politicians in particular. The ideas presented are often considered, if taken literally, as conspiratorial tactics applied to gain self-interest or play power-games. This may involve a purposeful and conventional misreading that naturally leads to a misconception. And accordingly, Lao Zi himself is often labeled a political conspirator. This is understandable to the extent that each reader is liable to form his own image of Lao Zi by reading personal or modern ideas and feelings into his book. This well explains why Lao Zi's thought can be renewed and revived from time to time. We tend to maintain that Lao Zi describes the interactions between all those categories simply in order to justify his conception of the inexorable transformation between opposites. According to Gao Heng, Chen Guying and many other scholars, Lao Zi is here talking about the *Dao* of Heaven or the natural law. Hence it is groundless to accuse him of being a conspirator.[9]

In fact, Lao Zi consistently holds on to his observation that everything has two sides, which seem to be in a state of continuous opposition and mutual transformation. That is to say, when one of the two sides involved develops to its extreme or acme, it will inevitably move over toward its opposite. A flower, for example, will naturally wither or close up (contraction) when it is in full blossom (expansion). Thus the latter can be viewed as a sign of the former. Conversely, an inchworm draws itself together when it wants to stretch out. Dragons and snakes hibernate in order to preserve life. It is therefore concluded that "Contraction and expansion act upon each other; hereby arises that which furthers." (see *Yi Jing Xi Ci* [*The Great Treatise* on *The Book of Changes*]).

This dialectical speculation is illustrated in Lao Zi's description of the interrelations and interactions between contraction and expansion, weakening and strengthening, destruction and promotion, as well as taking and giving. His analysis of the development of these matters and phenomena ultimately leads to his generalization that "Reversion is the movement of *Dao*." (DDJ, Ch. 40)

It is noteworthy that "reversion" (*fan*) is a dynamic term. It refers to the interrelation between opposites in one sense, and the return to the root known as the unity or union of opposites in another. The former reveals the state of being opposite, while the latter the state of transformation or change. A situation of this kind may be symbolized by the traditional sign of *Tai Ji* (Great Acme in literal translation) where the two forces known as *Yin* and *Yang* are always on the move, interdependent and interacting at the same time. Lao Zi was incredibly observant with regard to the changes that take place between and within things themselves, indicating that things are inclined to reverse to their opposite in any changing process. It is noticeable in both Nature and human society that everything is doomed to roll downhill once it reaches the summit: Things that are too lofty fall down easily; things that are too white stain easily; songs that are too pretentious have few listeners; reputations that are too high fall short of reality. All these vicissitudes seem to be in conformity with the Chinese conception of "inevitable reversal of the extreme." (*wu ji bi fan*) In addition, it is worth emphasizing that Lao Zi himself recognizes the objective existence of two extremes in the developmental process of a thing. However, he advises people not to cling to one side only because of the inevitable "movement" toward its opposite. Under such circumstances, one has to take into account both ends and keep an eye on the dynamic change that occurs on the verge or border district of interactions between the opposites. It is right there that one may grasp the chance and stay in an advantageous position.

A relevant and profound understanding of the principle that "Reversion is the movement of the *Dao*" is believed to be the key to the sagely wisdom mentioned above. This wisdom can be looked upon as the highest form of wisdom if the realization of sageliness is taken as the highest form of achievement of man. It provides enlightenment and guidance, visibly and invisibly, to human existence as well as spiritual nourishment. In view of pleasure-seeking, for example, the sagely wisdom sheds its light on the fact that "The five colors make one's eyes blind. The five tones make one's ears deaf. The five flavors cause one's palate to go stale. Racing and hunting cause one's mind to go mad...." (DDJ, Ch. 12) The negative and even destructive outcome is a moral lesson for those who indulge in sensuous enjoyment or hedonistic way of life.

Then, in view of fame-oriented love and wealth-directed acquisitiveness, the sagely wisdom tenders a significant message that "An excessive love of fame is bound to bring about an extravagant expense. A rich hoard of wealth is bound to suffer a heavy loss. Therefore, he who is contented will encounter no disgrace" (DDJ, Ch. 44) in one sense, and "be always contented" (DDJ, Ch. 46), "rich" (DDJ, Ch. 33) or happy in another. As can be detected in human society, what people desire and seek after are chiefly fame and wealth. They may go so far as to be alienated or enslaved by "the reins of fame and the shackles of wealth" (*ming jiang li suo*) as is metaphorically stated in Chinese. Hence Lao Zi advises people to be contented with what they have, and at the same time warns the avaricious rich and fame-thirsty people not to go to extremes. Thus the concept of contentment with what one has comprises part of the traditional Chinese attitude toward material possessions.

Subsequently, in view of the development of any thing or situation, the sagely wisdom maintains that "the hard and stiff are the companions of death, whereas the soft and tender are the companions of life." (DDJ, Ch. 76) Therefore, "The tender can overcome the hard, and the weak can overcome the strong." (DDJ, Ch. 78) This potentiality is dialectically asserted by Lao Zi in the notion that "Weakness is the function of the *Dao*" (DDJ, Ch. 40) Hence he recommends people to "keep to the tender and weak" because these are assumed to develop and surely conquer "the firm and the strong" in the end. To justify this assertion, he makes constant use of "water" as a simile when illustrating the potential and overwhelming power of "the tender and weak." At this point, nevertheless, one must be highly conscious of the problematic facet of his tendency to absolutize the function of "weakness" by cutting it off from actual and varying conditions. Yet, this does not negate the enlightenment contained, therein.

Furthermore, in view of the true and the beautiful social discourse interactions, the sagely wisdom tells us that "True words are not beautiful; beautiful words are not true." (DDJ, Ch. 81) This implies an intention to encourage people to become good listeners by distinguishing between the real and the false. Otherwise, they will run the risk of being swallowed up in a sea of "beautiful words" that is more easily available in a society or community less democratic and with less freedom of speech. Next, as regards fortune and misfortune, the sagely wisdom demonstrates a dialectical interrelationship between the two opposites. That is, "Misfortune is that beside which fortune lies. Fortune is that beneath which misfortune lurks." (DDJ, Ch. 58) As is known to all, fortune as the symbol of gain is what people like to embrace, while misfortune as the symbol of loss is what people try to avoid. Yet, people hardly realize that the two opposites go hand in hand, like twins. This again reveals the potential change or transformation to the antithesis at a certain point. The thought itself is naturally corresponding to Lao Zi's generalization that "Reversion is the movement of the *Dao*."

Finally, with regard to codes of social conduct, the sagely wisdom is exemplified through "the three treasures" advocated by

Lao Zi: "The first is 'kindness,' the second is 'frugality,' the third is 'to dare not be ahead of the world.'" It is proclaimed that "With kindness one can become courageous; with frugality one can become generous; and with not daring to be ahead of the world one can become the leader of the world." (Ch. 67) The whole idea is largely based on the viewpoint of "retreat" that seems to be somewhat defensive and passive. But Lao Zi assures that only the ability to fall back is bravery, the ability to shrink is to stretch, and that avoiding prominence and precedence makes one the first. He is convinced that any breach of these three rules of wisdom will bring about complete failure. That is why "the three treasures" are also proposed as possible solutions to such social problems as harsh human relations, insatiable desires and keen competition among the people in general, and among the rich and powerful in particular.

In short, practical wisdom and sagely wisdom work on different levels and have different orientations. They help people gratify their needs and fulfil their purposes. The pursuit of either of them tends to be influenced by at least two major factors: One is the predetermined objective linked with one's value system, and the other is the understanding of the principle that "Reversion is the movement of the *Dao*." Needless to say, this understanding varies in degree from person to person. As regards those who prefer to seek instrumental benefits more than anything else, they will only scratch the surface and focus on the pragmatic dimension of wisdom. Conversely, those who prefer to pursue possible self-transcendence can reach into its depths and concentrate on the sagely dimension of wisdom. I presume to argue that the experience and practice of the sagely wisdom turns out to be a process of artistizing the way of life, which in turn leads to absolute spiritual freedom and an independent personality. Yet, as far as I can see, the accomplishment of the process is not attainable, so to speak, unless a proper attitude toward life and death is adopted from the Daoist viewpoint.

III Path to Freedom: Attitudes Toward Life and Death

According to his observation and experience in China, Bertrand Russell once acknowledged that the Chinese people in general seemed to know well how to enjoy life even though they were immersed in poverty—living conditions mostly intolerable to most Westerners. Hence the longer you stayed with them, the more you began to like and appreciate them and their culture as a whole. There are many reasons for this. Yet, the most important reason lies, I believe, in their philosophically matter-of-fact attitude toward life itself. This attitude is usually expressed in plain language but in a poetic form: One lives life in the same way as the grass goes through autumn (*ren sheng yi shi*, *cao mu yi qiu*), implying that, like grass, life itself is a natural process, flourishing in spring (youth) and then withering in autumn (age). As an aphorism widely accepted and frequently mouthed by Chinese people, it contains a moral to indicate not only the commonplace trip from life to death, but also a hidden advice to those who are liable to fall victim to the cares and worries encountered in the life to which they cling. Such a notion is deeply rooted in the psychology of most Chinese people and stays influential because of its subtle enlightenment. It originated, as far as I understand, in early Daoism as a philosophy associated with Lao Zi and Zhuang Zi in particular.

As we know, the conceptions of both life and death are crutially important to all human beings alike. Almost all living beings are afraid to die, and especially so are human beings. The love of life and fear of death seem to be connected with the natural instinct or the life-and-death emotional complex in the case of mankind. These emotions hinder human beings from attaining true spiritual freedom. Accordingly, almost all philosophers, East or West, were and are preoccupied in one way or another with various outlooks on life and death. Lao Zi, as the founder of Daoism, asserts that both life and death are as natural as anything else in the world. Zhuang Zi, who continues this thought-way, holds that they are neither to be welcomed nor to be rejected. Therefore, these two thinkers view life and death as nothing but natural phenomena to the extent that the former is not to be overvalued and the latter not to be dreaded. Chapter 50 expounds on this theme as follows:

Man comes alive into the world
  And goes dead into the earth.
Three out of ten will live longer.
Three out of ten will live shorter.
And three out of ten will strive for long life
  but meet premature death.
And for what reason?
It is because of excessive preservation of life.
Only those who don't value their lives are wiser
  Than those who overvalue their lives.

I have heard that those who are good at preserving life
  Will not meet rhinoceroses or tigers when traveling the byways,
  Nor will be wounded or killed when fighting battles.
Rhinoceroses cannot butt their horns against them.
Tigers cannot fasten their claws upon them.
And weapons cannot thrust their blades into them.
And for what reason?
Because they are out of the range of death.

This chapter discloses a message that both life and death are nothing more than natural phenomena, apart from the implicit criticism of the matter-corrupted rich and nobility. The "excessive preservation of life" that will be most likely to end in premature death can be well attested by the exposure of the destructive effects related to the "five colors" that cause blindness, the "five tones" that cause deafness, the "five flavors" that cause loss of taste, and "racing and hunting" that cause madness (DDJ, Ch. 12). Observant and critical as he was, Lao Zi could do nothing to alter or improve the situation. He therefore stuck to his philosophy of plainness and simplicity by advising people to live in accordance with the principle of the *Dao*. Under such circumstances, the best way to preserve life is, according to Lao Zi, to live through one's natural term free from cares and worries by going beyond "the range of death."

"Man comes alive into the world and goes dead in the

earth...." (DDJ, Ch. 50) This statement is noticeably a manifestation of Lao Zi's attitude toward life and death. Its implied message aims to remind one (1) to live one's life as naturally as possible so as to enjoy it to the full; (2) not to be oppressed by a tragic sense of death that befalls all men alike; (3) not to overvalue life because it is in vain to strive for excessive preservation of life.

In Zhuang Zi's philosophy, there is frequent explication of the naturalness of both life and death. Once he even goes so far as to proclaim that life is a tumor and death as the breaking of the tumor. Elsewhere Zhuang Zi concludes that all living beings in the world are evolved from *qi* as the vital force. Thus one comes to be alive when this vital force becomes compact, and one dies when this vital force disperses. Zhuang Zi continues to remark that the earth offers one a paradigm of prime; he then toils throughout his life; he lives an easy life when old and retired; and he finally enjoys rest after death. Describing life and death as such a cycle, Zhuang Zi tells people not to welcome life when it comes along, and not to struggle against death when it befalls you. That thinking is vividly illustrated by the story of Zhuang Zi beating a drum and singing following the death of his beloved wife.

The Daoist position on death is that one can possibly achieve freedom in the pure sense of this term only when he sees through the essence of death as a natural and inevitable phenomenon. This argument is, of course, open to criticism and counter-argument as well. It is, on the one hand, somewhat shrouded in obscurity and paradox; thus it could be viewed as something pessimistically negative, leading one to be psychologically crushed by such a dark and tragic sense of death. The result might be the reduction of a person into a passive being due to the consciousness of the inevitability of death. In other words, he would set no aims but muddle through life simply because death is like a sword hanging overhead, ready to fall upon him at any minute. In short, he may have no drive to take any action, but simply wait for the coming of death. Such being the case, whether to be or not to be is no longer the question, simply because this kind of life is not distinct from death. This easily reminds us of the Chinese saying, "The suffering of misery is no worse than the death of the heart (i.e. loss of hope)."

On the other hand, this argument about death could possibly lead to a positive stance toward life itself. That is to say, with a high awareness of the inevitability of death, one may first of all work a meaning or a purpose into life as a natural passage from birth to death. Thus he may make the most out of it because he treasures every minute of the process. He knows well that time is on the wing and can never be recaptured once it passes by. (We therefore have an old saying that "He who is with high aspirations tends to sigh with a feeling that time is always too short.") Hence he would be ready to adopt a sense of mission or social commitment. Consequently he contributes and constructs more in his life and work. He expects that what he has achieved may extend the significance of his existence into society and history as well. Secondly, since he recognizes death for what it is, he will be able to make light of whatever hardships, difficulties, miseries and sufferings—all the negative experiences—he confronts throughout his life. This may be expressed in Nietzsche's phrase: He may be in a position to "laugh at all tragedies." Thirdly, since he recognizes death for what it is, he may devote or sacrifice his life to a cause or causes in case of need. For instance, revolutionaries, religious martyrs, etc., choose to die a hero's death for their ideals. Confucianism recommends that a *jun zi* (superior man) should give up his body for the asdvancement of humanity. This spirit of devotion obviously demands a positive conception of death as a natural phenomenon.

In a word, when we argue that one can be possibly free in the real sense of the term only by seeing through the nature of death, we are encouraged to face death without fear. Thus we have no reason to be either panicked or enslaved by death to the degree that we have to crawl under its imagined claws. We should accordingly be masters of our own fate and of death as well. In that case we could be able to improve our quality of existence in its spiritual dimension, and have access to absolute freedom in the pure sense of this term.

To close this discussion, there are three more statements to be made: (1) We tend to read the modern into the old when rediscovering such classics as the *Dao De Jing*. This is understandable due to the fact that the texts concerned are more suggestive than articulate on the one hand, and on the other, they remain open to new interpretations so long as the latter are justifiable in the textual and historical contexts. (2) The *Dao* of human existence is likely to swing or slant toward either the *Dao* of man or the *Dao* of the sage. The former appears more closely leagued with practical wisdom, whereas the latter consorts with sagely wisdom. (3) As regards Lao Zi's *Dao* of human existence, it is oriented toward the *Dao* of the sage, in association with sagely wisdom. The possible attitudes toward it can be broadly categorized into the three types explained by Lao Zi:

When the highest type of *shi* (i.e. literati) hear of the *Dao*,
  They diligently practice it.
When the average type of *shi* hear of the *Dao*,
  They half-believe it.
When the lowest type of *shi* hear of the *Dao*,
  They laugh heartily at it.
If they did not laugh at it,
  It would not be the *Dao*. (DDJ, Ch. 41)

Notes:

[1] A distinction is made between Daoism as a philosophy (*Dao Jia* or *Dao Xue*) and Daoism as a religion (*Dao Jiao*) according to the tradition of Chinese philosophy. Cf. Feng Youlan (Fung Yu-lan). "A Short History of Chinese Philosophy," in *Selected Philosophical Writings of Fung Yu-lan*. Beijing: Foreign Languages Press, 1991, pp. 193-198; also cf. Wang Ming. *Dao Jia Yu Dao Jiao Si Xiang Yan Jiu* (*Studies of Daoism as A Philosophy and A Religion*). Beijing: China Social Sciences Press, 1987.

[2] Ibid., (*Selected Philosophical Writings of Fung Yu-lan*), p. 205.

[3] Cf. Wang Keping. "Lao Zi's Doctrine of the Dao in Perspective," *Essays on Sino-Occidental Aesthetic Cultures*. Beijing: Tourism Education Press, 1998.

[4] Cf. Mencius. "Jing Xin Shang" (Chapter 7A), in *Meng Zi* (*The Book of Mencius*). Beijing: Zhonghua Shuju Press, 1988.

[5] Cf. Dong Zhongshu. "Yin Yang Yi" (The Meaning of Yin and Yang), in

Chun Qiu Fan Lu (*The Book of Dong Zhongshu*). Shanghai: Shanghai Gu Ji Press, 1990.

[6] Cf. Liu Shuxian. "You Tian Ren He Yi Xin Shi Kan Ren Yu Zi Ran Zhi Guan Xi" (*The Relations Between Man and Nature in View of Newly-Interpreted Heaven-man Oneness*), in *Ru Jia Si Xiang Yu Xian Dai Hua* (*Confucian Thought and Modernization*). Beijing: China Broadcasting and Television Press, 1993.

[7] Cf. Gu Di & Zhou Ying. *Lao Zi Tong* (*Complete Studies of Lao Zi*). Changchun: Jilin Renmin Press, Vol. 2, 1991, pp. 85-92; also cf. Gao Heng. *Lao Zi Zheng Gu* (*A Revised Annotation of Lao Zi's Dao De Jing*). Beijing: Zhonghua Shuju Press, 1988, pp. 56-58.

[8] Cf. Wang Keping. "On the Social Development and the Rediscovery of the Doctrine of Nature-Man Oneness," in *Research Journal*, Beijing Second Foreign Languages Institute, No. 2, April, 1995. (Note: The article is based on a paper delivered at the '94 Beijing International Symposium on "Social Development and Oriental Culture").

[9] Cf. Gao Heng. *Lao Zi Zheng Gu* (*A Revised Annotation of Lao Zi's Dao De Jing*). Beijing: Zhonghua Shuju Press, 1988, p. 81; also cf: Chen Guying. *Lao Zi Zhu Yi Ji Ping Jie* (*An Annotated and Paraphrased Version of Lao Zi's Dao De Jing with Commentary*). Beijing: Zhonghua Shuju Press, 1992, pp. 205-207.

Key References

A. Translated Works

CHAN Wing-tsit (tr. & ed.). *A Source Book in Chinese Philosophy*. Princeton, N.J: Princeton University Press, 1973.

CHUANG Tzu (ZHUANG Zi). *A Taoist Classic: Chuang-tzu*. (tr. Fung Yu-lan) Beijing: Foreign Languages Press, 1989.

CHUANG Tzu (ZHUANG Zi). *The Complete Works of Chuang Tzu*. (tr. Burton Watson) N.Y.: Columbia University Press, 1968.

FUNG Yu-lan. *A History of Chinese Philosophy*. (Vol. I) Princeton, N.J.: Princeton University Press, 1952.

—*Selected Philosophical Writings*. Beijing: Foreign Languages Press, 1991.

GONG Dafei & FENG Yu (eds). *Chinese Maxims*. Beijing: Sinolingua, 1994.

HUANG Di (Emperor HUANG Di). *The Four Classics of Emperor Huang Di*. (*Huang Di Si Jing Jin Zhu Jin Yi*). (ed. Yu Mingguang, tr. Zhang Chun) Changsha: Yuelu Publishing House, 1993.

KIU, K.L. *100 Ancient Chinese Fables*. Beijing: China Translation & Publishing Corp., 1991.

LAO Tzu (LAO Zi). *Lao-tzu Te-Tao Ching*. (tr. Robert G. Henricks) London: The Bodley Head, 1990.

LAO Tzu (LAO Zi). *The Lao Tzu* (*Tao-Te Ching*). (tr. Chan Wing-tsit), in *A Source Book in Chinese Philosophy*. Princeton, N.J.: Princeton University Press, 1973, pp. 139-176.

LAO Zi. *A Taoist Classic: Lao Zi*. (ed. Ren Jiyu, tr. He Guanghu et al.) Beijing: Foreign Languages Press, 1993.

SUN Zi. *The Art of War*. (tr. Pan Jiabin & Liu Ruixiang) Beijing: Military Sciences Press, 1993.

The I Ching or Book of Changes. (tr. Carry F. Baynes) Princeton, N.J.: Princeton University Press, 1980.

B. Untranslated Works

AI Qi (ed.). *Lao Zi Ba Shi Yi Zhang*. (*81 Chapters of The Book of Lao Zi*) Tianjin: Tianjin Academy of Social Sciences Publishing House, 1993.

CAO Lihua. *Zhong Hua Chuan Tong Mei Xue Ti Xi Tan Yuan*. (*An Investigation into the Origin of Chinese Traditional Aesthetics*) Beijing: Capital Normal University Press, 1994.

CHEN Guying. *Lao Zi Zhu Yi Ji Ping Jie*. (*The Lao Zi with Notes and Commentary*) Beijing: China Book Company, 1992.

—*Lao Zhuang Xin Lun*. (*New Essays on Lao Zi and Zhuang Zi*) Shanghai: Shanghai Chinese Classics Publishing House, 1992.

—*Zhuang Zi Jin Zhu Jin Yi*. (*The Zhuang Zi with Notes and Commentary*) Beijing: China Book Company, 1983.

CHEN Guying (ed). *Dao Jia Wen Hua Yan Jiu*. (*Daoist Cultural Studies* Nos 2, 3) Shanghai: Shanghai Guji Chubanshe, 1992, 1993.

CHEN Wangheng. *Long Teng Feng Zhu*. (*Flying Dragon and Phoenix: Chinese Aesthetics in Perspective*) Hangzhou: Zhejiang University Press, 1994.

DAI Jianye. *Lao Zi: Zi Ran Ren Sheng*. (*Lao Zi: A Natural Life*) Wuhan: Changjiang Literature and Art Publishing House, 1993.

FENG Dawen. *Hui Gui Zi Ran: Dao Jia De Zhu Diao Yu Bian Zou*. (*Return to Nature: The Dominant Tone and Variations of Daoism*) Guangzhou: Guangdong People's Publishing House, 1992.

FENG Qi. *Zhong Guo Gu Dai Zhe Xue De Luo Ji Fa Zhan*. (*Logical Development of Chinese Ancient Philosophy*) Shanghai: Shanghai People's Publishing House, 1993.

FENG Tianyu. *Zhong Hua Yuan Dian Jing Shen*. (*The Spirit of

Chinese Meta-Classics) Shanghai: Shanghai People's Publishing House, 1994.

Fudan University Journal (ed.). *Zhong Guo Gu Dai Mei Xue Shi Yan Jiu.* (*Studies of The History of Chinese Ancient Aesthetics*) Shanghai: Fudan University Press, 1983.

FUNG Yu-lan (FENG Youlan). *Zhong Guo Zhe Xue Shi Xin Bian.* (*New Edition of the History of Chinese Philosophy* vols 1-2) Beijing: People's Publishing House, 1992.

GAO Heng. *Lao Zi Zheng Gu.* (*A Revised Annotation of Lao Zi's Dao De Jing*) Beijing: China Bookstore, 1988.

GE Rongjin (ed.). *Dao Jia Wen Hua Yu Xian Dai Wen Ming.* (*Daoist Culture and Modern Civilization*) Beijing: People's University Press, 1991.

GU Di & ZHOU Ying. *Lao Zi Tong.* (*Comprehensive Studies of Lao Zi* 2 vols) Changchun: Jilin People's Publishing House, 1991.

HESHANG Gong (ed.). *Dao De Zhen Jing.* (*A True Classic: Dao De Jing*) Shanghai: Shanghai Chinese Classics Publishing House, 1991.

LI Zehou. *Zhong Guo Gu Dai Si Xiang Shi Lun.* (*Essays on The History of Chinese Ancient Thought*) Beijing: People's Publishing House, 1986.

—*Hua Xia Mei Xue.* (*Chinese Aesthetics*) Beijing: International Cultural Interflow Publishing Company, 1989.

LI Zehou & LIU Gangji (eds). *Zhong Guo Mei Xue Shi.* (*History of Chinese Aesthetics* Vol. 1) Beijing: China Social Sciences Press, 1984.

LIU Shu & LIU Hao (ed.). *Dao De Jing.* (*Dao De Jing of Lao Zi*) Hefei: Anhui People's Publishing House, 1990.

MIN Ze. *Zhong Guo Mei Xue Si Xiang Shi.* (*A History of Chinese Aesthetic Thought* Vol. 1) Jinan: Qilu Press, 1989.

NAN Huaijin. *Chan Zong Yu Dao Jia.* (*Chanism and Daoism*) Shanghai: Fudan University Press, 1993.

QIAO Changlu. *Zhong Guo Ren Sheng Zhe Xue.* (*Chinese Philosophy of Life*) Beijing: People's University Press, 1990.

QIN Xincheng & LIU Shengyuan. *Lao Zi Zhuan.* (*A Biography of Lao Zi*) Shijiazhuang: Huashan Literature and Art Publishing House, 1993.

REN Jiyu (ed.). *Zhong Guo Zhe Xue Shi.* (*A History of Chinese Philosophy* Vol. 1) Beijing: People's Publishing House, 1963.

SHA Shaohai (ed.). *Lao Zi Quan Yi.* (*A Complete Paraphrase of The Lao Zi*) Guiyang: Guizhou People's Publishing House, 1992.

SIMA Qian. *Shi Ji.* (*Historical Records*) Changsha: Yuelu Press, 1992.

SUN Yikai, QIAN Gengsin & LI Renqun. *Lao Zi Wai Zhuan Lao Zi Bai Wen.* (*A Story of Lao Zi and 100 Questions on His Ideas*) Hefei: Anhui People's Publishing House, 1992.

WANG Anshi. *Dao De Jing Zhu* (*Dao De Jing Annotated*), see *Zhong Guo Zhe Xue Shi Zi Liao Xuan Ji.* (*Some Highlights of Chinese Philosophy in Song, Ming and Yuan Dynasties*) Beijing: China Book Company, 1982.

WANG Bi (ed.). *Lao Zi Zhu.* (*The Lao Zi Annotated*) Shanghai: Shanghai Chinese Classics Publishing House, 1989.

WANG Ming. *Dao Jia He Dao Jia Si Xiang Yan Jiu.* (*An Investigation of Daoism and Its Ideas*) Beijing: China Social Sciences Press, 1987.

XU Fuguan. *Zhong Guo Yi Shu Jing Shen.* (*The Spirit of Chinese Art*). Shenyang: Chunfeng Literature and Art Publishing House, 1987.

XU Kangsheng. *Lao Zi Yu Dao Jia.* (*Lao Zi and Daoism*) Beijing: Xinhua Publishing House, 1993.

YE Lang. *Zhong Guo Mei Xue Shi Da Gang.* (*An Outline of the History of Chinese Aesthetics*) Shanghai: Shanghai People's Publishing House, 1987.

ZHANG Dainian. *Zhong Guo Zhe Xue Da Gang.* (*An Outline of Chinese Philosophy*) Beijing: China Social Sciences Press, 1982.

—*Wen Hua Yu Zhe Xue. (Chinese Culture and Philosophy*) Beijing: Educational Science Publishing House, 1988.

ZHANG Liwen (ed.). *Dao.* Beijing: People's University Press, 1989.

ZHANG Wenxun. *Ru Dao Shi Mei Xue Si Xiang Tan Suo.* (*An Exploration of Aesthetic Ideas In Confucianism, Daoism and*

Buddhism) Beijing: China Social Sciences Press, 1988.
ZHAO Jihui et al. (eds). *Zhong Guo Ru Xue Shi*. (*A History of Chinese Confucianism*) Zhengzhou: Zhongzhou Ancient Books Publishing House, 1993.
ZHOU Zhenfu. *Zhou Yi Yi Zhu*. (*The Book of Changes Paraphrased and Annotated*) Beijing: China Book Company, 1991.

Glossary

B

bai	the white
bian zhe	the eloquent arguer
bing qiang ze mie	an army will be shattered when it becomes strong
bo zhe	he who shows off his extensive learning
bo zhe bu zhi	he who shows off his extensive learning does not know
bu dao	be contrary to the *Dao*
bu gan wei	dare not to take any action
bu gan wei tian xia xian	dare not be ahead of the world
bu shan	the evil
bu shan ren	the bad man
bu yan zhi jiao	wordless teaching
bu yu	be free of desires
bu zheng	non-competition
bu zheng zhi de	the virtue of non-competition
bu zhi zu	discontent

C

chang duan xiang xing	long and short contrast with each other
chi zi	new-born infant
chong qi	interactions (between *Yin* and *Yang*)
ci	the feminine
ci (*ai*)	kindness

D

da bai ruo ru	the whitest appears as if soiled
da dao	the great *Dao*
da fang ruo yu	the squarest has no corners
da huan you shen	one has great trouble because of the body that he has
da qi mian cheng	the greatest vessel can never be completed
da shun	the great harmony
da wei	great hypocrisy
da xiang	the great image, the greatest form
da xiang wu xing	the greatest form has no shape
da yin xi sheng	the greatest music sounds faint
Dao	the *Dao* (*Tao*, the Way)
dao fa zi ran	the *Dao* follows the way of naturalness
dao ji	the law of the *Dao*
dao shan shi qie shan cheng	the *Dao* that initiates all things and bring them to completion
dao sheng yi	the *Dao* produces the One
dao sheng zhi	the *Dao* begets all beings
dao yin wu ming	the *Dao* is hidden and nameless
dao zhi dong	the movement of the *Dao*
dao zhi yong	the function of the *Dao*
De	*De* (Virtue)
de xu zhi	*De* fosters all beings
di	the Lord
di chu xuan jian	clean and purify your profound insight

E

er	the Two
er sheng san	the Two give rise to the Three

F

fan	reversion, return

fan zhe dao zhi dong	reversion is the movement of the *Dao*
fu	fortune
fu xi huo zhi suo fu	fortune is that beneath which misfortune lurks

G

gang qiang	the hard and the strong
gang qiang chu xia	the hard and strong stay in the inferior position
gao xia xiang qing	high and low distinguish each other
gong cheng er bu ju	he accomplishes his work but takes no credit for his contribution
gong sui shen tui	retreat as soon as the work is done
guang	generosity
guang de	far-reaching *De*
guang de ruo bu zu	the far-reaching *De* appears insufficient
gui	ghosts, spirits
gui de	to honor *De*
gui sheng	excessive preservation of life
guo zhi mu	the mother (*Dao*) of the country

H

he	harmony
hei	the black
hou	retreat
hu huang	the vague and the elusive
huo	misfortune
huo mo da yu bu zhi zu	there is no calamity greater than discontent
huo xi fu zhi suo yi	misfortune is that beside which fortune lies
hun er wei yi	the inseparable One

J

jian	frugality
jian de	the firm *De*
jian de ruo tou	the firm *De* appears timid
jian su bao pu	manifest plainness and embrace simplicity
jin dao	the *Dao* that advances
jin dao ruo tui	the *Dao* that advances seems to retreat
jing	the essence, spirit
jing dou	steadfast quietude
jing wei zao jun	the tranquil is the lord of the hasty
jue qiao qi li	skill is thrown away and profit ignored
jue ren qi yi	humanity is eradicated and righteousness abandoned
jue sheng qi zhi	sageliness is eliminated and knowledge discarded
jue xue wu you	get rid of learning and have no worries

K

ke	the defensive
kong de	the great *De*

L

li er bu hai	benefit all things and cause no harm
ling	become divine

M

miao	subtle, subtlety
mei	the beautiful, beauty
mei xing	good deeds
mei yan	beautiful words

mei yan bu xin	beautiful words are not true
Ming	Name
ming	wisdom (light, enlightenment)
ming dao	the *Dao* that is bright
ming dao ruo mei	the *Dao* that is bright seems dark
mu qiang ze zhe	a tree will be broken when it grows huge

N

nan yi xiang cheng	difficult and easy complete each other
ning	become tranquil
(*ning*) *jing*	tranquility

P

pei tian zhi ji	the supreme principle of matching Heaven
pin	the female (organ)
pu	simplicity

Q

qi	vital force (energy)
qian hou xiang sui	front and back follow each other
qing	become clear
qing jing	remain quiet and tranquil
qu ze quan	to yield is yet to be preserved wholly

R

ren yi	humanity and righteousness
ren zhi dao	the *Dao* of man
rong	glory
rou	disgrace
rou ruo	the soft and tender

rou ruo chu shang	the soft and tender stay in the superior position
rou ruo sheng gang qiang	the soft and tender overcome the hard and strong
ruo	weakness
ruo zhe dao zhi yong	weakness is the function of the *Dao*

S

san	the Three
san sheng wan wu	the Three bring forth the myriad things
shan	the good
shan fu wei yao	the good can suddenly turn into the evil
shan ren	the good man
shan zhe	the good
shang de	superior *De*
shang de ruo gu	superior *De* appears empty like a valley
shang li	superior propriety
shang ren	superior humanity
shang yi	superior righteousness
shao si gua yu	reduce selfishness and have few desires
she	the extravagant
shen	supernatural function, deities
sheng er bu you	he nurtures all things but takes possession of nothing
sheng ren	the (Daoist) sage
sheng ren zhe you li	he who conquers others is physically strong
sheng ren zhi dao	the *Dao* of the sage (the Daoist sage)
sheng zhi tu	companions of life
shui	water
si zhi tu	companions of death

T

tai	the excessive

tian di mu	mother of all things under Heaven
tian di zhi gen	root of Heaven and Earth
tian di zhi shi	origin of Heaven and Earth
tian wang	the net of Heaven
tian xia gu	the valley of the world
tian xia mu	the mother of the universe
tian xia shen qi	the state as a sacred vessel
tian xia shi	the principle of the world
tian xia xi	the ravine of the world
tian zhi dao	the *Dao* of Heaven

W

wa ze ying	to be hollow is yet to become full
wan wu sheng yu you	all things come from Being-within-form
wan wu zhi mu	mother of the myriad things
wan wu zhi zong	ancestor of all things
wang ze zhi	to be bent is yet to become straight
wei er bu shi	he promotes all things but lays no claim to his ability
wei er bu zheng	act for others but never compete with them
wei dao ri sun	the pursuit of the *Dao* is to decrease day after day
wei xue ri yi	the pursuit of learning is to increase day after day
wu ming	subtle light
Wu	Being-without-form
wu	have-nothing
wu ji	ultimate infinity
wu se	the five colors
wu shi	make-no-trouble, do nothing arbitrary
wu si	have no personal interests
wu wei	take-no-action, nonaction
wu wei	the five flavors
wu wei er wu bu wei	he takes no action and yet nothing is left

	undone
wu wei zhi yi	the advantage of take-no-action
wu wu	non-thingness
wu xiang zhi xiang	image without image
wu (yi)	the ugly
wu yu	innocent of desires
wu yin	the five tones
wu zhi yi wei yong	have-nothing creates utility
wu zhuang zhi zhuang	shape without shape

X

xi chang	the eternal
xi ming	the hidden light
xia de	inferior *De*
xian	precedence (advance)
xiang	the image
xiao ci	filial piety and parental affection
xin	the true
xin yan	true words
xin yan bu mei	true words are not beautiful
xiong	the masculine
xuan	deep and profound
xuan tong	profound identification
xu	vacuity
xu ji	complete vacuity
xuan de	profound *De*
xuan pin	subtle and profound female
xuan pin zhi men	gate of the subtle and profound female
xue bu xue	learn what is unlearned

Y

yan zhe	he who speaks
yan zhe bu zhi	he who speaks does not know
Yang	the *Yang*, the male principle

yao miao	the significant subtlety of the *Dao*
yi	the One
yi dao	the *Dao* (Way) that is level
yi dao ruo lei	the *Dao* that is level seems to be uneven
yi (qi) yong bing	an army should be operated in an (unusual) way
yi (zheng) zhi guo	a state should be governed in a (normal) way
yi sheng er	the One turns into the Two
Yin	the Yin, the female peinciple
yin sheng xiang he	sound and voice harmonize with each other
ying	become full
yong	courage
yong ren zhi li	the use of others' force
you	have-something
You	Being-within-form
You sheng yu Wu	Being-within-form comes from Being-without-form
you shi	do anything arbitrary
you wu xiang sheng	have-something and have-nothing produce each other
you zhi yi wei li	have-something brings advantage
yu bu yu	desire to have no desires

Z

zai ying po bao yi	keep the spirit and embrace the One
zhen	the concrete
zheng fu wei qi	the normal can suddenly turn into the abnormal
zheng yan ruo fan	positive words seem to be negative
zhi chang yue ming	knowing the eternal is called enlightenment and wisdom
zhi hui	knowledge and craftiness
zhi ren zhe zhi	he who knows others is knowledgeable

zhi zhe	he who knows
zhi zhe bu bo	he who knows does not show off his extensive learning
zhi zhe bu yan	he who knows does not speak
zhi de	the simple *De*
zhi de ruo yu	the simple *De* appears as if clumsy
zhi zu	contentment, he who is contented
zhi zu bu rou	he who is contented will encounter no disgrace
zhong miao zhi men	doorway of all subtleties
zhong wei qing gen	the heavy is the root of the light
zhuan qi zhi rou	concentrate your vital force
zi hua	self-transformation
zi ran	natural reason, naturalness, spontaneity
zi sheng zhe qiang	he who conquers himself is mighty
zi zheng	(of itself) be righted and at peace
zi zhi zhe ming	he who knows himself is wise
zuo er bu ci	he lets all things grow without his initiation
zun dao	venerate the *Dao*

图书在版编目(CIP)数据
老子思想新释:英文/王柯平著.—北京:
外文出版社，1998
ISBN 7-119-02229-6

Ⅰ.老… Ⅱ.王… Ⅲ.老子-哲学思想-研究
Ⅳ.B223.15

中国版本图书馆 CIP 数据核字 (98) 第 17194 号

责任编辑　赵　岚
封面设计　唐少文

外文出版社网页:
http://www.flp.com.cn
外文出版社电子邮件地址:
info@flp.com.cn
sales@flp.com.cn

老子思想新释
王柯平　著
*

外文出版社出版
(中国北京百万庄大街 24 号)
邮政编码 100037
北京外文印刷厂印刷
中国国际图书贸易总公司发行
(中国北京车公庄西路 35 号)
北京邮政信箱第 399 号　邮政编码 100044
1998 年(大 32 开)第 1 版
1998 年第 1 版第 1 次印刷
(英)
ISBN 7-119-02229-6 /B·12(外)
04800(平)
2-E-3293P